Mexican Social Movements
and the Transition to Democracy

A tod@s l@s luchadores sociales
de Tepoztlán y Atenco

Mexican Social Movements and the Transition to Democracy

JOHN STOLLE-MCALLISTER

McFarland & Company, Inc., Publishers
Jefferson, North Carolina, and London

LIBRARY OF CONGRESS CATALOGUING-IN-PUBLICATION DATA

Stolle-McAllister, John.
   Mexican social movements and the transition to democracy /
John Stolle-McAllister.
     p.   cm.
   Includes bibliographical references and index.

   ISBN 0-7864-1999-7 (softcover : 50# alkaline paper) ∞

   1. Social movements — Mexico — Tepoztlán.   2. Tepoztlán
(Mexico) — Social conditions.   3. Social conflict — Mexico —
Tepoztlán.   4. Tepoztlán (Mexico) — Politics and government.
5. Golf courses — Mexico — Tepoztlán.   6. Democracy —
Mexico — Tepoztlán.   7. Economic development — Social
aspects — Mexico — Tepoztlán.   I. Title.
HN120.T46S86   2005
303.48'4'097249 — dc22   2004022961

British Library cataloguing data are available

On the cover: FPDT activists, Atenco, July 2003, in front of Zapata poster

Manufactured in the United States of America

McFarland & Company, Inc., Publishers
  Box 611, Jefferson, North Carolina 28640
  www.mcfarlandpub.com

Acknowledgments

I am indebted to many people and organizations for their assistance in completing this project. Although, I cannot list them all here, I would be remiss not to mention the following.

First, I would like to thank the communities of Tepoztlán and Atenco. They have shown me that it is possible to organize, defend themselves, and to imagine different ways of being a community. They have struggled to make "the world one where all worlds fit." Their example serves as a reminder to me that no opponent is all powerful and that another world is possible. I am also deeply grateful to the many residents and activists who took time out of their busy lives to share with me their stories and their insights into social struggle, democratic reform and cultural change. I am privileged to have been able to get to know them and to be, at least temporarily, part of their communities. I hope that I have done them justice in representing them here.

This kind of project also required much intellectual and financial assistance. Many thanks for the generous support from the MacArthur Foundation, the Graduate School and the Department of Comparative Literature and Cultural Studies at the University of Minnesota, as well as the University of Maryland, Baltimore County, all of which provided me with the funds and the release time I needed to research, travel and write. I would also like to recognize mentors and friends at the Interdisciplinary Center for the Study of Global Change at the University of Minnesota, for providing a challenging and supportive environment that helped to shape this project from the beginning. More recently, the department of Modern Languages and Linguistics at UMBC has proven to be a good home for me while I finished this book, as it has provided me with an environment filled with creative and dedicated colleagues where interdisciplinarity and hybrid thinking are the norm. Although I do not wish to omit anyone, I would like to offer special thanks to Hernán Vidal, Bud Duvall,

John Mowitt, Carmen Tostada, Kathryn Sikkink, Salvador Guzmán, Bruce Campbell and Jack Sinnigen, who have provided access to materials and useful feedback to this project at various points along the way, helping to clarify my thinking and improve my writing.

I would also like to express my gratitude to the good folks at McFarland, who have been both efficient and professional in dealing with me and this project. Their suggestions and hard work getting the manuscript into its final form is much appreciated.

Finally, I need to thank my family for being so supportive through this entire process: my parents, who initially sparked my interest in social justice and my curiosity about other cultures and my children Georgia and Rowan, who constantly remind me of the need to create a better, fairer world. And, of course, Kathy, who besides accompanying me on various research trips, shared parental duties, and read and reread the entire manuscript as it evolved, giving me invaluable feedback and honest criticism. Most of all, she always believed in my ability to complete this project, even when I did not. Thank you.

Table of Contents

Preface

This book is about people who said "No" and meant it. They said no to big development projects. They said no to threats. They said no to assimilation. More specifically, this book details and analyzes the remarkable stories of how people in two small towns in Mexico built movements to defend their communities' resources and identities. What makes these stories so stunning is that in an age of apparent neoliberal hegemony, when transnational capital moves freely around the world obliterating all opposition, activists within these small communities were able to rally residents to oppose, at sometimes great personal risk, projects worth hundreds of millions, even billions, of dollars, because those projects threatened their livelihoods and their senses of self as a community. Concerned community members in Tepoztlán, Morelos, and Atenco, Mexico, built upon already existing identities and community organizations to strengthen residents' resolve, while weaving wider networks of solidarity and support to block the construction of an exclusive country club, in the first case, and a new international airport, in the second. The process of these movements led not only to victories for their immediate demands, but also to a greater sense of power among local residents and a larger questioning of democracy.

These movements are also important, because they represent forces of democratization that are not represented by economic and political elites negotiating Mexico's transition to democracy. The transition from below, embodied by these and other movements, forces questions of economic fairness and cultural diversity onto the agendas of political reform. The fact that these movements took place immediately on either side of Mexico's transfer of power from the long ruling Institutional Revolutionary Party (PRI) to Vicente Fox's National Action Party (PAN), yet had remarkably similar economic, political and cultural demands, suggests that the much discussed transition, while removing the PRI, has thus far

1

failed to find ways to represent large sectors of Mexican society. As much as these movements are political struggles over power and control of resources, they are also cultural struggles over identity and representation. They reject the monocultural premise of the Mexican elite and insist, instead, that political institutions, if they are to be democratic, need to be accountable to the pluricultural reality of contemporary society.

My interest in social movements in these times of transition coalesced in the early 1990s, while I was working in Cuernavaca, Morelos, as a coordinator for a U.S. study abroad program. Part of my job involved coordinating meetings between U.S. visitors and community activists, and I was always struck, not only by the activists' dedication to their causes, but also by the sense that their reality and the reality portrayed by Mexico's elite institutions were vastly different. They were not just arguing about policy differences or a better piece of the economic pie; they had radically different visions of what their society ought to be. The activists' discourses were almost always rooted in "community," mutual responsibility and a sense of an uncompleted historic mission, dating back to the revolution led by Emiliano Zapata at the beginning of the twentieth century or even beyond. Organizing around the 500th anniversary of Columbus's arrival on the continent and the subsequent revolt of Maya communities organized in the Zapatista Army of National Liberation (EZLN) helped put a name on this other vision of what Guillermo Bonfil Batalla called "deep Mexico." One of my friends, a retired gas station attendant and Christian Base Community activist, explained it clearly to me in 1996: "All this time, it has been the Indians. We *mestizos* didn't know how to pay attention to them. But they have known all along how to organize; they have been the strongest and most determined. We in the city need to learn from them and from our own heritage as indigenous people, too."

To say, however, that what was, and is, at stake in Mexico is simply the redress of grievances or the recognition of indigenous rights and culture oversimplifies the matter. This point struck me one day, again in Cuernavaca in 1996. I was standing outside of a storefront copy shop waiting to copy some documents. There were two people in line in front of me. One was a lawyer, dressed in a three piece suit with a cell phone on his belt. The second was an older campesino, dressed in ragged white pants and shirt and wearing worn *huaraches*, common among the state's indigenous peoples. And then there was me, a foreigner. It occurred to me that the cultural issues in Mexico were more complicated than simply an either/or conflict; instead, they entailed a much more circuitous process of mutual influence, change, and appropriation of values, practices and technologies. When the conflict in Tepoztlán exploded in 1995, although it was often framed in terms of either/or, visits there soon made apparent that the political and cultural struggle beneath the golf course involved a distinct combination, or hybridization, of various projects—modernity, indigenous self-determination, neoliberalism, environmentalism, zapatista ideology, liberation theology, and human rights among the most easily named. But through all of that potential confusion, the activists and other residents never lost sight of their attempts to define and defend their community. What was for me a confusing and contradictory mixture of cultural discourses, was for many residents a coherent and unified way of explaining their place in the world, a place from which they could project themselves and their desires into larger discussions of the common good.

I carried out my research in Tepoztlán most intensively between 1996 and 1999, living in the barrio of Santa Cruz in Tepoztlán for about a year of that time. I conducted interviews with movement leaders, participants and other residents about their memories of the conflict as well as their perceptions about how the conflict changed, or did not change, their community. I was also able to work in the archives located in the National Institute of History and Anthropology's site in Tepoztlán, which provided useful documentation toward understanding the community's past and its political and cultural composition. Finally, I was privileged to be able to participate in the events and rhythms of everyday life, which helped me understand the importance and challenges that community life holds for many individual Tepoztecos.

This book focuses primarily on the struggle in Tepoztlán, starting with a history and analysis of the anti-golf movement that began in 1995 and following up through political events into 2003. I then turn my attention to reconstructing some of the local discourses used by Tepozteco activists during the conflict, including the legend of Tepoztécatl, the legacy of Emiliano Zapata, and the importance of neighborhood religious organizations. Since no community, however, is completely isolated, I next consider global influences on both everyday life in Tepoztlán and its effects on movement organizing. I analyze, in particular, the ways in which community members appropriated the discourses of environmentalism and human rights as the movement entered into alliances with organizations promoting those causes. Finally, I examine how the movement benefited from and created political opportunities within the context of a national PRI divided over the question of democratization. This section documents how the movement contributed to the creation of activist webs within various public spheres, strengthening organizations of civil society and helping create a more democratic political culture by offering new forms of representation and participation.

The last chapter deals with the movement by *ejiditarios* in Atenco to prevent the federal government from expropriating their lands to build an airport. Despite the circumstances being quite different, the issues, strategies and tactics of the protesters were remarkably similar to those of the Tepoztecos. Although the PRI had been replaced in the federal government, the questions of representation and accountability remained the same, raising for me questions about the depth of the transition in Mexico as well as highlighting what I saw as the deeper cultural issues that motivated the protesters in Tepoztlán. I visited and stayed in Atenco several times in 2003, conducting interviews and gathering documentation about the movement. This final chapter, although a less detailed analysis than that of Tepoztlán, strengthens my findings about the complex cultural aspects of this type of social movement in relation to structural changes.

I have also included an appendix describing the theoretical framing behind my argument. Although this structure may be a bit unorthodox, I have organized the book this way to highlight the people in the movements, by putting their stories and my analysis of them first and including theory last. I believe that my arguments about contingent hybridity will be of interest to scholars of cultural studies, but the explicit theorization of it is not necessary to the discussion of the social movements and their relation to political and cultural change in Mexico.

Finally, I have chosen to identify only elected officials or movement spokespeople speaking to me on the record. All other interviewees are either anonymous or are represented by pseudonyms to protect them from any possible negative impact that their cooperation with this project might have had on their lives. All translations of interviews and documents from Spanish to English are mine, unless otherwise noted.

Introduction

Social Movements and the Political Transition

During the late 1990s, as Mexicans contemplated a new political system, a bit of fading graffiti that read "*sí a la democracia, no a las elecciones*" ("Yes to democracy, no to elections") appeared on a wall behind vendors in the busy market of Tepoztlán, Morelos. This seemingly contradictory message highlights the complexity inherent in this transition era in Mexican political life. It suggests that while there are important relationships between institutional changes and democracy, the latter is not necessarily reducible to participating in the political system simply through voting. Additionally, this particular piece of political commentary, written in a small community in the context of a protracted struggle over control of local natural and political resources, illustrates that political cultures develop within specific historic and cultural contexts. What began as community efforts to block the construction of an exclusive country club, evolved into a wide-ranging debate about local autonomy, ecology, human rights and democracy. The political culture that both fostered the conflict and was transformed by it was created by the interaction of the particularities of Tepozteco history with the generalities of national and global discourses. This unique blend of circumstances created an equally unique political culture that would engage national debates about the democratic transition by challenging many of the assumptions of that process, such as elections equaling democracy and political parties being the best mechanism for change.

Disputes over natural resources and cultural autonomy resulted in serious and sometimes violent conflict not only in Tepoztlán, but also among indigenous communities in Chiapas and Oaxaca throughout the

5

1990s and into the beginning of this century. Conflicts over economic and natural resources also led to profound political disputes in the state of Guerrero, where nascent guerrilla organizations appeared and local communities declared themselves autonomous. Even the ouster of the autocratic Institutional Revolutionary Party (PRI) from the presidency in 2000 did not end the types of conflict that result in loss of governability. Since the change in government, communities, such as those in Atenco in the state of Mexico, have boycotted elections and declared their autonomy in the face of a state seemingly determined to impose its will over local communities and appropriate natural resources for the highest bidder. These types of conflicts have all given rise to social movements, such as the one in Tepoztlán, that articulate a very different vision of what democracy could be. Furthermore, it is these locally based social movements, rather than centrally organized national political machines, that increasingly serve as the creative and organizational engines within the larger political system, because they give expression to the multivocal and heterogeneous demands being made upon the state. Although individually they do not mount a serious challenge to the overall stability of the system, they serve as important conduits for political thought and action because they are one of the means through which local people attempt to adapt to their changing political and cultural environments.

Although in a general sense, most liberal observers would take for granted that voting should be the building block of a functional democracy, in the highly charged case of Tepoztlán, as well as other areas throughout the republic, the act of voting is not necessarily synonymous with democratic practices. Voting is frequently seen as a capitulation to a centralized system that shows only contempt for local needs and desires. Worse yet, that system negates other kinds of potentially democratic practices, attempting to extinguish cultural and political diversity in the name of a monocultural, modern state system. Instead of simply accepting a cultural and political order devised from outside of their experiences, locally based social movements, such as the one in Tepoztlán, are able to adapt their beliefs and practices to incorporate parts of those outside discourses to their own unique experiences. This process of cultural hybridity, that is the fusing of different codes onto lived experiences, has been amply discussed in the realm of Latin American cultural studies. These kinds of social movements would seem to be excellent examples of this process as participants incorporate modern and non modern, local and global discourses into their identities and their concrete practices. Although this hybridity occurs routinely in everyday life, participants in social movements explicitly redefine their relationships to power structures by exploiting their abilities to transit different cultural regimes and create new ones based on those experiences.

While hybridity gives movement activists a great deal of flexibility and fluidity in dealing with both opponents and allies, it also ties them to greater and lesser degrees with the systems that they oppose. Their identities, beliefs and practices while assuming a contentious position, also come in part from the more general cultural system, so that even as they attempt to reposition themselves in relation to power structures, movement participants also act within the parameters of those relationships. They are simultaneously inside and outside the systems against which they are protesting, and therefore, they necessarily use the language, rules and symbolic codes of the general system, even when they give them more unique meanings. One of the ambiguities of hybridity is that it formulates uniqueness even as it reaffirms likeness. Although movement activists often contend that their struggles reflect directly and only on their particular historic reality, they necessarily do so as participants within more general social relationships, which excludes complete isolation. Their experiences both before and during the movement are, therefore, simultaneously local, global and national, which is reflected in their seemingly contradictory demands both for autonomy and for greater inclusion.

This fluidity of position intersects with the transition to democracy by making the entire question of transition less clear. From what and to what, exactly, is Mexico transitioning? On the one hand, social movements have been integral in pushing for democratic reform of the Mexican state, and at the same time, they appear to function outside of the immediate control of the state, often assuming antagonistic postures toward state agencies, political parties and institutional processes. They incorporate the language of democratization into their own discourses, but because their positions are also grounded quite explicitly in beliefs and experiences with non-modern, non-liberal origins as well, the definitions and practices of democracy that they are advocating are quite different than those proposed by liberal reformers. Although many of the political and economic disputes through the transition period have revolved around the questions of electoral versus participatory democracy, social movements also embody an altogether different proposition — one that incorporates the rhetoric of liberal democratization with practices of a different origin. In that sense, it is not entirely clear into what the Mexican system is transitioning. The political classes of various ideological stripes negotiate possible projects of nationhood, while the women and men who are participating in locally based social movements offer a slightly different, hybrid version of what that national project might be.

Participation in social movements represent one of the ways in which political culture was being formed in Mexico at the end of the twentieth century and the beginning of the twenty-first. In some ways, the term political culture is redundant, since the distinction between politics and culture is really an artificial one. All politics is cultural and all culture is political. Often times we limit the study of politics to the actions and motivations of institutional actors and formal structures. But, politics is really about the flow of power, often channeled through these institutions, but also exceeding them. Politics is about who makes decisions, how they make those decisions and how they transform those ideas into concrete practices. Similarly, culture is often limited to objects, art, literature, rituals and the like, making culture into a seemingly static set of social relationships and values. Culture, of course, however, is dynamic and always in motion. It refers to the production of meaning and the sensibilities that order our lives. Culture necessarily changes as material reality evolves, even as it contributes to the direction of that evolution. It is, therefore, like politics, about the flow of power, as it simultaneously determines difference and arranges hierarchies.[1] Since culture constructs the systems of meanings in which we live our lives, it is profoundly political in that it contributes to the ordering of social relations and the distribution of power.

Specifically, *Mexican Social Movements* chronicles and analyzes the community of Tepoztlán's successful efforts to stop a transnationally connected development company from building a golf course and country club within their town. Although, and because, it is a very local story, it is also emblematic and constitutive of the larger context in which it takes place. In an attempt to protect their natural resources from outside exploitation, activists organized their community to take, in the end, very radical steps to protest and eventually derail this project. They simultaneously built internal cohesion by drawing upon locally circulating discourses and practices of difference, while reaching out to national and international groups to build an effective web of solidarity. In the process, they highlighted the incapacity of the state to articulate believable narratives of justice and inclusion and showed its lack of legitimacy as an arbiter of social disputes. It was in many ways, therefore, emblematic of the disintegration of PRI hegemony as well as contributing, at least a small part, to the broader debate about what a true democracy ought to look like. The no election graffiti mentioned above, therefore, reflected the perspective of many Tepozteco protesters in that they saw elections as legitimizing an otherwise spent political system. For these individuals, to be a true democrat meant one had to work outside of the state system in all of its manifestations.

The movement in Tepoztlán, which began as an attempt to stop the construction of a golf course, shows how members of a small community could successfully challenge flows of power by asserting their unique perspective and organizational skills, and by articulating another possible history. Through the course of their protest against the country club, movement participants expressed and enacted ideas about the role of government and the definition of democracy that varied greatly from officially sanctioned definitions and practices. They drew upon local traditions and invoked their right to employ "uses and customs" to name their own political leadership, in defiance of state authorities. This case is indicative not only of the state of governance at the end of the PRI, in which party operatives were no longer able to control important sectors of society, but also illustrates the tensions of cultural adaptation at work in local communities during this time. Town residents were torn between assimilation and autonomy as they organized their community and articulated their position not only against the project but also in relationship to larger social and political structures. Although these tensions were indicative of the downfall of the PRI, they have continued past the end of PRI rule. The continuation of these deeply embedded disputes suggests that a new, perhaps more democratic state will face issues that will require a profound rethinking of the power relationships between the center and the periphery and between the various cultural groups within the country. Returning, again, to the skepticism about elections, it would also appear that resolving the problems of equality and participation will require more than just reform of electoral institutions.

Because the Tepoztlán movement and its immediate political fallout span the last few years of PRI rule and the beginning of the new administration, it illustrates important political and cultural processes during this time period. One of the reasons that the PRI was unable to continue governing was that its populist model was unable to exert meaningful influence over, or create viable political narratives about, an expanding and heterogeneous civil society (Cornelius, Eisenstadt et al. 1999; Meyenberg Leycegui 2001; Williams 2001; Olvera 2003; Urías German 2003). It was both a political failure, in terms of institutional incapacity and a cultural failure in terms of being unable to construct meaningful discourses about what it means to be a part of the Mexican nation. If the PRI, therefore, could not hold onto power in part because it could not incorporate a multitude of Mexican identities and communities into a governable nation, then how is the current administration with its continued allegiance to neoliberalism to forge such a nation? Can it consolidate a democratic regime without engaging in meaningful dialogue with the various social and cultural sectors that hold serious disagreements with that model?

This dual political and cultural problematic is quite evident in Tepoztlán, where the state's institutions were able neither to resolve the conflict nor to control the social narratives being told within the community. What began as a dispute over land-use issues quickly developed into a more far-reaching conflict over local democratic governance, human rights and environmentally sustainable development. Beginning in 1994, a transnational real estate development corporation, Kladt-Sobrino (KS) proposed building the exclusive golf resort within the municipality's limits. Alarmed by potential environmental problems as well as perceived threats to their community's livelihoods and sense of self, activists organized townspeople to oppose the project. When, despite promises to the contrary, local officials issued changes in land-use permits to the developers, the community denounced them and removed them from office. The movement, headed by the Committee for Tepozteco Unity (CUT), soon organized elections for a new municipal council, citing their rights under Mexico's Constitution and the system of "uses and customs." In this process, which was never recognized by the state government, they made use of neighborhood networks, developed and maintained by the town's religious *mayordomo*[2] system, in order to identify candidates and to guarantee the transparency of their effort (Rosas 1997). The use of these networks was not only efficient, as they were well established and respected by the community, but also served as an affirmation of their local cultural identity, and its relationship to their political rights (Corona Caraveo and Pérez y Zavala 1999).

While activists were securing internal cohesion by emphasizing local differences with the larger Mexican nation, they were also weaving national and transnational discourses into their overall political strategy (Rabasa 2001; Stolle-McAllister 2004). Images and claims of authenticity about the meanings of Emiliano Zapata, the Revolution and the Constitution could be found throughout publications and pronouncements of activists during this period. Likewise, the movement actively sought allies in national and global environmental and human rights networks to assist them in building a viable coalition against the state and its aggressive and increasingly violent policy of support for the golf course project.[3] These alliances also led to the adoption by many people in Tepoztlán of the titles of "environmentalist" and "human rights defender" and the appropriation of parts of those discourses to local symbolic networks and practices. The movement, in other words, adopted an organizational strategy that looked both inwards toward affirming a unique *Tepozteco* identity and political practices, and outward toward building coalitions with national and transnational organizations. The conflict over the golf course became a visible manifestation of the community's negotiating of the contradictions of an increasingly globalized society. It synthesized national and transnational discourses within the context of its particular historic experience, in a process of cultural adaptation that successfully allowed activists to move between different cultural regimes, and to speak simultaneously to the logics of local relationships, state-centered discourse and global activist networks.

These kinds of movements, therefore, play an important role in the transition to democracy, not only because they oppose the imposition of a particular project or model of development, but also because they alter the social and cultural terrain that citizens inhabit. In the case of Tepoztlán, the impact of the conflict continued to be felt years after KS suspended the project. The movement substantially marked the narratives and practices of residents concerning participation in government by fostering assertive citizen identities and by proving that saying no to unwanted projects could be effective. Furthermore, local officials were more accountable to citizen demands and Tepoztlán witnessed highly competitive local elections and internal debates about the desired roles of political parties in a participatory democratic process. Citizens were also more active in the judicial system, demanding that it fulfill its role as a check on an arbitrary administration, as they successfully sought to have charges against them dropped and to have the courts return their communal land to them. At the level of everyday life, the movement left many Tepoztecos with a deeper sense of strength and pride in local identities and capabilities. Many people, for instance, reported a greater personal and collective meaning to their rituals and festivals as a means of fortifying community ties. In more general terms, the strengthening of the power of the local, both in terms of political practices and identities, challenges the idea of a unified national project, which in turn forces central authorities to consider other identities and practices in their construction of a democratic state.

The timing of the Tepoztlán movement, along with, of course, the Zapatistas in Chiapas and the myriad of other contentious movements occurring simultaneously and autonomously around the country, strongly suggests that the question of Mexico's democratic transition needs to be considered outside of and in relation to institutional reforms. The fact that such movements have continued despite the change in office, as demonstrated most visibly by the anti-airport movement in Atenco in 2001 and 2002 (and analyzed at the end of this book), further suggests that the political cultural processes underway in Mexico correspond to something other than just institutional reform. That is, the question of democracy, participation and equality are not captured exclusively in more transparent and accountable electoral practices. While the liberal notions of equality and effective suffrage are clearly important, there are quite obviously non-liberal cultural discourses, which also have claims to democracy, circulating through various sectors of Mexican society. These other discourses and practices need to be accounted for in the current process of constructing political cultures, and point to the complexity of democratic political cultures within a heterogeneous population. How can centralized institutions exert power and formulate policies while still respecting the rights, needs and desires of communities with values and practices that sometimes clearly contradict the overall national economic and political project? Is it possible, or democratic, for central authorities to impose on or convince very different groups of the legitimacy of a particular national project? How do diverse communities envision and practice internal social relations and how do they reach out to and interact with other outside groups?

The emphasis in this book on the specificity of a particular movement serves to critique a model of political analysis that focuses almost exclusively on institutions while ignoring the ways in which non-elites develop and practice their own political culture. By not acknowledging the agency of non-institutional actors, many analysts fail to account for the complex ways in which political hegemony is constructed, contested and maintained. Such an absence not only voids the importance that various social movements have played and continue to play in constructing a multicultural society, but also obscures the political transformation currently underway by ignoring the important cultural processes that take place as part of people's everyday life. Social movements provide a means whereby non-elites not only imagine themselves as political actors, but also create concrete mechanisms through which they negotiate their relationships with more powerful institutions. Because individuals engaging in contentious politics develop new political practices and articulate different social identities, they are able to more persuasively assert their agendas in national political discussions (Johnston and Klandermans 1995). This, in turn, changes the terms of discourse between civil society and the state and may ultimately contribute to larger institutional changes by participating in the process of altering the contours of civil society (Calderón 1995; Brito Velázquez 1997; Alvarez, Dagnino et al. 1998; Olvera 2003).

Grassroots activists are caught within the cultural contradictions of Mexico's pluricultural society, and, as was the case in Tepoztlán, must be able to successfully navigate those contradictions by appropriating and articulating various discourses that are relevant and useful to their lives. Such a strategy of hybridization seeks compromises with dominant institutions, while holding out the possibility of giving voice to marginalized voices as well. At the same time, however, these very same activists also tend to seek autonomy from those institutions (Fox and Hernández 1992; Cornelius 1999). That is, they simultaneously look into the specificities of their own historic experience and attempt to define their difference from the national system, which justifies their enactment of a unique, locally controlled political process, while demanding that their concerns be taken seriously within the realm of national policy making.

Translated into the world of on the ground politics, therefore, the Mexican transition faces the problem not just of the institutional consolidation of reform, but must also find a way to negotiate among the multiple communities of the nation in order to arrive at a social consensus concerning governance. This still to be defined shared understanding of the rules of social and political interaction must take into account the processes being worked out between negotiation and differentiation inherent in these expressions of political and cultural desire from various social sectors, illustrated most vividly through social movements.

"The movement made us a community"

Although these processes need to be seen as necessarily partial and incomplete, as there are also innumerable other factors shaping people's identities, perceptions and actions, participation itself comprises an important aspect of the political-cultural project of these movements. The crises that give birth to movements force those involved to rethink their relationships to other actors and institutions. Opposing a project of the dominant sector also forces them to articulate, and attempt to put into action, a different set of understandings and rules by which to live. Movement participation helps to create new public agents and renovated senses of community.

In Tepoztlán, for instance, even years after the conflict ended, pride at having defeated the golf course continued to be an important element in discussions about those turbulent months as many residents assumed an identity based at least in part on their rebelliousness. Across the political spectrum residents noted that despite internal differences and antagonistic party affiliations, they collectively would never allow an outside entity to impose a project on them again. Some leaders of the movement, furthermore, transformed themselves from social activists into formal political actors, as a means of furthering the struggle and consolidating their vision of local democracy, by winning hard fought elections and running the town's municipal government from 1995 through 2003.

Despite political and ideological limits, these movements exemplify and embody important cultural factors at play in shaping Mexican public life. Although they do not have the capacity to carry out deep structural reforms, and it would be illusory to impute revolutionary aims onto each of these movements, they give expression to different visions of democracy and governance.[4] Furthermore, they provide a concrete means through which individuals and groups, acting as cultural producers, reshape their environments of meanings and practices to create signifying formations that orient their lives and that contest the hegemonic intentions of more powerful sectors. Even when they do not actually hold formal political power, they make impossible the kinds of discursive closures that dominant sectors intend to impose on the population in general by refusing to cooperate and by espousing other possibilities. They defy predetermined notions about who "Mexicans" are and how they ought to behave. They give proof to the fact that rather than a Mexican nation, there are various. Rather than a singular type of state, the multiple cultural practices and visions of the Mexican peoples demand more heterogeneous political relationships between local populations and central authorities.

Furthermore, participation in movements drastically alters the self-identification of participants (Melucci 1995). It is not that the activists themselves simply pull out predetermined identities and strategies for negotiating power, but rather the acts of protesting and proposing, themselves, contribute to the construction of those oppositional and differential identities. One of my interviewees in Atenco eloquently summed up the importance of participating in collective social action in the process of creating identities and of defining local culture, by noting that before the movement, many of them in this relatively small town "didn't even know each other. We met in the movement and really it was the movement that made us a community. We are like a family now. Even with things not related to politics, we go to each other's houses or help out when someone needs something. It's really been very beautiful" (2003). Again and again in my interviews with movement participants in both Tepoztlán and Atenco, I was told things like, "I never expressed my opinion in public, before the movement. But, after going to a couple of neighborhood assemblies, I got brave and spoke up. People liked what I said and thought what I said was correct. They wanted me to represent them. I never thought I would be involved with politics" (Interview, Tepoztlán 1999). Or, "I never participated in anything. I never went to any meetings of any kind. Most of us never did. I never even bought the paper. But now I am always here, always participating and supporting" (Interview, Atenco 2003).

Movements, therefore, in many ways, act like catalysts. Not only in the sense of motivating and providing the means through which people might act in the public sphere, but also in forging sometimes different cultural systems together. Because of the greatly different experiences and backgrounds within the Mexican population, there are many cultures circulating within the national territory and even within relatively small communities. Because these cultures come into constant contact and conflict with one another, they are continually renovating themselves and adapting to changing material circumstances. This process of cultural hybridity is an ongoing negotiation of power and meaning, which sometimes smoothly blends different cultural codes and sometimes creates friction between competing groups and competing senses of common identity and common purpose (see the Appendix for a more detailed discussion of cultural hybridity). One of the biggest sources of this friction is between cultures that have developed over generations around profoundly local beliefs and practices, articulated, of course, with national and increasingly transnational sensibilities as well. Although this conflict is often referred to as traditional versus modern or even postmodern, it is more productive to view it as local versus cosmopolitan, because the identities of both cultural groups share many points of mutual articulation (García Canclini 1995). Even the separation between local and cosmopolitan, however, is relatively artificial, as local and global cultures are mutually constitutive (Robertson 1992; Bueno Castellanos 2000; Guidry, Kennedy et al. 2000). Hybridity, therefore, is a useful categorization in that it recognizes that the global or cosmopolitan influences do not simply replace local diversity with an imposed homogenous culture and that there is no linear evolution between different cultural codes; rather they exist simultaneously and interactively.

The struggle between competing cultural discourses, furthermore, has as much to do with ideological differences between tradition and modernity as it does with autonomy and control over natural resources. Social and political conflicts arise primarily around struggles over material goods, distribution of wealth and control of natural resources, all of which are intimately connected with understandings of self and group identity. Does the state, because it represents the nation, have the right to control natural resources and decide how best to administer the national society? Or do local groups, who understand the world in a slightly different manner, maintain the right to protect their own natural and cultural resources and, in that effort, maintain their difference within the larger group to which they belong? These confrontations over material goods, therefore, find echo in cultural differences between local and national or global expectations.

Movement participants inhabit a space that is marked by the confluence of these material and discursive differences. Since movements aim not only to imagine how they might fit into such a heterogeneous world, but to actively change that world, they must not only combine ideological differences, but material ones as well as they seek out creative resolutions to the contradictions of contemporary life. Social movements, for instance, need to be able to communicate between and among the different perspectives and practices of their local communities as well as with the potentially homogenizing forces of national and transnational institutions. For the most part, successful movements, those that get their demands met and achieve high levels of internal cohesion and support among wide networks of other activist, have been remarkably adept at not only existing among these contradictions, but also at creating new cultural formations based on combing those discursive differences to meet their needs.

Mexican Transition and Social Movements

The meanings and implications of this moment in Mexican political history, which is often referred to as the transition to democracy, are highly contested among activists, politicians and academics. Even the timeframe for when the transition began is not agreed upon. What does seem to be common ground is that by the end of the twentieth century the state designed and operated by the PRI became inoperable for social, political and economic factors. Like all hegemonic formations, the PRI's political control over the country was an ongoing process of negotiation among various social sectors. In general terms, however, the PRI maintained control through three interrelated strategies. Ideologically, the PRI positioned itself as the inheritor to the revolutionary project begun in the early twentieth century. Materially, the PRI arbitrated economic disputes in populist fashion by providing financial incentives to labor and *campesino* organizations in return for their support of the party. When economics and ideology failed to guarantee support, the PRI-State also turned to selective repression and targeted violence to help contain dissent.

Levy and Bruhn (2001) argue that the PRI was successful for so long in part because it was able to provide economic growth and stability in exchange for a lack of democratic practices. It built a corporatist state by fulfilling populist demands and incorporating important social sectors into the party hierarchy. By providing material rewards for loyalty and positioning itself as the only possible heir to the Mexican Revolution, even after it had long abandoned any revolutionary aspirations, the PRI successfully governed the country for seventy years. However, over time, and with changing economic circumstances, the PRI was able neither to maintain its patronage networks nor to make believable claims about advancing the most marginalized sectors of society. Social movements appeared as both symptom and agent in the demise of the PRI-era, because they took root in the public spaces that the PRI's corporate organization was not able to effectively colonize, and they articulated demands that the PRI-State would ultimately be unable to fulfill.

Various kinds of social movements found their way into these hegemonic fissures, gradually forcing them open into a more general crisis. Although the lineages of these movements could be traced back much further, as each movement builds on the experiences of previous ones, the most recent cycle of social movements can easily be linked back to the student movement in the 1960s. Dissatisfied with the closed political structures of the PRI and highly skeptical of the state's economic priorities, the mostly middle class student movement reached out to and formed cross-class and cross-organizational alliances with other social sectors as they demanded more openness and fundamental changes in Mexican society. The rapid growth and effectiveness of the students' organizing capacities apparently startled government elites, who, when they could not co-opt the movement leadership, opted for repression. The massacre in Tlaltelolco on 2 October 1968 remains one of the darkest and most controversial days in recent Mexican history. Although the repression did effectively stop the movement, it also scattered its members some of whom quickly took up their organizing again, although in a more quiet and local fashion.

The 1970s saw various kinds of local movements grow, some of which took up arms against the state. In general, however, this was a time of reassessment and regrouping as movement leaders worked with smaller communities to develop strategies and create increasingly strong local and at times anti-systemic identities (Vélez-Ibañez 1983). Although the oil boom of the 1970s allowed the PRI to fortify its patronage system and to strengthen its grip on power through a combination of repression and of co-optation aimed at various movement leaders, PRI elites feared losing their waning legitimacy because of complaints about the dirty war tactics being employed to control rebellions and because it had run unopposed in the 1976 presidential election. To counter its growing authoritarian image, the PRI opted to legalize the Communist Party and increase the number of seats allotted to minority parties in the formula of proportional representation in Congress. This reform is often pointed to as the second important point in the transition, because the state recognized the need for plurality and provided an institutional opening for the opposition.

Because of its built in limitations, which guaranteed the PRI with a super-majority in Congress, it also demonstrated the party's desire to maintain control of the process even as it appeared to be making concessions to the opposition (Urías German 2003).

The 1980s saw a spike in movement activities, as the economic crisis of 1982 severely curtailed the PRI's ability to secure the loyalty of potentially dissident sectors. The inability of the state to oversee continued economic growth or to soften the blow of economic hardship led to a generalized awareness that independent organizations could, and in fact would have to, play a greater role in developing and implementing public policies (LaBotz 1995). The crisis required the state to make steep cuts in government spending, forcing many to begin looking to each other and to non-governmental organizations for assistance. This created a structural crisis for the PRI as marginalized sectors began searching elsewhere for redress to their exclusion and for the means through which to construct their identities. Furthermore, the depth of the crisis also caused great stress on middle class sectors, as it shook their faith in the PRI's ability to administer a viable program of economic growth.

The next big jolt for the state and qualitative leap forward for the growth and prominence of social movements came three years later. The 1985 earthquake, besides leaving much of Mexico City in ruins, also shattered the state's already dubious image of being able to care for the country's citizens. Groups of civilians organized rescue operations and openly challenged and defied the government's attempts to control relief and rebuilding efforts. Citizen groups faced off against armed police and army units and entrenched bureaucrats in what Carlos Monsiváis (1987) characterizes as "an enormous civil rebellion in the name of human rights and respect for life" (50). The earthquake fanned the growth of the Urban Popular Movement (MUP) throughout the late 1980s in which urban groups, unassociated with any political party or state entity successfully made demands for basic services and increased respect for human rights (Castillo, Patiño et al. 2001). This movement also played an important role in changing people's perceptions of self-government eventually leading to the first elected government in Mexico City in 1997 (Tavera-Fenollosa 1999).

Three years after the earthquake, the 1988 national elections saw the formation of a coherent and broadly based opposition bloc, the National Democratic Front (FDN), headed by ex-priista, Cuauhtémoc Cárdenas. This coalition was heavily supported by the urban popular movement, and is believed to have carried Mexico City by a wide margin and to have won a slim majority of the votes cast nation-wide in the general elections.

Although Carlos Salinas officially won the election that year, there remain many doubts as to the legitimacy of that victory. Electoral fraud was rampant and brazen throughout the campaign and the counting of the ballots, exemplified by the suspicious and convenient crashing of the computer system tabulating the votes when it appeared that Cardenas was headed for certain victory. The government's refusal to allow the ballots to be publicly recounted only further convinced many that the elections had been stolen. Proceeding from the election, however, leaders of the FDN founded the Party of the Democratic Revolution (PRD), and attempted to provide a space for the political participation of a wide array of movements organized within civil society. Institutionally, the PRI was forced to give up some control of the Federal Electoral Institute, which had lost most of its credibility by awarding the election to Salinas.

The Salinas government worked hard to win legitimacy and rebuild its patronage networks in light of the 1988 election debacle. Politically, in the late 1980s and early 1990s, the PRI permitted the loss of several important governorships in northern Mexico through negotiated settlements of elections with the PAN, as it came to a tactical and ideological alliance with its more conservative rival. Socially, the Salinas administration embarked on an ambitious infrastructure and community oriented development plan, the National Solidarity Program (PRONASOL). PRONASOL, which was primarily funded through the massive privatization of state enterprises, provided money to community-based organizations for projects that they deemed important. These funds were distributed directly from the Office of the Presidency and were meant, in part, to rebuild the electoral support among marginalized groups that the PRI had lost over the previous decade (Dresser 1991). In the short term, this strategy was effective as the 1991 mid-term elections saw an increase in support for the PRI, while it derailed some of the demands of social movements and slowed the growth of the PRD, which had hoped to regain what the PRI had stolen from them in 1988.

PRONASOL and the Salinas administration, however, were not able to completely halt the demands for greater democracy and greater participation that social movements represented. By the mid 1990s, two important, and very different types of movements had gained national attention. First, the Barzón Movement, a group of farmers and middle class debtors was organized to protest high interest rates on all kinds of consumer debt. It gained many adherents and became a national movement after the December 1994 peso crash sent interest rates soaring, making most people's debts virtually unpayable. The widespread outrage at economic mismanagement, with perceived benefits going to a tiny elite of capitalist speculators at the cost of the vast majority, who were saddled with high interest rates and plummeting real wages, quickly pushed the Barzón from local to national political importance (Torres 1999; Williams 2001). Leaders of the Barzón Movement gradually expanded their sphere of influence to include a presence throughout much of the country. Many of their demonstrations have been marked by creative use of public spaces and direct attacks of neoliberal economic policies, as well as public appearances and statements of mutual support from seemingly unlikely allies such as the Zapatistas in Chiapas. This time period was also characterized by a growth in more conservative middle class associations, which, like Barzón, advocated less radical issues, but which, were, nevertheless, demonstrating both their dissatisfaction with the PRI-State, as well as their autonomy from it (Ramírez Sáiz and de la Torre 2003).

Perhaps the most important and visible opposition movement of civil society in recent years, however, has come from the rebellion of indigenous communities in the southern state of Chiapas. The January 1994 insurrection demonstrated that despite the assurances of the PRI technocrats, Mexico was not on the verge of making a qualitative leap into the industrialized, overdeveloped world. The political, social, economic and cultural demands of the Zapatista National Liberation Army (EZLN) illustrated the profound contradictions haunting Mexican society. The lack of viable democratic institutions, the abandonment of marginalized groups, economic policies that furthered that marginalization and the inability to acknowledge the pluricultural reality of the Mexican nation were all evidenced in Zapatista demands. Although the EZLN used force in getting attention for its demands, the movement has been characterized by its ability to organize among civil society and it has reached well beyond the indigenous communities from which it arose.

When Ernesto Zedillo took office at the end of 1994, he was faced with escalating economic and political crises and mounting pressures for serious reform. 1994 was a very destabilizing year for the PRI. Besides the Zapatista rebellion, its candidate for president Luis Donaldo Colosio was assassinated, the President's brother Raúl Salinas was implicated in drug trafficking and the murder of another high ranking official of the PRI and the peso crashed at the end of the year, resulting in an acute economic crisis beginning in 1995. To complicate matters, in February 1995, President Zedillo ordered a failed attempt to capture the EZLN leadership, leading to even greater organizing and protests within an already disenchanted civil society. In order to build up the party's legitimacy, Zedillo enacted a series of reforms designed to decentralize the state and to end PRI control over the electoral process. The IFE was granted autonomy from the parties and the Electoral Tribunal was granted authority to investigate and prosecute violations of federal and local electoral law. A major complaint about the 1994 presidential elections was that the PRI received most of the public financing (73 percent) and dominated the media, hampering competition. An important part of the 1996 reforms, therefore, was a 600 percent increase in public financing for political parties and a formula that shared those revenues based partially on percentages of votes won in the previous elections (Urías German 2003). Finally, rules governing electoral coalitions were loosened and the threshold for political parties to hold onto their registry was lowered to 2 percent, while the level for awarding seats for proportional representation was fixed at 3 percent. As a result of these reforms, the PRI hierarchy lost not only its majority in the 1997 Congress, but also control over its own party, sectors of which, often referred to as the dinosaurs, were disillusioned with the reforms (Meyer 1998; Cornelius 1999). For the first time in modern Mexican history, the President could not count on automatic approval of his initiatives and was forced to seriously negotiate with other parties. Equally important, Zedillo refused to use the tradition of the *dedazo* (big finger) to name his successor in 2000, opting instead for a public process to select the PRI's next presidential candidate.

Vicente Fox of the PAN picked up on this political momentum for change, and was able to put together a coalition of political actors from across the ideological spectrum determined to end PRI control over the state (Levy and Bruhn 2001). The success of his "Change" campaign hinged not necessarily on adherence to his neoliberal economic plan, but on the hope that removing the PRI would serve as an important step toward consolidating a transition to democracy. In some ways, it has been an important step toward strengthening a more open, competitive and transparent process. In other ways, however, Fox has been sharply criticized for not fulfilling his promises on economic growth, human rights improvements and substantial transformations of state structures.

The elections, in other words, did not end the transition process. Again, the Zapatistas provided the clearest example of how the transition had failed to incorporate dissatisfied social and political sectors into the process. In their 2001 March to Mexico City to demand the passage of a set of laws guaranteeing indigenous cultural rights and political autonomy, the Zapatistas demonstrated the depth of support for their movement by attracting huge crowds wherever they went. Their highly publicized campaign not only made explicit connections with the multitude of other locally based movements that they encountered on their journey, but also quite forcefully put the question of cultural difference on the national agenda. The indigenous movement since the 1990s has consistently insisted that there are many Mexicos within Mexico. Although the cultural and political differences between the indigenous communities and mainstream Mexican society are quite pronounced, many other movements have adopted this notion of cultural difference in articulating their demands with the state and with the rest of society. In Tepoztlán, for instance, protesters claimed to be using the notion of "uses and customs" to legitimize holding their own elections, despite the fact that Tepoztlán is really not an indigenous community, by most definitions of indigenous. Likewise other identity based groups, such as gays and lesbians, women etc. articulate their demands as cultural difference. Zapatista leader Subcommander Marcos (2001) paid homage to this strategy in his speech in the Zócalo of Mexico City in March 2001, by addressing himself to, "Brother, sister, indigenous, worker, peasant, teacher, student, *colono*, home maker, driver, fisher, longshoreman, office worker, employee, vendors, gang members, unemployed, media worker, professional, religious, homosexual, lesbian, transsexual, artist, intellectual, party member, activist, sailor, soldier, athlete, legislator, bureaucrat, man, woman, child, young person, elder," as a means of recognizing the differences inherent in the population and the implicit hope that people can work together while respecting those differences.

Despite the debates about the relative significance of each of these events, they point to a steady confluence of economic, social and institutional trends that are mutually influential. Economic crises, institutional reform and dissatisfied groups seeking redress to both material and ideological demands all constitute part of this transition period. What is not clear, however, is how what has thus far transpired contributes to the solid foundation of a necessarily democratic state, or even what a democratic state might look like. Political elites, it would appear, have been reacting to a series of crises, but have not been able to outline, much less put into practice, a vision that would incorporate the multiple demands of social movements or construct an economy that would meet the needs of the country's most marginalized citizens (Ramírez 2003). Gregorio Urías (2003) himself a PRD legislator, critiques the leadership of the three main parties for being so focused on presidential succession that they have not fostered the kinds of dialogue necessary to create a suitable political environment for a true transition. In their quest to seek power, he contends, the parties have not debated the necessary changes to the structures of the state that would more adequately provide for citizen representation and participation. This lack of serious dialogue and willingness to reach consensus among the political parties represented in state institutions hampers similar discussions within civil society about what constitutes democracy.

Although many perspectives about democracy circulate within various public spheres, two poles of debate have emerged over the past decade. One side of the debate, represented by a liberal view of democracy is that, while imperfect, Mexico is moving toward consolidating a democratic state based in the rule of law. Indeed, in many ways, formal Mexican democracy by these standards is making progress. Since 1988 a number of parties have competed in elections at all levels, and the processes through which those votes are counted and certified have become increasingly transparent. Political parties receive substantial governmental subsidies, which guarantee at least some media access for even the smallest of officially recognized parties. Balloting is generally considered to be free and fair, with a transparent process for registering complaints and investigating irregularities. A formula of proportional representation also ensures that all parties receiving at least three percent of the vote will have representation in government, even if they fail to win an outright majority in any district.

Supporters of the current transition process argue that democracy needs to be understood as a limited and very specific form of government that functions under the precept of representation based on one person, one vote (Aguilar Rivera 2003). Democracy can only function in an environment in which freedoms of information and assembly are guaranteed, in which the rules of the political game are clearly established and in which there exists a transparent process for selecting officials and peaceful transfers of power. They argue that Mexico increasingly fits those criteria and discount arguments concerning social equality, group rights and culturally relative forms of leadership selection as irrelevant or even contradictory to a functioning democracy.

On the other side, the transition to democracy is harshly criticized for only focusing on parties alternating in office and not on questions of participation, social equality and dismantling the authoritarian structures left by seventy years of PRI rule. Jorge Alonso (2003) argues that democracy cannot exist in any meaningful way until the vast social and economic inequalities that run through the nation are addressed in a serious manner. He criticizes the emphasis placed on institutional reforms and on guaranteeing elite competition as a means of evading the more difficult questions of structural inequality. How can people who have to struggle just to survive participate effectively in a political system that seems to have little interest in resolving their problems? The record 60 percent abstention rate around the country for the 2003-midterm elections suggests that popular interest in the political process is declining, as citizens see little connection between formal politics and the conditions of their lives. As Julio Hernandez Lopez suggested in the Mexico City daily *La Jornada* shortly after the July 2003 elections, Mexico is quickly becoming a "democracy without people" (1).

Within this context of an unsettled and unclear transition, social movements give voice to other versions of democracy that explicitly include meaningful and direct participation in decision making, and local control over cultural and natural resources. The specificity of their demands represent the continued fragmentation within Mexican society and serve as important outlets for the contentious political and cultural discourse that parties and state institutions are unwilling or unable to produce. Their existence and success deepens and complicates national discussions about the design and implementation of democracy by continually challenging the limits of reform that political parties attempt to impose. They refuse to be bound to the limitations of political subjectivity that elites are attempting to create through the transition process, and because of that refusal offer a proposal, as partial as it may be, which demands that locality and specificity play important roles in national and general discussions. They are not willing to be simply abstract citizens in a state system, but rather continually insist on their own protagonism and demonstrate their adaptability to changing circumstances.

The growth in social movements, both in terms of number and depth of identity construction, mirrors the PRI's take-over by technocratic elites represented by its last three presidents, de la Madrid, Salinas, and Zedillo. Its whole-hearted embrace of neoliberal ideology from the 1980s onward made the populist model of government untenable. The PRI's abandonment of land reform in 1992 alienated most of the poor agricultural sector, and in 1994, the Zapatistas characterized Mexico's joining of NAFTA as a "death sentence" for indigenous communities. Facing an exploding crisis in legitimacy, the PRI was left with an anachronistic system of leadership selection and an increased tendency to use violent repression both to settle internal scores and to thwart perceived external threats. Although selective repression had always been part of the PRI's ruling arsenal, by the end of the 1990s it lacked the ideological cover to justify such measures. This internal break down was further deepened by international pressures, which continually criticized the use of violence and torture by Mexican officials.

Heather Williams (2001) contends that although contentious politics has a long history in Mexican public life, the rapid transformation of the Mexican economy from 1982 onward dramatically altered the ways in which protest manifested itself. As the federal government retreated from direct involvement in fiscal programs, industrial production, and the regulation of prices, protesters were faced with the dilemma of deciding to whom they ought to protest (15). On the one hand, the federal government was no longer directly responsible for distributive demands, but local officials continued to be dependent on federal agencies for budgets, severely limiting their abilities to meet demands. Mexico's market transitions, therefore, have made the state fundamentally unstable, forcing protesters to alter their strategies and tactics. As Williams argues:

> Because state-level agents who deal with protesters have unclear jurisdictions and variable budget lines, struggles over micro-level issues tend to last for very long periods of time and require repeated and costly mobilization on the part of protesters. As a result, insurgent groups must find ways of externalizing the cost of protest itself. They do this by making deals with political parties, by courting the sympathies of the media and portions of the public, and even by altering the internal practices of the group [15].

The breaking of the PRI's control over economic matters, in other words, led to a diffusion in the types of protests that materialized. Given the state's commitment to market reforms, the PRI was simply unable to meet the material demands of many sectors, resulting in a myriad of new ways for unsatisfied constituencies to make demands for more equitable distribution of resources. Furthermore, since immediate resolution of issues was becoming even more complicated by the changing and uneven nature of the Mexican state, protesting groups sought out allies among political parties, NGOs, the press and other communities, making for a more thickly associated civil society. No longer were disputes simply between a small group and the federal government, but now those small groups were forced to seek out and make common cause with other sectors as well.

This shift in the material relationships between the state and nonconforming sectors of civil society, as well as within civil society itself, was closely matched by the PRI-State's loss of control over its ideological apparatus. Williams points out, "The opportunity for protest occurs when a particular narrative of good and evil becomes available to a group of people *at a moment when* the state cannot produce an effective counternarrative" (16). The social movements that have appeared in the past twenty years have not only capitalized on the state's abandonment of its supposed revolutionary goals, but have in fact turned the state's narratives of legitimacy and nationalism against it. Movements frequently invoke revolutionary images and slogans popularized by years of PRI-State indoctrination to legitimize themselves. The Zapatista movement is perhaps most obvious for their appropriation of Emiliano Zapata as the pure revolutionary; the human rights movement continually calls upon the state to respect and enforce its own laws and constitution; indigenous groups point to the "indigenous" part of *mestizo* ideology, et cetera. What all of these current social movements have in common is the use of various narratives of justice accompanied by the state's inability to counter with a credible alternative. Recycling old rhetoric was no longer a viable strategy for the PRI, given its material abandonment of those ideals and given the fact that the opposition was more effectively using that rhetoric to attack the PRI-State itself.

The PRI was ultimately defeated as the hegemonic power in Mexico, therefore, because its populist project became both materially and ideologically incapacitated. Economic crises and neoliberal reforms made it increasingly difficult for PRI operatives to maintain their patronage systems as the state was continually forced to cut its intervention in the economy beginning in the early 1980s. As those financial mechanisms of control and co-optation became weaker, so did the PRI's ability to even nominally incorporate marginal sectors into the populist fold. This weakening of control made the PRI's ideological claims to be fulfilling its revolutionary legacy even less believable. Increasingly large numbers of people came to believe that the technocratic elites running the PRI were more interested in serving transnational corporate interests rather than urban middle and working sectors or rural small landholders.

Removing the PRI from government, therefore, was the result not only of elite bargaining and institutional pressures, but also due to the PRI's capitulation of its material and ideological foundations. This transformation of the PRI, from revolutionary heir to neoliberal technocrat, created the conditions for the kinds of protests and movements that have developed over the past two decades. These movements are not only a symptom of structural opportunities, but have also dramatically contributed to the ways in which various sectors of Mexican society identify themselves and make demands of the state. The process of transition, therefore, is not only about changing institutions, but it is also about changes in peoples' everyday lives and the ways in which they symbolically and materially organize their communities. In the last decade, in particular, these kinds of changes have led to a deepening sense that Mexico is a pluricultural nation. The increasing importance of indigenous communities in national politics is only one example of the kinds of multivocality being created in contemporary Mexico. The unified nation, which was envisioned beginning in the nineteenth century by elites and found a formation in the populist, post-revolutionary state, is quickly being replaced by competing visions of what it means to be Mexican (Villoro 2001). This newly assertive multivocality challenges state reformers to adopt more inclusive decision-making processes. At the same time, however, because movements tend to remain skeptical of political parties, they refuse to give up autonomous development as a price for their inclusion. In this sense, these types of small social movements are of paramount importance in understanding not only how and why the PRI became undone, but what challenges a potentially democratic Mexican state faces.

Structure of the Book

Mexican Social Movements has an unusual structure that both reflects the hybrid nature of its subject matter, and places the voices and stories of people involved in creating their political cultures before the voice of the analyst. Although I certainly do not pretend to be absent from the representations of the movements and the actors that I have produced here, and analysis necessarily cuts through description and reporting, I have placed the more explicitly abstract analysis as an appendix for both strategic and intellectual reasons. On the one hand, the stories and voices of the participants of these movements in Tepoztlán and Atenco illustrate important tendencies within Mexican public life that will be of interest to an audience more generally interested in contemporary Mexican politics and popular culture. Although the theoretical framework balancing adaptation and differentiation is present throughout, these readers may not be interested in the intellectual route that I have taken to get there. The book is understandable and coherent without an explicit summation of the cultural argument.

These same processes, however, do provide important insights into debates among practitioners of cultural studies, particularly within the U.S. academy. Identity politics, cultural resistance, hybridity, and subalternity are all important topics of discussion within U.S. cultural studies. Although there does not seem to be consensus on exactly what cultural studies is, there is a general sense that it constitutes an attempt by intellectuals to connect their work with the flows of culture and power within society. As it has been constituted, most objects of cultural studies involve the mass media, literature and cinema, with the ethnographic side of culture generally ignored, leading Sonia Alvarez, Evelina Dagnino and Arturo Escobar (1998) to observe that, "Despite the interest of cultural studies scholars in examining the relations between cultural practices and power and their commitment to social transformation, 'cultural politics' often refers to disembodied struggles over meanings and representations, the political stakes of which for concrete social actors are sometimes difficult to discern" (5). This book is an attempt to make the political stakes for concrete social actors more easily discernable. The ethnographic and political data, therefore fits with the theoretical chapter on hybridity and subalternity by providing a concrete footing for the abstract discussion of how political subjects are created and transformed by their circumstances even as they attempt to change those circumstances. It is logical, therefore, to place this discussion after having examined the stories themselves. For those readers, however, who are interested in the framing of the arguments first, they should begin with the appendix and then proceed from there.

Theoretically, as I have been suggesting through this introduction, the political and cultural arguments that I make in the book are framed by the tensions between hybridity and subalternity, and how that tension is manifested through the contentious politics practiced by social movements as the structures of the Mexican state are questioned and reformed. By hybridity I refer particularly to the notion put forth most influentially by García Canclini (1995) in which he argues that contemporary Latin American culture is marked by the constant articulation of differing cultural discourses. This has been quite evident in the practices of these movements in which local, national and transnational, non-modern and modern are continually interwoven. One of the organizers in Atenco exemplified this, perhaps superficially, when questioned about communication. She responded, "If we need to get everyone together, we fire three rockets and ring the bells in the church, just like for festivals. And, well, of course, cell phone, too" (Interview, Atenco 2003).

The theoretical problem with hybridity, however, is that in the end it dissolves difference. If people continually combine elements of the cultural codes with which they have contact, in the end there will be no difference. The activists in both of these movements, however, despite their abilities to move through different cultural terrains and combine them in useful manners, still maintained their difference as an important element of their identities. They understood themselves as being on the margins of the larger social order, and although they were making demands to be given a voice in decisions affecting them, they continued to see themselves fundamentally as outsiders. Their identities and practices, therefore, were partially dependent on them not being assimilated into a larger system, and they drew their strength, ironically, from their relative weakness. Cultural theorists concerned with this notion of subalternity, or marginalization, have drawn upon this desire for autonomy and the abilities of peripheral actors to use and imagine alternative histories and forms of organization to articulate ways in which marginalized peoples exercise agency in their dealings with power (Beverly 1999; Moreiras 1999; Rodríguez 2001). They argue that people from colonized or otherwise marginal social sectors engage in all kinds of resistance, and because they remain outside of dominant epistemological and cultural systems, they maintain parts of their knowledge and identities that are not open to assimilation by dominant social sectors.[5]

Social movements embody elements described by both theories, but the tactics and strategies deployed by activists are dependent both on their abilities to work within the system and with other groups, as well as their abilities to articulate an identity of themselves that is different. I use the phrase contingent hybridity to describe the processes both creating and created by social activists. In particular, the use of ethnographic work to connect the beliefs and practices of everyday life to larger issues of political organization, reinforces previous studies that have likewise attempted to show that politics is not just practiced in the voting booth or in governmental offices, but is woven throughout a range of quotidian cultural and social practices and beliefs (Bennett 1995; Rubin 1997; Stephen 1997; Alvarez, Dagnino et al. 1998; Gutmann 2002). In the particular case of Mexico, locally based social movements continue to pull at the transition's untidy ends. If the transition cannot accommodate the hybrid world-views and political practices developed by the Mexican population and expressed through social movements, then it is highly questionable that the political elites will be able to consolidate a truly democratic state.

The first chapter is a detailed description of the town of Tepoztlán and its struggle against the golf course project. Tepoztlán provides a compelling example of the contradictions that the PRI government faced as it attempted to reform itself by the end of the twentieth century, because of the tensions between local, national and global identities as well as disparities in the distribution of power and material goods. In Tepoztlán, many residents claim to have a very unique cultural identity, one that makes them different than their compatriots, demonstrated by a general interest in local history, myths and ritual practices. At the same time, because of its location just outside of Mexico City and its natural beauty, people from all parts of the country and many different areas of the world frequently visit Tepoztlán. Added to this exchange, many Tepoztecos travel as far as the U.S. for work, and professional education and employment have been the goals of many Tepozteco families for their children. Residents combine and adapt these different influences to produce a specifically hybrid culture that allows them to move in and about the various social terrains of their lives.

When the Kladt-Sobrino group proposed building the golf course, the community was uniquely positioned to articulate an opinion about the project, and then to act forcefully to oppose its construction. Activists, many of whom had experience with other social conflicts, were able to take advantage of shared community experiences and organizations in order to forge a strong alliance against the project. In addition to overcoming the many internal differences within the community, activists were also able to engage with national and transnational activist and media networks in order to broaden their base of support and to apply pressure to the state government to end its support for the project. In the course of articulating this double discourse, simultaneously looking in and out, the movement contributed to creating a locally hybrid culture.

After several months of intense conflict, which saw the deposing of local authorities, the officially unrecognized selection of new ones, the imprisonment of several leaders and the assassination of another, the Tepozteco movement succeeded in forcing KS to withdraw the project. The political fallout of the movement continued to be felt for years afterward as activists struggled with their relationship to political parties and attempted to fashion a locally participatory democracy within the larger context of a faltering authoritarian state. The example of Tepoztlán suggests that within the parameters of gradual state reform, local activists were challenging the limits of democracy and change by drawing upon the specificities of their unique historic experience and blending it with the more general discussions of reform. Furthermore, it shows that democratic change was not something that was occurring only within formal institutions, but was also being encouraged and formed by ideas and practices beyond the immediate control of those institutions.

Since residents continually claimed that they were motivated to resist the golf course and stand up to the government out of their love for Tepoztlán and because they considered themselves to be a unique community, the second chapter analyzes the movement by examining some of the discursive threads of that local identity. The pyramid overlooking the town and the ubiquitous use of Nahuatl names for places, suggests that an important place to begin would be with the community's understanding of its pre–Columbian legacy.

An important element of communal life in Tepoztlán is the annual reenactment of the Challenge of the Tepozteco King. The myth is well known, and as with most oral histories has many versions. In this chapter, I focus on one collected by town historian Angel Zúñiga, as it seems to encompass many of the disparate tales of the legendary king. Tepozteco is the son of the wind god, Ehecatepetl, and born of a young princess. He is raised by a humble family, and with the help of his father, defeats the monster Xochicalcatl and humiliates the pompous kings of the surrounding communities. He later converts to Christianity, convincing many of his followers to do the same, and helps to build the Cathedral in Tenochtitlán. He leaves Tepoztlán after the community disobeys him, warning them to protect their lands and their traditions. Residents of Tepoztlán referred often to this myth in explaining who they were and why they were so adamant in defending their land and their identity. KS was easily compared to Xochicalcatl, and the arrogant state governor to the humiliated nobility. They pointed to this founding myth as proof of their natural rebelliousness, as well as their willingness to participate in making their country a better place, just as Tepozteco had done through his conversion and his assistance with the cathedral in Mexico City. Likewise, his final departure served as a continual warning for residents to remain steadfast in their protection of the community.

The second major mythical figure to appear repeatedly throughout the struggle in Tepoztlán was that of Emiliano Zapata. The revolutionary's image accompanied protesters to all events and his symbolic capital as the uncompromising revolutionary served as moral guidance for movement activists. Despite some contradictory testimony from actual participants in the Revolution, Zapata is widely seen as an unblemished icon. Like Tepozteco, Zapata has a strong local draw, as he was from the state of Morelos and often used Tepoztlán as a base of operations. Of equal importance, however, is also Zapata's stature as a national icon. By claiming to be heirs of Zapata, the Tepozteco activists were challenging the state over the meaning of that symbol, turning an important state symbol back against the state itself. It also served to reinforce the notion that despite the importance of being Tepoztecos, they were also Mexicans and were, in fact, living up to the nation's highest ideals.

Finally, the chapter shows how these notions do not exist simply as ideas, but are also embodied through concrete practices. A notable feature of social life in Tepoztlán is the importance of neighborhood. Each neighborhood has clearly defined borders, an animal mascot and, importantly, a colonial era chapel. These chapels are maintained through a system of *mayordomos*, who are selected through an annual assembly to see to the chapel's maintenance and to organize the patron saint's festivals and any community work that needs to be done. Many residents claim that this system is a legacy of the pre–Columbian *calpulli* organizations that directed work and spiritual life. Although many anthropologists dispute this idea, noting that the neighborhoods themselves were colonial creations, it nevertheless serves as a concrete bridge to other non-modern identities that are important to people in everyday life. Furthermore, the notion and practice of collective work also come from these pre–Columbian origins. Many residents explicitly linked community service with Zapata, as another practitioner of Mesoamerican culture. These beliefs and practices served not only to ideologically prepare people to participate in the movement, but they also provided conduits for communicating and organizing.

Despite the importance of locality to the movement, it was not an isolated political event nor is Tepoztlán somehow disconnected from the rest of the world. The third chapter considers how everyday life in the community is clearly marked by influences from outside. The movement itself took advantage of these outside connections to build alliances with transnational environmental and human rights organizations, resulting not only in a more effective movement, but also in changed local identities. Many participants began identifying themselves as environmentalists or as human rights defenders. But, as one of my interviewees in Tepoztlán noted, they were "not environmentalists as you understand them in NGOs or in the university" (Interview, Tepoztlán, 1999). Rather, the global discourses that movement participants adopted were also modified to fit the needs and experiences of their particular circumstances.

This combination of local and global world views and practices exemplifies the contradictions inherent in the many processes of globalization, and the ways in which the Tepozteco activists got caught up in those processes also suggests that locally based people can use the tools and opportunities of globalization for their own ends. Using the conflict in Tepoztlán as an example, this chapter deconstructs the notion that globalization is a homogenous process, demonstrating instead that there are several, uneven processes of globalization taking place. Furthermore, the starting point for understanding globalization ought to be at the local level, since people's lives are simultaneously local and global, but they live their lives in concrete, locally defined circumstances.

Beginning, therefore, with the influences of a heterogeneous globalization, this chapter analyzes how the Tepozteco activists, already living in a community deeply affected by globalized relationships, used their experiences with outside ideas and practices to create an effective movement. The movement leadership was able to take advantage not only of their expertise in local organizing and communication, but also tap into those wider networks of activists to recast their land dispute as an environmental one. Likewise, their conflicts with local authorities were easily translated into the language of human rights, as those authorities increased physical and psychological pressure against them and stepped outside of the norms established by the rule of law. Despite, however, their increased contact with these global discourses of social change, the Tepozteco activists never lost sight of the local nature of their conflict and of their identities. They did not, in other words, become generic environmental activists, but very specifically Tepozteco environmentalists. Environmentalism, for most of them, although certainly connected with larger issues of sustainability, biodiversity, etc, was focused on the locally specific issues of conserving resources, preventing outsiders from exploiting and despoiling their land and keeping a lid on the urban sprawl creeping toward them from Cuernavaca and Mexico City.

The fusion of local and global discourses in the movement and in the evolution of participants' identities was a vivid example of cultural hybridity. People drew upon and were influenced both by their contacts with the outside world and their uniquely local experiences. These two different fields, of course, become increasingly entwined, and in the case of this conflict, people were able to mold them to help shape the outcome of their struggle.

In the fourth chapter, I argue that the melding of distinct discourses and appropriation of uses and customs to serve the needs of the movement occurred within a particular political context. Although at the time, 1995–1996, participants obviously could not know that the PRI had only a few years left as the dominant political power, it was obviously weakened as a hegemonic power, and the movement took advantage of the political opportunities inherent in that moment of weakness. The ideas that the movement was advocating resonated with larger debates about democratization, civil society and local autonomy, while the success of their actions were at least partially dependent on the limited capacity of the state to resolve conflicts. The PRI, in this case, was able neither to produce a viable narrative that included the angry protesters, nor to provide the financial and material support needed by party operatives to distribute in communities like Tepoztlán in order to insure compliance. Furthermore, the decentralization of the party and state apparatus, undertaken as part of the Salinas and Zedillo reforms, made it difficult for the PRI to control its own members, as it was unable to moderate the governor's position and behavior, even as he became an increasing liability in the conflict. The Tepozteco activists, therefore, were working within these structural fissures to advance their goals.

The movement in Tepoztlán, furthermore, illustrated many of the complex issues involved in the creation of political cultures within civil society. Its supporters generally labeled the movement as an exemplary model of civil society in an almost epic battle against the state, even though this framing failed to account for the complexities of civil society. Although this type of argument corresponded to the long history in which the PRI-state had essentially eliminated autonomous organizations, it portrayed civil society as a unified actor. This was problematic because civil society is a field of many different actors with shifting interests and loyalties, as could seen by the rapid disintegration of the movement. Rather, the significance of the movement lay in the ability of participants to negotiate a common agenda and to devise strategies that allowed them to effectively communicate with state actors.

Within the larger context of the transition then underway, the movement in Tepoztlán and other contemporary movements raise the question of to what exactly Mexican political life was, and is, transitioning. Democracy was certainly a prominent theme of discussion, both locally and nationally. The distrust that the movement demonstrated toward the political parties and the uneasy alliance it eventually formed with the PRD, underscored the larger national debates about what democracy actually is. The existing political structures, however, also limited the possibilities for Tepozteco autonomy. Although some members of the community wished to continue with the experiment in participatory democracy and municipal autonomy, the majority, in the end, opted to compromise with the state, and to work within the system. Different visions and hopes for democracy, in other words, needed to be altered to accommodate other political forces. It was not possible for one side to simply impose its vision over all the others.

While the debate between electoral and participatory democracy was certainly not new, the injection of a Mesoamerican ideology by Tepozteco activists (borrowed in no small part from Zapatista discourse in Chiapas) added a new dimension to the debate about a different kind of Mexican state. As the electoral reforms of 1997 and the PRI's loss of the presidency in 2000 have pushed one type of transition to the forefront of national discussion, there remains serious debate about what a democratic state ought to look like. Most specifically, it raises the thorny issue of how to construct a singular state that represents the pluricultural reality of Mexico.

The final chapter considers how these issues of democracy and local sovereignty continued past the election of Vicente Fox in 2000. When the new democratic government attempted to expropriate the *ejido* lands of campesinos in the town of Atenco, it set off a social explosion that demonstrated that the issues involved in the Tepoztlán dispute were not limited to Tepoztlán, nor were they limited to the deficiencies of an autocratic government. Rather, they are dependent on deeper cultural and social divides that the current power arrangement is not capable of resolving.

From the beginning of its tenure, the newly elected government of Vicente Fox gave high priority to the construction of a new international airport, citing the size and safety inadequacies of the current Mexico City location. It carried out a highly publicized search for a new site, and in October 2001 named the *ejidos* in and around Atenco as the designated site. The *ejiditarios* and other residents, who had not been consulted and who were offered seven pesos (seventy U.S. cents) per square meter, were incensed and quickly formed an organization, the Front of Towns in Defense of the Land (FPDT), to oppose the expropriation. They rallied internal support for their cause, claiming that their families had occupied those lands since before the Spanish Conquest, and questioned how they would support themselves once they lost their land. Movement leaders quickly began legal proceedings to stop the expropriation, but as they had little faith in the courts' ability to protect them, also began organizing increasingly loud and disorderly protests. They marched frequently to Mexico City, brandishing their machetes, as symbols of their livelihoods, to demand that the expropriation be cancelled. In July 2002 the level of conflict increased greatly. Atenco residents confronted government officials and private contractors beginning survey work on their lands, despite injunctions against any work being done, held them prisoner and confiscated their equipment. On 22 July, state police, many of them in civilian clothes, attacked a group of Atenco marchers, injuring many and capturing the movement's leadership. Activists regrouped in Atenco, blocked the highway, took government officials hostage and threatened to blow up two gasoline trucks if their members were not released. After delicate negotiations, the stand off was peacefully resolved.

On 1 August, President Fox cancelled the expropriation orders, citing the growing chaos in the region. As in Tepoztlán, however, the cancellation of the project was not the end of the story. The Atenquenses soon declared themselves to be an autonomous municipality and demanded that criminal charges against the protesters be dropped. This stance led to electoral violence and the cancellation of elections in March and July 2003. At issue, ultimately, as in Tepoztlán, were the questions of local autonomy and cultural difference from the mainstream political institutions.

This case serves as a validation of my thesis that the cultural politics of social movements is not entirely dependent on formal political institutions, but instead correspond to other cultural influences as well. Through this example, and in relation to the analysis of Tepoztlán, I argue that instead of understanding political change through the homogenizing lens of national institutions and discourses, Mexico must be seen as a multicultural country and the project of building a viable nation rests on the ability of a national state to recognize and negotiate between quasi-autonomous yet interdependent communities.

Lastly, the appendix is a detailed discussion outlining a critique of both hybridity and subalternity in which I propose that both need to be read against each other in terms of the historic and political contingencies of specific circumstances. The contingent nature of hybridity is illustrated by strategies developed by social movements as they negotiate the cultural and political differences between their members and the state and elite economic sectors of society. The revision of both approaches is necessitated by the partial abilities of each to describe the situations, but the incapacity of either to fully account for the actual practices of the marginalized sectors they aim to describe. On the one hand, although these movements are undoubtedly hybrid, the desires and abilities of activists to maintain themselves as outsiders to the system and to draw upon histories that have not been assimilated by dominant sectors suggests that while cultures are hybrid, actors within that culture have some ability to control the process and to select useful aspects of different discourses to meet their needs. It is not an automatic process created simply by the juxtaposition of different kinds of cultural inputs.

This is where subalternity provides an important theoretical foothold for grounding an oppositional standpoint for marginalized actors. Subalternists broadly argue that dispossessed, excluded and colonized sectors maintain their autonomy through a number of strategies. Below the surface of their obvious subjugation, these groups, referred to as "social majorities" by Gustavo Esteva (1998), resist their oppression through periodic rebellion, non-cooperation or simply ignoring the demands of dominant social sectors. In other words, subaltern groups maintain a part of their culture that is neither understandable nor open to assimilation by dominant sectors. This would also seem to describe the strategies and desires of participants in local social movements. The theoretical problem with subalternity is that it imputes an almost automatic rebelliousness to marginalized social sectors. As social movements demonstrate, that is not the case. Rebellion and resistance are the result of painstaking political work, convincing, talking, organizing, compromising and coalition building. Furthermore, movements base their success on their abilities to communicate with other groups through a hybrid communication network. The Zapatistas, to name the most obvious example, have been successful not only because they are well rooted in the Maya communities of Chiapas, but also because they are able to communicate with much wider audiences and are able to insert their demands into larger debates about democracy, human rights and sustainable development. Their insurrection was not spontaneous, but rather the culmination of years of work and the incorporation of other discourses, such as women's rights, into traditional discourses of indigenous identity. Instead, local communities are able to develop hybrid cultures that are grounded in their historic circumstances. They are able to maintain their difference, even as they incorporate outside influences and communicate with potential allies outside of their immediate networks. This ability to maintain difference while working with other communities represents a challenge to the reformulation of the Mexican state, because as it is currently being restructured, the state maintains a monolithic approach to regulating social relations. The elites driving the transition have thus far not been able to incorporate the pluricultural realities of the Mexican people, and until they are able to do so, social movements will continue to represent the fragmented interests of various communities and will continue to challenge the state's attempts to force their conformity with a system that ignores their difference and their demands for local control over resources. The social movements represent, therefore, different perspectives and possibilities for democracy and sociability in Mexico.

1

Tepoztlán's "No al Golf"

This has gone way beyond the golf course.
Tepozteco activist, March 1996

Tepoztlán, Morelos, is a small, picturesque town nestled in the Ajusco mountain range, about 30 miles south of Mexico City. Most of its streets are cobbled stone, and each of its eight neighborhoods has a colonial era chapel and its own patron saint. Looking up from the town's main church, dedicated to the Virgin Mary, one can easily make out the pyramid of Tepoztecatl, which sits atop a leveled mountain. The striking beauty of the area, as well as its easy access to the larger metropolitan areas of the Federal District and Cuernavaca, have made Tepoztlán a prime tourist destination. Many wealthy families maintain weekend houses in the municipality, and the Sunday market draws thousands of visitors each week, filling the town's many restaurants, shops and hotels. Its proximity to Mexico City and its preservation of many festivals and traditions has also made it the object of many anthropological studies through the past century.[1]

History is an important part of everyday life in Tepoztlán. The pyramid and Nahuatl names remind people of their indigenous heritage, and the churches of their colonial legacy. Rituals and festivals help form bonds between residents and between the past and present. The Revolution, which resulted in the depopulation of the town at the beginning of the twentieth century, plays an important role in the collective consciousness of Tepoztecos, who have built a reputation for being independent-minded and rebellious. This rebelliousness is not limited to the distant past or to glorifications of revolutionary violence, but is strengthened by the participation of many Tepoztecos in a wide variety of social struggles, both locally and regionally. Tepozteco activists, in recent years have stopped the construction of highways, railroads and cable cars, all supposedly designed to increase tourism to their home. Tepoztlán has also been prominent for producing or being home to human rights activists, popular educators and socially committed artists and intellectuals. The town has been a site of visible support for the Zapatista movement in Chiapas, offering shelter to traveling Zapatistas and filing a motion in the Supreme Court to have the 2001 reform laws on indigenous rights overturned, after it failed to meet Zapatista expectations.

In the late 1990s, Tepoztlán attracted the attention of national and even international media, human rights and environmental activists and scholars, because of the political conflict created by the town's resistance to a country club and golf course. The battle, dubbed the Golf War by some observers, pitted local residents against a powerful transnational development company and a corrupt and violent state government. The conflict attracted much attention, not only because of the unlikely success of the Tepoztecos, but also because it highlighted many of the struggles taking place in Mexico at this time. The struggle of the Tepoztecos embodied debates about democracy and limits on governmental authority within the context of declining PRI control. In a more general sense, it highlighted the dynamic tensions between center and periphery as residents negotiated changes in their economic and political relations amongst themselves and with the larger urban areas of Cuernavaca, the state capital, and Mexico City as they attempted to breach the culture clash between neoliberal discourse and community-based identities.

The dispute with the Kladt-Sobrino (KS) development company over the construction of a multi million-dollar resort, although built upon years of distrust of development projects, galvanized local residents in August 1995, when local officials' acquiesced to KS and state government pressures for permission to begin building. Townspeople, feeling betrayed by their elected authorities, forced them to flee the municipality and eventually named their own interim government. Their continued refusal to cooperate with KS or with state officials led to increasingly violent confrontations with the state government and eventually to the death of one and the imprisonment of several protesters. At stake, however, was more than just the construction of a golf course. By the end, townspeople were questioning the legitimacy of state authorities and were one of the most visible manifestations of larger national conflicts concerning control of natural resources. Although their prime objective was to prevent the golf course, the protesters in Tepoztlán brought to the fore debates circulating in Mexican public life about the nature of democracy, the need for the protection of human rights, finding the balance between economic growth and sustainable development, and the rights of local people to maintain autonomous control over internal matters.

In 1994, when the conflict began, Tepoztlán was a municipality of approximately 27,000 people. The municipality consisted of the county seat, by the same name, in which sixty percent of the population lived and where most governmental and economic activity took place, as well as six smaller villages. It had a diversified economic base, with agriculture, commerce, construction and tourism all playing important roles in providing income for residents (Benet 1996). The population of the town consisted primarily of people born and raised there, with an increasing number of people moving away from traditional *campesino* lifestyles, by seeking higher education and professional employment (Lomnitz 1999). Since Oscar Lewis conducted his famous studies of the town in the 1940s and 1950s, the population had linguistically shifted from majority Nahuatl speaking to almost exclusively Spanish speaking (particularly in the more urban areas of the county seat), while the percentage of people making a living through traditional agriculture had dropped considerably. Over the past several decades, tourism had become a very important and dynamic sector of the local economy, and the town had attracted a number of outside residents including, migrant agricultural workers and artisans, a number of national and international artists and intellectuals, and wealthy Mexico City residents who maintained large weekend homes. Those outsiders who tried to adapt to Tepoztlán's uniqueness and who were respectful of its customs and traditions were welcomed as "*tepoztinos*," those who did not would be forever "*fuereños*." If one's family was not from Tepoztlán, however, one could never become a true Tepozteco.

Until the movement succeeded in dislodging the PRI from its stranglehold on power in Tepoztlán and until national reforms sought to incrementally increase municipal autonomy, the governing system in Tepoztlán was tightly controlled by powerful members of the PRI based in Cuernavaca. The municipal president and council (*ayuntamiento*) constituted the local authorities. Although municipalities were theoretically autonomous and decentralized administrations, in practice they were very much part of a centralized, dependent system, because the state legislature oversaw and approved all municipal budgets. During the years of PRI political dominance, the governor traditionally dictated, or at least had a great influence over, the selection of local officials.[2] Historically, state governors had kept local governments weak by allowing the opposition to win some of the seats in the *Ayuntamiento*, so that decisions were difficult to carry out, thus making the municipal president dependent on his patron, the governor. In Tepoztlán, this structural weakness was further extended by the existence of the Commissioner for Communal Land Holdings, who oversaw the use of communally held land, which accounted for about 85 percent of municipal lands. This created an interesting dilemma for local politicians, because the municipal government could not carry out any projects on that land without the permission of the Commissioner of Communal Lands. Likewise, the Commissioner was dependent on the President and *Ayuntamiento* for funding. Historically these two entities, themselves characterized by internal corruption, had been at odds with each other over how to proceed, or how to split political and economic spoils of office, and thus, had contributed to keeping local government weak and dependent on the state government.[3]

As the golf course conflict in Tepoztlán came to a head in the mid 1990s, these historic divisions and structural weaknesses played important roles establishing the political environment. In the 1994 elections Governor Jorge Carrillo imposed Alejandro Morales as the official candidate for municipal president. Although a visible member of an important and apparently reformist political group in Tepoztlán, Morales nevertheless did not have the necessary support within the community or even within the local PRI to be a consensus candidate for office. The governor ignored the municipal PRI committee and backed Morales, who was forced to run under the registry of the Party of the Authentic Mexican Revolution (PARM), a satellite opposition party controlled by the state PRI. Maria Rosas (1997), who chronicled the conflict in Tepoztlán, speculates that "the governor had brought him to the presidency for the only reason of approving the Club and for putting a lid on the opposition as best as he could" (22). The opposition was headed by the PRD-endorsed Adela Bocanegra, who would later become the spokesperson for the anti-golf movement. Although she won the county seat outright, where fraud was harder to commit, she lost in the outlying villages where the state PRI machine reportedly bought votes for Morales in exchange for building materials and fertilizers. The absence of genuine local support, total dependency on the governor and strong opposition in the county seat greatly weakened Morales' political influence and would make the anti-golf movement bolder in its challenges.

The imposition of candidates was certainly not unique to the state of Morelos, and the challenge that the Tepoztecos would be able to mount to it was illustrative of political changes occurring in Mexico through the 1990's. While the PRI had successfully governed the country through an elaborate, corporate system of controls and rewards, that system was under great pressure by the end of 1994. The populist state was seriously weakened by neoliberal economic reforms that drastically reduced its ability to intervene directly in the economy, and subsequently its ability to provide for the various sectors of its political machine. At the same time, a growing pro-democracy movement headed institutionally by the PRD and various organizations in civil society were challenging the PRI's traditional methods of manipulating elections and applying repression on dissident activists. The emergence of the Zapatista Army for National Liberation (EZLN) in Chiapas in the beginning of 1994 and the ensuing organization of civil society to defend it, placed a further challenge to the PRI-State's ability to dictate the terms of political discourse. Finally, the peso crash of December 1994 and the economic chaos that followed raised serious questions about the wisdom of neoliberal economic reform and the direction for which the technocratic elite in Mexico City had opted. In other words, the rebellion in Tepoztlán would take place within a national context of growing and vocal dissatisfaction with the PRI model of governance.

The conflict also took place among global trends that were articulating demands around questions of difference and the fragmentation of national identities. Tepoztecos were certainly not immune to these tendencies. Although many Tepoztecos have a great deal of contact with people from outside their community either through work, interactions with tourists, or the media, there is a palpable ambivalence toward outsiders. Although this distrust has been documented for generations, it is clearly expressed through people's attitudes about tourism, which by the 1980s had become one of the most important and dynamic sectors of the local economy. On the positive side, tourism generates a considerable amount of income and jobs for townspeople. The entire town is literally transformed on weekends and holidays as thousands of people come from Mexico City, Cuernavaca and other areas. Also, the desire by outsiders to build weekend and vacation houses in the municipality has considerably elevated the price of land, and created many construction jobs. Many townspeople have taken advantage of this situation to increase their incomes, either through providing needed services or through selling overpriced real estate. Furthermore, the tourist industry, for the most part, continues to be locally owned and operated, meaning that much of the economic benefit and control over its development stays within the community. Finally, since some of the tourists who come to Tepoztlán are economic and political elites from the capital, many local politicians have been able to foment relationships with them in order to help them further themselves and make improvements in the town.

There are, however, many negative sides to the increasing importance of tourism as well. High real estate prices, for instance, while advantageous to the seller, make buying land out of reach for many Tepoztecos. Local planning authorities note that this selling of land has caused a scarcity of places for local inhabitants to live, putting pressure on delicate environmental areas as the "urban stain" creeps up into the mountains (Ortiz Rivera 1999). There are also frictions between tourists and local people in that tourists tend to be much richer than most Tepoztecos and many are foreigners, leading in some cases to serious misunderstandings and bad feelings. Some Tepoztecos complain that tourists, while welcome, often cause problems by not honoring local customs. As one resident explained, "Tepoztlán is a 'magical place' and has much to offer. What I don't like is when they leave trash behind and are disrespectful, but I don't think that they shouldn't come" (Interview 1998). This ambiguity has played a key role in debates within the town over the past 30 years as to how to best develop its natural resources, and would prove to be a pivotal issue in the town's approach to the country club problem.

The opening of the town to outside influences and new residents has contributed to the construction of a local "hybrid culture." It is not so much that tourists come and go, but rather that the extended contacts with other parts of the country and the world that tourism facilitates, along with the contacts that labor migration and mass communication create, has had a fundamental impact on the development of local culture in Tepoztlán. In many ways, Tepoztlán represents a highly diverse, multicultural community. People from a number of social positions and experiences live and work together constructing a multivocal cultural system. Within the region, there are *campesino* families who continue to speak Nahuatl and who participate in agricultural and small commercial ventures. At the same time, however, there is an increasing importance on professional education, and many families place great emphasis on their children's education as a means for them to get ahead in life. It is said around town, that every family has at least one member teaching some where in the state of Morelos and one member working somewhere in the United States as a day laborer.

The changing demographics and class status for long-time families is further complicated by a great increase in the municipality's population from outside sources. There is a sizable colony of working and poor families from Guerrero and Oaxaca who come to work as agricultural laborers or to sell artisan work in the sprawling tourist market. At the other end of the economic spectrum, a large number of families from more privileged backgrounds keep vacation homes in town, and many artists and intellectuals have found Tepoztlán's relative tranquility desirable for their work. Finally, followers of new age or hippie philosophies have come attracted by the natural beauty and alleged energetic properties of the mountains. These diverse sectors of the local population are constantly interacting with each other, each modifying the others' cultural logic and producing a unique local culture.

This local culture, of course, is not without its contradictions. In particular, and as would become very apparent during the conflict, there is much distrust of outsiders (even those that have lived there for years), and attempts by long time residents to distinguish between "true" Tepoztecos and more recent inhabitants.[4] Despite, or perhaps because of, these divisions and tensions between new and more established community members, there is a great deal of emphasis in Tepoztlán on maintaining what are seen as authentic traditions. Many view the practicing of these traditions as a means of maintaining a unique identity versus a tendency toward homogenization produced by state policies and global mass media. This nostalgia for tradition, however, is also very much influenced by people's more cosmopolitan experiences, which constantly renovate local customs and rituals and compete for the attention of younger residents.

The Proposal and Its Doubters

Against this backdrop, the Kladt-Sobrino Group (KS), a multinational real estate development corporation based in the state capital, Cuernavaca, drew up plans to build a mega tourist project centered on an exclusive country club and golf course. From the point of view of investors, the location was ideal as it was about an hour's drive outside of Mexico City in an area with a national reputation and infrastructure for tourism. The plan called to use 187.5 hectares of land purchased (with some dubious legality) by KS's predecessor Montecastillo in the 1960s. The $500 million endeavor was to include an eighteen-hole golf course designed by Jack Nicklaus, an 8,000 square meter clubhouse, 800 luxury hotel and condominium units, a heliport, an artificial lake and shopping areas. An office building dedicated to data processing to be built and operated by U.S.-based GTE, represented the project's attempt to integrate itself more fully into the growing information technology industry. KS quickly secured investors willing to purchase stock at U.S. $500,000, as the project seemed sound and the timing ideal for this type of investment. Additionally, KS worked diligently to sell the advantages of the club to local residents and to secure the needed regulatory assistance from public officials.

Although most local residents would not be able to take advantage of these new amenities, as the daily minimum wage in Morelos in 1995 was 17 pesos (approximately U.S. $2.25), the area would reap several important benefits. KS and the state government estimated that the country club would create 13,000 temporary construction jobs and almost 3,000 permanent jobs once the club opened. Fiscally, the company was committed to remitting to the municipality over 10 million pesos between the time construction was to begin in 1995 and the year 2000, after which the municipality would profit from nearly 800,000 pesos yearly in taxes. The company promised to update and improve the municipal infrastructure by constructing a 30,000-kilowatt electric substation, and regularizing the water, drainage and road systems.

State officials lauded the project as a development pole for the region. The governor, ex-general Jorge Carrillo Olea, wrote to the investors that, "my government will support all aspects of projects, such as this one, which join economic development with social benefits and ecological preservation. Support will consist of, among other things: 1.) the granting of state and municipal permits and licenses; 2.) the coordination of social groups; 3.) the necessary federal support. This project is a model for Morelos" (*Ayuntamiento* 1). This enthusiasm for the project was expressed in the context of a severe economic crisis in Mexico set off by the 1994 peso crash. Investments of this magnitude promising the levels of employment that it did were few and far between. Furthermore, it was being proposed for an area with few other comparative advantages with which to compete in the increasingly difficult world market. The state government, therefore, saw in this project a unique opportunity to align economic development more closely with transnational capital, hoping that such an alliance would facilitate future development.

In addition to the purported economic benefits, golf course supporters argued that the project would also bring substantial environmental improvements to the area. The third of three environmental impact statements commissioned by KS (the first two found serious ecological problems), concluded that, among other things, the golf course would reclaim land that had already been deforested and essentially abandoned. It argued that the golf course would not replace native plants, which had been destroyed long ago by previous agricultural and extractive practices, and that the new grass and tree plantings would help fortify the local ecosystem. It countered previous studies' assertions about potential harm, arguing that proposed pesticides posed no risk to the human, animal or plant populations. The golf course, it claimed, would not seriously affect the local water supply, nor would the moving of tons of rock and construction of walls negatively affect the environmental balance (Icaza Longoria 1995). The state's environmental protection agency also supported the project in terms of its environmental benefits for the area. Pointing out that golf courses are industries without smokestacks, Ursula Oswald, the head of the agency, declared in a radio interview that "golf clubs are magnificent for the environment," in that they create more humid conditions through evaporation, provide for the flourishing of different plant species and allow a space for birds and other animals to prosper (Rosas 1997, 69). KS and its supporters, therefore, were able to call theirs an ecological project, designed to reclaim unused and degraded lands that were unable to support other types of profitable activities.

Even the conservative bishop of Cuernavaca, Luis Reynoso Cervantes called the project "a gift from God" for the town and the region (Rosas 1997, 32). Rumored to be an avid golfer himself, the bishop continually backed the state government's and KS's attempts to win support for the project. As the conflict intensified, he openly criticized the roles of the parish priest and the Base Ecclesial Communities, who were adamantly opposed to the project, for promoting "unrest and violence" in townspeople. He urged people to make a "rational" choice and to not turn this heavenly gift away, because it would provide numerous economic, social and environmental benefits to the town.

Many Tepoztecos were originally intrigued by the idea, particularly as they considered short-term economic gains for themselves. KS approached groups of people and tried to convince them that the project would benefit their particular interest. Certainly, builders would benefit from the construction, taxi drivers from having a base there, and local restaurants from having a branch inside the club. In the beginning there was only limited opposition. In a climate of generally bad economic news and poor job prospects, the possibility of a multimillion-dollar investment in their town and the promise of thousands of jobs appealed to many residents.

A politically and socially influential faction within the town, which had successfully defeated several other big tourist development projects over the past thirty years, however, had their doubts about this project. Their skepticism was further fueled when they saw how quickly and profoundly the state government was backing the project.[5] Beginning with a group of eight, the opposition began researching the potential pitfalls of this kind of project and organizing against the club. This original group in many ways reflected the changing face of the Tepoztlán community. Among its members were a doctor, who had worked for years in another state, a teacher, a taxi driver, a small landholder, a law student, and a community organizer who worked for a statewide group in Cuernavaca. Chronicler María Rosas describes the root of the opposition as, "Only the old *campesinos*, communal land holders, and some women; only in some teachers and a few professionals, in some social activists, was there a deep concern from the beginning about the club, and a capacity to see it as if it were already built" (Rosas 1997, 19). As people began talking to each other many questions began to arise, however, and there was increasing concern about the sustainability of the project. What would happen to the jobs after the construction? What kinds of permanent jobs would really be created? Would people actually get the higher paying construction jobs, after all, "nobody comes and just offers you a job, you have to go out and find it" (Cedillo Méndez 1999). People expressed great concern that they had invested considerable effort in providing professional education for their children, and believed that the kinds of manual jobs that KS was offering were not adequate to provide for the sustainable growth of the town's inhabitants. As one person expressed, "they were not promising the management and accounting jobs, just the cleaning and grounds keeping ones" (Interview 1999).

There were also troubling questions about the land. KS was proposing to build the golf club on parts of the Tepozteco National Park and the protected Ajusco-Chichinautzin Ecological Corridor. Also, much of the land that KS owned had allegedly been acquired illegally. The company's predecessor, Montecastillo had purchased the lands in the 1960s, but much of the territory was considered to be communal and, therefore, could not have been sold in the first place. Furthermore, small private landholders claimed that they had been fraudulently forced to sell to Montecastillo under threats of having their parcels enclosed and not granted access to them. Some people began questioning how putting up walls and fences would change the culture of the town. The Tepozteco Park and the communal lands had always been opened and shared, and by separating them off, they would be profoundly altering the ways in which people related to the land and to each other.

Finally, and perhaps most importantly in the end, there was great concern about water (Giménez 1995).[6] Tepoztlán suffers from an approximately eight month dry season each year, when there is virtually no rain. Providing enough water for town residents is already a very serious problem by the end of the dry season, when it is drastically rationed. The amounts of water that the golf course and the accompanying housing and industrial units would require equaled about one half of the town's daily water supply. People simply did not believe company and government reports that showed how they would acquire water from different aquifers. Using that much water to keep grass green seemed foolish, at best, to most town residents. International environmental groups, such as Greenpeace and the Global Anti-Golf Network, began advising the growing opposition movement about water use and other ecological pitfalls of golf courses and luxury resort development (Cedillo Méndez 1999). Activists collected information about pesticide and fertilizer use and their subsequent run-off into local food and water supplies to bolster their arguments against its construction.

Citing their concerns about land and water use, therefore, activists, calling themselves the Committee for Tepozteco Unity (CUT) began publicly voicing their opposition to the golf course in late 1994. The group grew beyond its original eight members to include about thirty people, representing different occupations, political parties and geographic areas, and they divided their work among committees for communication, research, logistics, legal matters, negotiation and organizing. Because the core group of activists was so diverse, they were able to access the media and solidarity networks outside of Tepoztlán, as well as take advantage of internal communication networks by convincing neighborhood religious leaders, the *mayordomos*, of the justness of their cause. They met privately and then in increasingly large demonstrations with the municipal president, Alejandro Morales, and the rest of the municipal council to make sure that they would not issue needed land-use permits. The land that KS wanted to use was technically designated as agricultural or forest land. In order to build on it, therefore, its designation needed to be changed and the municipal council was the only governmental entity with the authority to make those changes. At the same time, activists pursued other means to ensure that the club would not be built. Lawsuits were filed in civil and agrarian court citing the illegal acquisition of communal land thirty years earlier. Although the suits were initially dismissed, they slowed the process down by issuing temporary injunctions against construction.[7]

While the courts were contemplating the land ownership question, the CUT publicized contradictions within the various environmental impact studies done for the project. Two studies were done for KS in 1994, and in both cases the project was rejected because of its effects on the local water table and its disruption of the ecological corridor were deemed to be unacceptable. In July 1995, however, the National Ecological Institute (INE), approved a study prepared by the Autonomous University of the State of Morelos (UAEM), the Metropolitan Autonomous University — Xochimilco (UAMX) and the Mexican Institute of Water Technology (IMTA), which found that the project would bring ecological and social benefits to the area, and discarded the earlier findings that the water consumed by the golf course would endanger the water supply to the valley.[8] Because of these findings, and despite the continuing legal concerns, however, INE issued a temporary permit to Tzematzin, KS's construction company, to allow them to begin construction as soon as the municipal council issued a change in land-use permit. With that decision, the opposition's legal channels to stopping the golf course rested solely on the Municipal President and Council denying the needed permits.

Distillation of Opposing Political Cultures

In this moment before the conflict resulted in a profound disruption of everyday life, we can see the alignment not only of various political forces, but also the distillation of several key cultural positions. KS and the state represented the neoliberal project, in which they imputed meaning on places and practices through the mechanisms of the marketplace. They believed that social relationships were all ultimately economic ones, and that actors should make rational decisions based on the logic of self-interest. Although residents in Tepoztlán were, of course, also embedded in those discourses of modernity, the CUT made arguments against the golf course which were simultaneously modern, that is dependent upon scientific and economic rationale, and markedly non-modern as well, having to do with relationships developed outside of the market place. In their equations of costs and benefits, the Tepozteco opposition explicitly included not just economic matters, but also issues of social relations, cultural heritage, environmental sustainability and history. These cultural alignments can be seen very clearly in the ways in which the parties approached the question and meaning of land in this dispute.

To begin with, the golf course involved not only the legal but also the symbolic control over a large expanse of ostensibly public land. As noted above, many people in Tepoztlán considered the property to belong to a larger body of communal land, and did not recognize the legitimacy of KS's claim to it. Furthermore, parts of the property are within the national park and therefore are, and ought to be, open to public use. Many people used those public, open and undeveloped lands to graze animals or to travel through on their way to work their own fields. What was at stake, therefore, in the meaning of this land had to do with a fundamental conflict between private and public (or communal) property.

The corporation, KS, was attempting to mark this space as private, as a part of the modern world in which land is a commodity that can be bought, sold and owned. They intended to carry out this marking in several ways. First, they were going to physically alter it to fit the needs not of the people who usually live there, but rather those who could pay to use it. They were going to level it, plant specific kinds of imported grass and other plants, build dwellings, roads, a helipad, a pond etc. In doing so, they were responding purely to market demands. Since the Tepoztecos did not have the money to instill or preserve those meanings on it that they attributed to it, the market would dictate how this land should be signified.

Secondly, they planned to build a wall around it. A wall is, of course, a construction with a rich symbolic heritage. It is simultaneously an artificial attempt to contain natural space and processes like the spread of certain plant and animal species, while at the same time it makes a clear distinction between human populations. It contributes to a sense of mystery, a further othering, of two distinct peoples: those who live inside (but who can go out) and those who live outside (but who cannot come in). This class distinction has become increasingly prevalent in Mexico (and most of the rest of the world) throughout the last several decades. Although class markers of separation circulate continually throughout various social interactions and can be seen in dress, language, food, consumption etc., the building of walls was an attempt by KS to add this physical space, which was public but which was to become private, to that list of class markers. It served as another reminder of distinction and of the impossibility of meaningful and egalitarian interaction.

The construction of a luxury golf course in the middle of an otherwise relatively poor area highlighted the extreme differences in wealth that have been made more acute in Latin America because of neoliberal restructuring of the region's economy. A golf course, itself, epitomizes a global bourgeois culture that attempts to impose itself regardless of territorial limitations or local concerns. KS was proposing, in effect, an enclave community that would be separated from the rest of the population. This insulated community would enjoy all of the benefits of an elite culture (golf, green space, comfortable accommodations, shopping and restaurants) without having to interact with the rest of the local population, other than in terms of employer/employee. The way in which KS proposed its project to the townspeople further underscored its connection with global capitalist culture. The benefits to the town were delineated in terms of money and jobs. Groups of people were approached and sold on the idea, based on how it would benefit them personally. In its presentations to various groups of Tepoztecos, KS "never asked for opinions nor much less for the support of Tepoztlán. These were merely informative meetings that already took for granted the realization of the project without any commitment from the town" (Demesa Padilla 1998, 27). In other words, KS was using a top-down model of development, one in which control of capital granted it the right to make all of the decisions. Francisco Kladt further illustrated this attitude in a meeting with the Commissioner of

Communal Lands, Abraham López Cruz, in which López Cruz offered to back the project if the holders of communal lands would receive some financial benefits in return. This money would allow them to build and operate green houses and nurseries to offset the ecological damage of the club. Kladt responded to his offer of partnership by sarcastically asking him, "what money are you going to use to get in?" (Rosas 1997, 18). With that snub, López Cruz and the organization he controlled joined the opposition (temporarily, anyway). While capital defines corporate relationships, many townspeople had other criteria for establishing and evaluating their social relations.

The golf course and the meanings associated with it were meant to signal progress for the area. By mediating relations between townspeople and global capital, it was presented as the best way to resolve deep economic and social problems. From the perspective of KS, the only way for society to go forward was to support the kinds of progress associated with this penetration of capital into otherwise apparently undeveloped local communities. Movement leader, Gerardo Demesa, a teacher and leader of the teachers' union, reports that in one of the meetings to which he was invited in early 1995, an official of KS accused him of being a bad teacher for "opposing the progress of his town," by not backing the construction of the golf club (Demesa Padilla 1998, 28). This sense of progress, which has no space for dissent, also has little concern for the past. Neoliberal ideology looks primarily for short term gain, and therefore in their attempted sale of the project, KS officials never mentioned the town's history nor wanted to engage in questions of long term sustainability. Global capital is a mobile entity, and therefore in terms of costs and benefits, long term costs and old debts tend to be ignored, because the owners of capital can always move it someplace else if local communities become uncooperative.

The state likewise showed an adherence to this neoliberal ideology. Governor Carrillo indicated clearly that the position of the state was to approve necessary paperwork and control social mobilizations in order to guarantee a safe climate for investment. His lack of respect for internal democratic processes also fit with the overall approach toward social relations of global capital and an authoritarian political system. While he placed a great deal of emphasis on superficial legalities, his willingness to impose a weak political leader so as to be able to manipulate him and, he hoped, control the situation, points to a fundamental disrespect for local decision making. Rather than engaging the opposition to the golf course in a dialogue about municipal development, he engaged in a series of attacks on them, charging them with doing "a great deal of damage to

Morelos." He lamented in an interview, "it makes me sad that this project today, another one tomorrow and another one the day after will fail because of the manipulating protagonism of small groups ... that are playing with the generation of jobs ... by people who have nothing to do with the need for employment" (Miranda Rodríguez 1995, 7). Furthermore, according to Gerardo Demesa, the state government attempted to control these opposition forces by convincing "natural leaders" of the town to back the project. When these leaders insisted that a general assembly was necessary to approve the project, for instance, one of the officials "stood up furiously and yelled 'we aren't playing, the Golf Club will be built, like it or not!'" (27). For the state, the short term goal of jobs and investment outweighed the concerns of local residents about long term sustainability and maintenance of long standing social and cultural relations. In the view of state officials, a small group must have been manipulating the opposition for some undefined purpose, as opposition itself was necessarily illogical and irrational. For the state, opposition to this investment project amounted to something that had to be controlled and eliminated, rather than a force with which to negotiate or take seriously.

The underlying meanings of the construction proposals and the state's support for the project were not lost on the Tepozteco opposition. Although they were concerned about a number of aspects of the project, one of their clear objections was that they were going to be stuck between two wealthy enclaves. The southern part of the municipality had been effectively colonized by Mexico City elites over the previous generation. These part time residents had little contact with other Tepoztecos, except for acquiring supplies and services. People complained that they did not participate in community relations, and they resented that lack of participation. They feared that construction of this resort in the northeast sector of the municipality would further strain those internal social relations, which most residents highly valued. They saw, therefore, in the construction of the project, an inscription of class and other cultural values that were incongruent with ways in which they defined their community. The building of the wall around the resort would not only have prevented them from using a significant part of what should be the public space of the national park, but it also emphasized the exclusionary nature of a deeply polarized economy and society. To make matters worse, the bulk of the land that KS wanted to signify with this neoliberal notion of "private property" was allegedly communal. Since so much of the territory of Tepoztlán is considered communal, publicly owned space plays an important role in determining Tepozteco identities of collectivity (Lomnitz 1982, 65; *Batalla* 1995; Rosas 1997, 19). Communally owned land, in effect, strengthens all

Tepoztecos' connection to land issues and to each other, because they bear collective rights and privileges to it. The attempts of KS to convert it into private property by declaring ownership to it, altering its appearance and use, and physically separating it from the rest of the communal property was clearly seen as a threat to a way of life constructed over the meaning inherent in collectively and publicly owning land.

Similarly, the fears expressed by Tepoztecos about the use of water reflected both pragmatic concerns as well as those centered on the *meaning* of water. Like land, water was generally understood to be a public resource. By laying claim to half of the town's water supply to irrigate their course, KS was attempting to privatize, that is take out of circulation, a significant proportion of this public good. Residents were concerned that this lowering of the town's water supply would cause hardship for people who need to use it in their everyday lives, particularly given its scarcity during the long dry season.

At the same time, however, there is another story about water and communal identity that KS ignored in its attempts to secure exclusive use of it. In the 1960s, the federal Hydraulic Resources agency hoped to meet increased needs for water by installing a new piping system that would deliver water directly into people's homes. Previous to this, residents collected water from public taps. Although there was widespread skepticism from the beginning that such a system would work, doubt turned to anger when, after a few weeks of operation, the whole system ran dry. The spring from which they drew their water simply could not handle the demand caused by the newly constructed estates with their swimming pools and extensive gardens. After the agency refused to stop pumping water from the spring, townspeople took over the installation and destroyed it (Lomnitz 1982, 205).[9] KS, in its proposal to use large quantities of water for a very private population, therefore, not only threatened people's access to it, but it also touched upon an issue of signification, in which people associated access to water as a public and collective right, which was being continually threatened by the influx of population associated with exclusive development projects.

The opposition at this time, therefore, was beginning to stake out its political concerns and cultural positions in terms of collective rather than individual rights. While the golf course at first did appeal to people individually and in terms of short-term gain, as they began talking to each other, they began to have doubts. The opposition to the golf club, in other words, started revolving around collective, rather than individualist perspectives. Many activists involved from the beginning pointed to their need to hold public meetings to decide what should be done. This contrasts sharply with the divided and backroom deal-making with which the company and the state attempted to resolve questions. Rather than pressure public officials with secret promises and threats, activists convoked a public meeting in March 1995. Five thousand people, representing different geographic and social sectors, attended and witnessed the president and *Ayuntamiento* sign a document promising to oppose the golf course and explicitly pledging not to authorize any changes in land use permits (Ayuntamiento Libre 1996; Rosas 1997; Demesa Padilla 1998).

This use of democratic decision-making not only corresponded to the political juncture in Mexico, in which opposition groups and leading media figures were hotly debating the need for and the possible forms of democratic change, but also to deeper cultural processes. Issues of attachment to the land and mountains of Tepoztlán, both as a means of identity as well as a means through which family incomes and posterity are guaranteed, began to circulate and gain currency among members of the opposition and the general population as well. In the statement signed on 18 March 1995, the popular assembly noted that KS has been holding meetings with government officials and other citizens "arguing the benefits ... for the company without caring about the ecological, social and political damage, not to mention the economic damage that the project will bring with it to this municipality" (Ayuntamiento Libre 1996). As KS intensified its campaign, "Communal landholders, *ejiditarios* and some others elaborated informative flyers that made use of the decrees which protect the Tepozteco (National Park)" (Rosas 19). People in the town who were associated with protecting the land, in other words, began to remind their fellow community members of their collective inheritance and responsibility toward the land. "People were talking about their communal lands, more than 80 percent of the lands of the whole municipality, that, lost and recovered in a process of centuries, are their inheritance and their patrimony" (Rosas 1997, 19). This close association with local concerns began the process of positioning people in the town to oppose the construction of the golf course not only in terms of resource protection, but also in terms of preserving who they were. It brought to the fore the ambiguities associated with tourism, and lead to the crystallization of a Tepozteco identity that sought the furtherance of democratic control over those decisions that had a direct impact on people in their daily lives.

Betrayal and Rebellion, August–September 1995

These tensions building around the golf course throughout 1994 and 1995 erupted into open revolt on 24 August 1995. Despite repeated promises to the contrary, municipal president Alejandro Morales and a majority of the municipal council quietly approved the necessary land use permits for KS to begin construction on the golf course and subsequently for federal and state agencies to issue building permits that same day. Word spread quickly of this decision and within hours of the permits being signed, thousands of angry townspeople had gathered in the plaza in front of the municipal offices. Although Morales and the Council had already fled Tepoztlán out of fear for their safety, the gathered crowd quickly made effigies of their elected officials, with signs calling them traitors hanging around their necks and pesos spilling out of their pockets, and hung them from the building,

From that day, until late April 1996, the town began to meet in assemblies nightly to decide on their next steps. As a community, the assembly decided overwhelmingly to reaffirm their opposition to the golf course and to take whatever steps were necessary to prevent its construction. They also decided to authorize the CUT to be their representative to the government in negotiating an end to the stand off. A nightly guard was formed to address the fear that the state police would try to enter the town to either arrest movement leaders or provoke some sort of violence. Each of the town's eight neighborhoods took one night to gather a patrol and take charge of security. The CUT named a team of negotiators to meet with the governor and other state officials in order to convince them to officially dissolve the municipal council and to call for new elections as soon as possible. The government, however, refused to negotiate on this point, instead threatening townspeople with legal actions for trespassing on government property.

On the morning of 3 September, rumors began to run through the town that state riot police had taken up positions around the house of the Commissioner of Communal Landholdings, Abraham López Cruz, and that an assembly of Tepozteco Communal Landholders was taking place. This came as a great and troubling surprise to many of the actual landholders, who had not been informed of the meeting. People turned out in great numbers, armed with rocks and sticks to find out what was going on. As they became aware that there were a number of state officials at the meeting, as well as written and broadcast press, the protesters realized that the meeting was being held to approve the use of communal land for the construction of the golf course. After a brief skirmish with the police, the townspeople chased off the alleged *comuneros*, who had been brought in from other areas of the state to pose for the press as Tepoztecos who supported the golf club and to ratify the change in land use permits. They also captured four high ranking state and party officials and held them captive for two days while the CUT negotiated with the governor.[10] As a result of police complicity in the meeting, the police and other state officials were expelled from the town, because residents believed that they would be unsafe with them operating within municipal limits.[11] Also, the CUT built stone and barbed wire barricades to all of the town's entrances to monitor visitors and ensure that police were unable to enter unimpeded. These barricades were staffed night and day by both men and women armed with poles, spoons and rocks.

In exchange for the prisoners, the governor agreed to relieve Alejandro Morales of his duties, dissolve the municipal council and convoke new elections. Furthermore, he conceded to suspend legal action against activists on charges of kidnapping and illegal use of government property and to begin discussing the cancellation of the golf course. The "guests" were released on 5 September, and the governor promptly reneged on all of his promises. Instead, more arrest warrants were issued, while judicial police[12] snuck into town to spy on people and to provoke incidents attesting to the lack of law and order. Alejandro Morales, who barely escaped capture on the 3rd, was given an office in Cuernavaca, where he assured the press that "the troublemakers will be beaten in a few days" (Rosas 1997, 28).

It became apparent that the state government would not negotiate in good faith, both through the governor's unwillingness to keep his promises and because he sent negotiators of "third and fourth rank," with no ability to make decisions (Demesa Padilla 1998, 41). The CUT had been carrying out the negotiations on behalf of the town, but since it lacked any legal authority, the municipal-wide assembly decided to hold elections to name a provisional president and municipal council to continue negotiations, and see to the day-to-day business of government in town until the situation was resolved. CUT leaders had both ideological and pragmatic reasons to push for a provisional government. On the one hand, some state officials and their supporters in the press were accusing them of being a front for the PRD, interested only in gaining the political power that they had failed to win in elections the previous year. They wanted, therefore, to prove that they (the leadership) were not trying to win power for themselves. None of the thirty or so leaders of the CUT, therefore, ran for office. Pragmatically, they saw running the municipal government and running the protest movement to be two distinct, although perhaps related, tasks. By forming a municipal government, they hoped that they could restore some sense of normalness to the running of everyday life, while allowing movement leaders to continue focusing on their protest strategies. Given the lack of response to the multiple petitions to call for new legal elections, the CUT set new elections for 24 September. They based their action on Article 39 of the Constitution, which affirms that, "national sovereignty resides essentially and originally in the people. The people have at all times the inalienable right to alter or modify their form of government," and on the Mexican legal tradition of "uses and customs," under which indigenous communities are allowed to select their own leadership according to their specific social and cultural norms.[13]

The week before the elections, *mayordomos*, who had been giving moral and communicative support to the movement, used their prestige to convoke neighborhood assemblies to nominate representatives to be placed on the ballot. In the elections, the seven highest polling candidates from a field of twenty-eight would be named to the municipal council. The person to receive the most votes would automatically become municipal president. The ballots consisted of photographs, names and addresses of the candidates. Party affiliation was not placed on the ballot, and candidates were not allowed to represent any political parties. Each night, during the changing of the guard at the municipal palace, candidates were given an opportunity to introduce themselves and to explain their vision of municipal government and their strategy for fighting the Golf Club. The balloting was held according to federal election norms in which registered voters had to present their voting credential and, upon voting, had their thumbs dyed in indelible black ink. Ballots were secretly marked, deposited in clear plastic boxes, and publicly counted as soon as the polls closed. Civic Alliance, a non-governmental organization dedicated to protecting a free and fair vote, witnessed the elections at the request of the CUT and attested to their fairness and transparency.[14] After the state refused to recognize the validity of their elections, "in a general assembly the town determined that it was autonomous and that the Provisional Council would be the Free, Constitutional and Popular *Ayuntamiento* of Tepoztlán" (Demesa Padilla 1998, 41). The new officials were sworn in on 30 September, and the *Ayuntamiento Libre* began its tenure as the governing body of Tepoztlán.

The seating of the *Ayuntamiento Libre*, however, did not help in stabilizing the situation in Tepoztlán, as the crisis deepened over the next several months. The points of contention between the residents of Tepoztlán and the state government continued to grow. To the cancellation of the golf course, the CUT now added the dropping of criminal charges against protesters and the recognition of the *Ayuntamiento Libre* as the legitimate governing body in Tepoztlán. The state, arguing that a small handful of radicals had manipulated the situation in Tepoztlán, refused to concede to any of their demands, claiming that the protesters had disrupted the rule of law, and that a return to legality was needed before any substantive discussions could take place. For the Tepoztecos, who were now using the slogan "All of Tepoztlán is the CUT," the conflict had moved beyond a very local dispute about land use issues, to now call into question the right of centralized authorities to dictate the rules of the political game. The conflict, as one activist noted at the time, had indeed moved beyond the golf course problem, and would require a more comprehensive solution.

The activists in Tepoztlán were very much aware that they were precipitating a breach in everyday life by occupying the *Ayuntamiento*, taking hostages, holding elections and swearing in new officials. This disruption was a deliberate means to protest the inadequacies of the asymmetrical power relationships that had led to the conflict. By breaching accepted norms of behavior, they were contesting the routines of everyday life and forcing everyone involved to explicitly interrogate the meanings behind the subconscious acceptance of authority and the inequality of social relations. But, part of the goal of movement participants, besides the fulfillment of their immediate demands, was also a return to normalness; that is, a resolution of the conflict that would allow for the smooth functioning of everyday life, something that the present situation made impossible.

In order to force the more profound resolution that activists were seeking, it was necessary to clearly define sides and to force other residents, as well as state officials, potential allies and consumers of mass media to stop everyday life in order to consider the meanings and social relationships often times disguised by routine. If everyday life, with its obedience to authority and procedures, were allowed to continue, the golf course would inevitably be built, because regular citizens had no automatic or clear voice in those decisions. Gerardo Demesa, one of the leaders of the CUT, describes the decision to take over the municipal offices:

> In that meeting, the council had given written permission for the Golf Club to begin construction, betraying their town.... The Committee (immediately) ... convoked the town to a public assembly to let them know about this betrayal. From then on the town was alert and waiting in every sense, and as a concrete response decided to take the municipal palace and to disown the municipal authorities. This act took place on the 24th of August 1995 and in this moment guards were mounted 24 hours a day in the neighborhoods, *colonias* and communities.... Banners were then hung on the municipal building that expressed the rejection of the construction of the Golf Club. In this way, from the fabricated betrayal of the council, an insurrec-

tionary movement rose and the idea of total struggle began [Demesa Padilla 1998, 30].

Demesa's description clearly shows that those on the inside of the movement leadership realized that they were crossing a boundary that would seriously disrupt the day-to-day functioning of the town. His qualification of Morales' actions as a "betrayal to the town"[15] clarifies the antagonistic relationship that existed between the citizens and the state, represented by the "traitorous" municipal council. This antagonistic relationship implies that normal relations would not be possible. His next description of the population as being "alert" and "waiting" suggests that the passivity associated with everyday life had now passed. In our everyday lives, while we may be alert, we generally feel relatively certain that we will be secure in our persons and that the day's events will unfold in a routine manner. We do not generally go about our normal routines anxious about the rules of the game, not knowing what to expect next. The "concrete response" upon which the Tepoztecos embarked deepened the sense that everyday life would become elusive. Taking over the municipal palace, while a common tactic particularly around issues of electoral fraud, both in Tepoztlán and in many other municipalities, indicated that the norms of behavior between civil society and the state had been disrupted. Rather than the building being occupied by the state, it was now occupied by elements of civil society who were opposed to the state's vision of nation and order. The banners that were hung and the graffiti that was applied to the building further changed the meaning of the building. Rather than representing the bureaucratic control of the state over the population, the building quite literally expressed the rejection of that "normal" relationship.

Furthermore, the disowning of the municipal authorities in this case was an extralegal maneuver, one which would not be recognized by the state and one which would further deepen the split between the state and civil society in the quotidian functioning of relations. By breaking their relations with the state system, the Tepoztecos blocked the recognized channels of mediation between themselves as a civil society and the state. This would result in a very hostile response from the state government, including the cutting off of funds, the disruption of services and eventually legal and physical assaults against townspeople. Again, under the rules of everyday life, although the state may not necessarily be friendly, there are certain assumptions, upon which people depend, particularly that the state will not turn its repressive forces against them and that it will abide by the rule of law. The dismissal of the municipal council permitted the state to ignore those normal rules of behavior and target the entire population for retribution and discipline.

Finally, in Demesa's description, he places the formation of civil guards as an integral part of this break with the state. While there were certainly some well-grounded fears of a police intervention in the town, he places such importance on this aspect of the breach to further indicate that the usual rules of the game had been suspended. He is indicating the seriousness with which the town had disrupted every day life, namely to the point that they needed to protect themselves from reprisals. He is also highlighting that citizens were taking on some of the prime functions of the state, particularly the protection of law and order. Not only, therefore, had there been a disruption of everyday life, but there had even been a reversal of usual roles: instead of the state protecting citizens and monopolizing the legitimate use of force, citizens were protecting themselves from the state and assuming for themselves that legitimacy.

A second symbolically laden and illustrative event was the inauguration of the *Ayuntamiento Libre*, which again underscored the break in routine state-society relations and showed the Tepoztecos' desire to affirm their autonomy and establish some sort of normalcy.[16] They reworked the state rituals of the transfer of power to reflect the cultural specificity of their community and to symbolically enact the right of the population to name their authorities regardless of the state's desires. The ceremony was presided over by the Tepozteco King, the foundational figure in the town's mythology. In this ceremony, the King processed through the main square, accompanied by an entourage of young "maidens" bearing burning incense, and took his place on the stage. After saying a few words of greeting in Nahuatl, the ceremony was turned over to the moderator who addressed the large crowd, and informed them that because the state government was unwilling to participate in this process, it was up to the townspeople themselves to administer the oath of office. He reminded the audience that the only reason that they had gotten this far was because of the "unified and dignified voice" that said "no to the golf course," and since they were the ones responsible for bringing democracy to the town, they should administer the oath. The newly elected officials were to serve the citizens of Tepoztlán and it was they, the citizens, who were ultimately responsible for the success or failure of the democratic experiment. The audience then became active participant in the ritual by reading out loud the oath of office, to which the new officials swore. The Tepozteco King then gave a speech in Nahuatl, which was translated into Spanish since most of the citizens only speak Spanish. In his speech, the King warned the citizens and the new officials to protect the town from outsiders, to "be aware of lights that are not stars" and in so doing to honor their ancestral gods which have protected them and their land for so many centuries. He then turned his mace, as the symbol of political authority, over to the new municipal president, Lázaro Rodríguez, who promised to not give up in his fight against the golf course. Rodríguez, it is important to note, bears a resemblance to, and came dressed as, the revolutionary hero Emiliano Zapata, as a reminder of the important radical Zapatista heritage in the region.

This scene composes a snap shot of the symbolic reinscription of public spaces and rituals being undertaken by the CUT. The appearance of the Tepozteco King and his use of Nahuatl in the ceremony, rather than just being a simulation of some long past history, speaks to what Bonfil Batalla (1987) describes as "deep Mexico," those non–European symbols and practices which continue to be an important part of Mesoamerican culture despite five centuries of European colonialism. Although it is usually a submerged identity, movement activists brought it out into the public here as a means of reminding people that they are different from those who are trying to impose their economic and political projects on them. Although indigenous culture may not always be a very public one in Tepoztlán (in fact it represents a very small minority of the municipality's population), it nevertheless is a part of a complex hybridized culture, and the movement was trying to raise it out of its often times hidden environment to highlight it as an important aspect of people's identity.

Standing next to the king, the municipal president was very clearly and obviously invoking Zapata. The image of Zapata accompanied the Tepoztecos in all of their public demonstrations, and, in general, is a highly charged figure whose meaning is constantly contested between the state and opposition groups. He represents the great liberator of the poor in both official nationalist discourse as well as local mythologies. Rodríguez's representation of Zapata here was a demonstration of the public taking of power by those traditionally oppressed and marginalized sectors of society with whom the movement was attempting to identify. It was, in other words, a public reclamation from the state of this important national and local icon.

Finally, surrounding the stage was an audience of regular people who had been converted into active participants in this drama. This public involvement of the audience/witness broke simultaneously with the usual codes of theater and politics, by directly involving them in the unfolding of the drama, thus reinforcing the newly inscribed political meanings of public spaces by non-elite social sectors. It also dramatized the Zapatista slogan, "lead by obeying," that was popular among social activists in the wake of the Chiapas uprising.

The appearance of the public space in which these events was taking place was also transformed by the movement, as the CUT attempted to inscribe new meanings onto the commonly shared areas of the town. The Municipal Palace served not only as the place from where the new government was operating, it was also the focal point of many public activities. By the end of September 1995, almost every available space on the building has an anti-golf or pro–Tepoztlán slogan spray-painted on it. Writing on the walls declares that "Tepoztlán will win, because it is within the law" and warns that "If Zapata were alive, Carrillo wouldn't be." Banners are hung from the pillars and windows with similar slogans; most are souvenirs from the many marches that the town has undertaken to Cuernavaca and Mexico City. The former municipal officials hang in effigy, with signs saying "traitor" hanging around their necks. There are also two murals painted near the main entrance by the prominent political cartoonists El Fisgón and Rius. One shows KS as the devil playing golf with Carrillo as his caddie. The other has a Tepozteco saying that "Dignity is worth more than a damn golf course," and "If it is so urgent, let them build it at Los Pinos" (the President's official residence). Inside the *Ayuntamiento*, the governor's portrait has been removed and there is a painting depicting Zapata, Che Guevara and Subcomandante Marcos together. Besides the business of the nightly assemblies, the *Ayuntamiento* has been the stage for many other performances including musicians and even comedians who have come to help keep up the spirits of the Tepoztecos in their struggle. It has in many ways become a true public space in which community members come to express themselves, debate options and to make decisions, despite historical internal differences.

This creation and use of public space became a way in which partisan political manipulation was kept to a minimum, because secretly negotiated deals were not accepted. Government proposals were explained and examined carefully, and no decisions were made until the assembly ratified them. Many times, negotiating teams brought back what they though were good proposals, only to be told, "Tell the government that these are not advances; we'll continue like we are, *¡Qué viva el No al Club!*" (Rosas 1997, 95). They reaffirmed their mission and continued to deepen their identities as united, rebellious Tepoztecos. In other words, the political actions of defying the state government and searching for a democratic alternative found themselves expressed in the very use and appearance of public space.

While the nightly assemblies certainly served extremely practical purposes as a means to disseminate information, to build support and to debate strategies, they also served important symbolic functions. The

Top and bottom: Municipal offices, Tepoztlán, March 1996.

popular assembly has traditionally served the Tepozteco community as a means to make difficult decisions and to overrule decisions of the municipal president. It is very much linked to the history of collective land ownership in Tepoztlán, and as such the assembly served to enforce that bond of distinction that the CUT was utilizing in its rhetoric. As one activist explained, through the assemblies "we were recovering our democracy and our dignity by going back to our old traditions, the uses and customs of our ancestors" (Interview 1999). They strengthened the sense of community that had brought people together in the first place, and came to symbolize the larger issues of democracy that underlined the issues in the conflict.

At a more pragmatic level, they provided the community with the means to practice direct democratic politics. Within the parameters of being against the golf course, everyone's voice could be heard and everyone could share in the sometimes-anguishing decisions that needed to be made. Particularly at the beginning, the popular assemblies served as the mechanism for airing opinions and arriving at decisions. In the month between the taking of the municipal offices and the seating of the *Ayuntamiento Libre*, Quero (2003) notes that, "The assembly developed on the plaza with wide participation of the people but with a great deal of disorder, without a previous agenda or a general theme ... at this time, representative groups were being put together, tasks were split up, guards and checkpoints organized, reports given about the latest actions and diverse political questions, from opinions to rumors to the latest news" (158). It is also in this early phase that the CUT clearly became the organizing force and representative of the assembly. Furthermore, the location of these assemblies was of fundamental importance. By taking place in front of the *Ayuntamiento*, they further emphasized the new, democratic, signification in contrast to the old politics represented by the PRI and the deposed municipal council. Politics, in other words, took place *in front of* rather than *inside of* the building. By holding their assemblies outside of the building, the Tepoztecos were distancing politics from the closed-door style with which it is often associated. Public space became the appropriate place to discuss and practice politics.

The space that was occupied by the assemblies, besides being directly in front of the *Ayuntamiento* is also the area occupied by the biweekly market and the zócalo. It is a space that is associated with, and used for, the purposes of carrying out the routines of everyday life. Everyone in town passes through the market to purchase their supplies, and the zócalo is a common meeting place for different people throughout the day. Under the pressures of the movement, these spaces were also inscribed with the

meanings associated with important political decisions as well. This association between the routine of everyday life and the extraordinary importance of the decisions being made at the assemblies further emphasized
the importance of regular people in the acting out of explicitly political
situations. Just as the community had displaced the state in the centrality
of public life associated by their taking of the *Ayuntamiento*, they also col-
lapsed the differences between political and non-political routines of everyday life by using this important, quotidian communal space to practice a
kind of direct democracy.

Finally, it is important to note who was filling these newly signified
spaces. Gathered at the popular assemblies were women and men, young
and old, professional and laborer. There were groups that spoke to each
other in Nahuatl, and others who came late as they got home from work
in the fields or from Cuernavaca or Mexico City. The majority of atten-
dees were those who are generally excluded from the political process,
those who usually do not have a very well heard public voice. Politics as
usual is commonly carried out by politicians who may or may not consult
with their constituents, but who, in the end, work behind closed doors and
within institutional channels controlled by the state. In the case of this public sphere created by the movement, it was the voices of the professional
politicians that had been marginalized allowing for other, generally peripheral voices to come forth. That is not to say that local politicians were
absent, but rather that they spoke as peers and neighbors and not as representatives of political parties. There was an attempt to let everyone's
voice be heard and to debate the merits of differing strategies.[17] The negotiators for the CUT and the *Ayuntamiento* reported to everyone on the
progress (or lack thereof) of talks with the state government and solicited
a mandate on an approach for the next day's rounds of discussions. In this
process of dialogue, movement leaders attempted not to impose a fixed
program, but rather to air a variety of possibilities.

Daily Life and the Suspension of Normalcy — October 1995–April 1996

The changed appearance and meanings of these public spaces in
Tepoztlán, as well as the physical and political displacement of the state
government affirmed that the routines of everyday life had been profoundly
disrupted. Many participants reported that besides ridding themselves of
unwanted politicians, this suspension of everyday life had some positive
effects. To begin with, many residents claimed they felt a resurgence in

community spirit. The nightly meetings at the *Ayuntamiento* gave people a chance to see each other on a regular basis. Despite the ever-present feeling of danger, people also enjoyed a sort of party atmosphere in which there was free food and music or other entertainment before and after each night's business. The rotating guard duties served to cement neighborhood unity and helped many young people feel involved and important in the town's business. Older residents often openly complain about the seeming disinterest of young people in the town's traditions, and worry that they will lose them to the fast paced and alienating worlds of Mexico City and Cuernavaca. The movement, however, provided young people with a way of connecting with their community in a meaningful way. As one high school student explained, "Those against it (the golf course) always talked about being Tepoztecos and their fathers and grandfathers. That they were trying to protect what was theirs. We (youth) united against the golf course. Before, we were a number of small groups that were always fighting with each other. But, we got together to support the movement however we could" (Interview 1999). The barricades put up around the town delineated the edge of the "normal" and the "special" of Tepoztlán. One resident likened crossing the barricade to crossing into "liberated territory," in which the rules of oppressive and corrupt Mexico had been suspended. The suspension of the rules of everyday life, also gave people more superficial pleasures like driving the wrong way on one-way streets, having a reason to be wandering the streets late at night or chasing off suspicious strangers.

There were, however, also high costs to be paid for the breakdown in everyday life. A type of paranoia set in among town residents. The constant awareness that the police might enter either through outright force or clandestinely increased suspicion of outsiders. The PRI's manipulation of much of the press, particularly of the broadcast media, made it difficult to trust reporters. Many journalists were in fact banned from town because of misleading and outright untruthful reports (Martínez Zúñiga 1999). In February 1996, citizen patrols had captured two federal judicial police and the assembly that night had to decide what to do with them. There were many who were advocating lynching them, but, fortunately, cooler heads prevailed and convinced the assembly that killing them would only be an excuse for the army to occupy the town. After the officers had been interrogated, town leaders were convinced that they were attempting to execute warrants on issues unrelated to the Golf Club. Their weapons were confiscated and they were turned over to officials of the Federal Attorney General's Office on the highway outside of town later that night. The incident shows how far the rules of everyday life had been suspended, in that a public assembly seriously argued about executing federal officers for essentially carrying out their duties.

The state responded to the Tepoztlán crisis by cutting all funding to the new government, and refusing to recognize any of the paperwork (such as birth certificates and marriage licenses) issued by the municipality. This seriously impeded the local government's ability to function. Public works came to a virtual stand still, municipal employees went unpaid, and people could not be legally married or register births or deaths. Other civil registries, such as the one in Cuernavaca were told not to issue any licenses or certificates to any citizens of Tepoztlán, further complicating the lives of municipal residents and adding to the uncertainties that accompanied the suspension of everyday routines

In addition to these inconveniences, the state government turned ever more repressive and violent in its actions toward the Tepozteco activists. Eventually over one hundred arrest warrants were issued for citizens of Tepoztlán on charges ranging from destruction of government property, interference with police business, kidnapping and murder. In one of the most serious incidents, Pedro Barragán Gutiérrez, an uncle of the former municipal president, was killed. While the police and attorney general's office obscured official details of the case, many witnesses have reconstructed this story (Ayuntamiento Libre 1996; Comisión Nacional de Derechos Humanos 1997; Rosas 1997). Barragán and several other family members and friends, who supported the golf course, came into town armed and angry on the morning of 2 December. Earlier that day, Diana Ortega, the PRI leader of Tepoztlán and an ardent Golf Club supporter, had been detained for pulling out a gun during a dispute with other merchants. Barragán's group decided to rescue her. They began firing into the plaza and then in all directions. One of the men accidentally shot Barragán. "When Pedro Barragán fell wounded, say those who saw him, he was saying in surprise 'My own brother got me'" (Rosas 1997, 78). Citizen patrols quickly captured his associates and turned them over to the federal attorney general's office to be charged with the shooting and with possession of high caliber weapons. Pedro Barragán was brought, semi-conscious, to a hospital in Cuernavaca, where he died two weeks later.[18]

This incident quickly became the means through which the state increased the pressure on the Tepozteco movement. Instead of charging any of the people who had been firing weapons that morning, government officials quickly released them from custody and issued dozens of arrest warrants for CUT members instead. On 26 December, Fortino Mendoza, who was in charge of town security under the CUT/*Ayuntamiento Libre* was arrested by state judicial police and charged with Barragán's murder.

A week later, José Carrillo was also arrested and charged with the same crime, despite the fact that he held a federal injunction against his arrest. On 18 January, teacher and long-time activist Gerardo Demesa was arrested at his job at the National Education Workers' Unions (SNTE) in Cuernavaca. He describes his arrest:

> I arrived at my work place as usual at about 10:00 in the morning and some fifteen minutes later, while I was carrying out my duties, a great disturbance was heard as a crowd entered, throwing and kicking everything that they found in their path. They made their way upstairs to the office where I was, kicking in the door and, with an excessive amount of force, and with their weapons in hand they grabbed me by the hair and pushed me out the door. The steward of the union tried to help me by holding onto me, so they could not take me. One of the cruel subjects responded by arming his weapon, and putting it in the chest of the steward said, "let him go or I'll fuck you over...." The steward immediately let go and backed away. One of the men took me by the legs and dragged me approximately ten meters down the stairs. During the trajectory, I received serious blows to my head and body against the stairs. They brought me to the State Attorney General's office, where I was in the custody of the judicial police. They held me for more than two hours tied and covered with my own jacket... [1998, 49].

Demesa's account of his arrest further shows how the crisis in quotidian relations made everyday living very difficult. He went to work "as usual," but this would obviously be no usual day. He knew that there had been an arrest warrant issued for him, but decided that he did not want "to be a prisoner in my own town," (48) and so he tried to carry out his everyday function — going to work — even though he knew that he would be leaving the protection of Tepoztlán.

This was one of the most serious examples of how state officials took advantage of the suspension of normal behavior, as it began a series of illegal actions under the guise of protecting law and order. It was very clear, for instance, that Demesa had nothing to do with Barragán's death, as he was not in town on the day of the incident. The National Commission for Human Rights found later that the statement that Pedro Barragán supposedly made to police just before his death, in which he implicated Demesa, could not have actually happened, given the amount and types of medication that he was on at that time (CNDH). The state, in other words, took advantage of the fact that the Tepoztecos had broken the norms of state-civil society relations, which supposedly keep the state from interfering in citizen's private lives without due process of law, to carry on a campaign in which it deliberately violated the rights that it is obligated to protect.[19] As a result, Demesa would serve 28 months in state prison for this crime that he did not commit

Demesa's arrest, along with other flagrant human rights violations and criminal activity of the Carrillo administration, lead to the conflict in Tepoztlán becoming a wider social crisis in the state.[20] The teachers' union, for instance, temporarily shut down the public schools and sponsored one of the largest demonstrations ever in Cuernavaca to protest Demesa's arrest and the violation of their union's office. Tepoztlán became the focal point for a great deal of organizing, as groups felt safe to meet there and wanted to show their support. A statewide organization, the Unity of Morelos Social Movements, was formed demanding the resignation of the officials responsible for Demesa's imprisonment.[21] In light of this breach becoming a more general social crisis, the state had an increasingly urgent need to find a solution to the problem in Tepoztlán.

Throughout this unstable time of the disruption of daily life, there was a constant attempt to return to normal. The CUT attempted to have the state resolve the issue (to their liking, of course), by legally dissolving the municipal council and calling new elections. When that failed, they named their own government, so that daily functions could continue, and they used the rituals of the state (swearing in ceremony, occupying the municipal building, and quoting the Constitution) to give legitimacy to their actions, suggesting that the goal in many ways was to repair the breach and to return to normal. Even leaders of the CUT such as Gerardo Demesa, attempted to go about their daily business as best they could, only to find the breach that they had provoked made this impossible. Besides showing how strong the drive to the normal is, it also shows that it was impossible for the Tepoztecos to simply resolve the issue themselves. The problem, and therefore the solution, involved forces and actors outside of the municipality, and they needed, therefore, to find a way to negotiate acceptable relations with those outside social actors. The state, likewise, had a desire to return to normal. The municipal government was completely beyond the governor's control and therefore the usual workings of government could not continue. Likewise, the golf course could not be built so long as the people in the town continued to live outside of the parameters of acceptable, predictable behavior. Investors were not interested in putting large sums of money into projects in which they could not reasonably predict a profitable return on their investment. The stability and predictability that comes with the unquestioning acceptance of the rules of everyday life are essential to the smooth operation of various projects, and the state needed to regain control of this machinery of normalness in order to efficiently administer society and to carry out its projects.

Martyrdom and Cancellation, April 1996

The resolution of the crisis in Tepoztlán would require a sacrifice on the part of the Tepoztecos. On the morning of 10 April 1996, a caravan of several hundred people left for "Zapata's March," the annual commemoration of the revolutionary hero's death. On the highway outside of Tlaltizapán, where President Zedillo was giving a speech and where the Tepoztecos had hoped to present a letter petitioning him to intervene on their behalf, a large contingent of riot police stopped and cut off the convoy. The police had blocked the road with sugar cane trucks, making it impossible for the caravan to turn back. They ordered the Tepoztecos to get out of their buses, trucks and cars. The Tepoztecos refused, citing their right to free passage. The police made violent threats. Rocks were thrown. The police then opened fire on the caravan. One man, 65-year-old Marcos Olmeda was shot. His body was thrown into a pick up truck and driven away. It would later be found in the city of Jojutla, a good distance from the incident. The rest of the caravan was physically forced out of their vehicles and made to sit without food or water in the hot April sun for the rest of the day. Although many people were injured in the attack, the police would not allow the press, other citizens or medical help to pass through the roadblock to assist them in any way.

In a press statement that night, the government reported that some 150 people from Tepoztlán had interfered with a routine operation of the state preventive police. Two people had been slightly injured and 34 people arrested as "they destroyed four patrol cars and were carrying illegal firearms. It should be noted that the police officers were not armed" (*La Jornada*, 12 April 1996). Later on, the government claimed that two police officers were seriously injured when they were run over by the Tepoztecos. The government accused the Tepoztecos of intending to cause a disturbance at President Zedillo's appearance, and dismissed charges that Marcos Olmeda had been injured or killed in the incident, claiming that he had not even been there.

These claims, however, were quickly refuted by a video that one of the Tepoztecos had taken that clearly showed that the police were armed and that they had fired on the crowd. It showed Marcos Olmeda being killed. The video also captured a high-ranking state police official, Captain Ariño, pulling out his handgun, suggesting that the incident had been well planned and approved at the highest levels of the police hierarchy. As the story quickly spun out of the government's control, it was forced to acknowledge that the police had been armed, and that they had shot at the crowd. Several of the officers involved were charged in the incident. Ariño was also charged with abuse of authority and disobeying orders for his leading of the attack and sent, briefly, to prison. In the end, forty-eight police officers were charged with crimes related to the attack, and in the end all forty-eight were released with a small fine for disobeying orders. No one was ever formally charged with Olmeda's murder.

Governor Carrillo now had a serious problem on his hands, which he needed to resolve quickly, because he was losing his ability to govern the state. As María Rosas notes, "the time had now passed for talking about golf, tourism, progress and million dollar investments. And because Morelos is Tepoztlán, but also Yautepec, Jonacatepec, Puente de Ixtla, Cuautla, Huitzilac and other places that Carrillo Olea was losing ground every day, the state government needed to find a fast way to close the Tepoztlán case" (114). Groups were quickly coalescing in the "Organization of NGOs of Eastern Morelos State" (ONGROEM) to work for Carrillo's impeachment because of the ambush and the accumulation of other human rights abuses throughout the state (*La Jornada*, 14 April 1996). He responded to criticism by assuring the press that "...the CUT is not Tepoztlán and Tepoztlán is not Morelos" (*La Jornada*, 15 April 1996: 8), as a means not only to diffuse the idea that he was losing control of the state, but also to reinforce his rhetoric that the movement in Tepoztlán was being manipulated by a handful of radical troublemakers. While the Governor's stance was to deny accusations in the ambush, and then to revise those statements when confronted with evidence to the contrary, he also publicly made overtures to the Tepoztecos. On April 15, Carrillo stated that, "We'll sit down and have a beer and some *sopes*, the Tepoztecos and the Governor, to restart the dialogue" (*La Jornada*, 16 April 1996: 1). Although his invitation to dialogue continued to show his client-patron attitude toward politics, as well as the lack of seriousness with which he viewed the police attack and assassination, he did nevertheless send a neutral envoy to Tepoztlán to begin negotiations. It was a tacit recognition that the policy of physical and psychological pressures had failed and that a new path would need to be taken. He was also, however, insisting on doing politics as usual, through back-room deals and negotiations with a small number of representatives. He allowed the implicit and explicit threats to the personal safety and integrity of activists to remain unresolved as a means of strengthening his negotiating position. Although the meeting with "beer and *sopes*" never took place, because the Governor would be unwelcome, to say the least, in Tepoztlán, his representative, Ana Laura Ortega, did make some progress in negotiations over the next several months, by winning the trust of some of the Tepozteco negotiators.

KS, for its part, suspended the golf course two days after Marcos

Olmeda's death. In a press statement, the company cited the general lack of governability in the town, noting that the social unrest seriously compromised the security of its investments. In its press release, KS reiterated its position that it had wanted a peaceful resolution to the conflict, but that had turned out to be impossible. They insisted that the project sought

> ...to contribute to the improvement of the quality of life of the Tepoztecos and to be part of the urban and social reordering of Tepoztlán. The social impact in the municipality would be a benefit for society at large, since it would have contributed to the true vocation of the municipality, which is tourism, commerce and services, seeing that the land no longer has an agricultural use given its high level of erosion [*La Jornada,* 14 April 1996: 5].

Here then, while the company was conceding that it could not build the golf course in the town (for the time being), it nevertheless continued to reinforce the modernization discourse that it had employed earlier in its proposals. Development for them is a top-down endeavor, in which the company knows what is best for Tepoztlán. They wanted to "reorder" the urban and social relations of the community along the lines of its "true" calling. Nowhere in this statement is there an allusion to a partnership with the community, nor a process that involves community members to determine what is really the "true interests" of the town. There was no consideration of the peculiarities of the town's history, nor thought given to why they might want to retain the social relations that they had developed there over time. Knowledge and, therefore, decision making, lay with those who control capital. Furthermore, since the project was the height of rational planning, its rejection must be due to some irrational current. A few days later Francisco Kladt offered "an apology to the 'true' Tepoztecos that had supported the idea of the golf club," and was certain that the majority in Tepoztlán supported the project because it meant an important source of employment for the region (*La Jornada* 16 April 1996: 17). He concluded his press conference by noting that the company had strictly followed the law and had acquired the legal right to do what they wanted on their land. Nevertheless, forces outside of the laws of the state and of the market interfered with the project and caused it to be indefinitely suspended.

The movement also used this moment to reflect on the causes of the conflict and to articulate its stance given the course of events. Once the body of Marcos Olmeda was finally found, it was brought back to Tepoztlán where it rested in state at the *Ayuntamiento.* His murder forced many to reflect on how far the struggle had gone and to reaffirm their dedication to its principle causes—cancellation of the Golf Club and recognition of their political leadership. When news spread that KS had suspended the Golf Club, "there were people crying in the assembly because this was the last straw. How is it possible that we have to die so that they understand? How is it possible that they think that with that they go and are clean of the violence?" (Rosas 1997, 115). Marcos Olmeda became the symbol for the struggle. A long time social activist and founder of the PRD in Tepoztlán, he represented the genuineness of social struggle. In the tightly knit movement and community, his death was strongly felt, and many commented that "part of us died with him" (Rosas 1997, 113). Reflecting on his death, María Rosas realizes,

> We are wiped out; since 10 April time is continuous, without night or day.... Long hours at the wake and of looking at each other with the clear awareness that this time the government has gone too far, that it is not possible, it is inhuman, irrational and unjustifiable to come to the point of murdering so that a gang of business people can fatten their wallets. The government went too far, now what? In the nightly assembly women wrapped in their *rebozos* look fixedly at the ground.... Without moving from their place, one of them says, "Let all of Mexico know what Carrillo has done to us." Other voices complement: "And let them know that not even with this, will we back down" [113].

This passage illustrates very clearly how the movement used this moment to strengthen its positions, but also indicates, that it was beginning to feel spent. While clearly the "government had gone too far," there is also the underlying sense that the movement may have gone too far as well. No one intended for there to be a martyr to this story. Marcos Olmeda was not just a social activist, after all, but he was a friend. Rosas reports that "we are wiped out," but it is not just because of the events of the past few days, but also because of the tremendous stress under which the movement and the town were operating for the previous eight months. The uncertainty was beginning to catch up to them, and the "irrationality" and "inhumanity" of their opponents who have "gone too far," took them by surprise, leaving them to ask, "what next?" While the need to resolve the issue was becoming more urgent for the Tepoztecos as well as for the state and the company, the Tepoztecos were also reaffirming their previous positions. They cite their unity and defiance "let all of Mexico know what they did to *us*" and "we will not back down." In his funeral address, the parish priest and movement supporter, Filiberto González, praised "the genuineness of this popular struggle, that does not seek power or money, but rather the well-being of the community" (*La Jornada*, 13 April

1996: 7), as a means of cementing the positions taken by the movement which sought to cast the Tepoztecos as a unified group entirely focused on the common good as opposed to the greed and self-centeredness of the KS investors. Movement activists, while acknowledging their exhaustion and implicitly their need to resolve the conflict, also reiterated their constitution as a collective organization seeking goals other than short-term enrichment.

All three parties to the conflict, in this moment of redress, were contesting the "true nature" of the Tepoztecos and of the movement. The Governor insisted that the "CUT is not Tepoztlán." KS apologized to the "true Tepoztecos" who have supported the project, implying, of course, that those who opposed it were some how false Tepoztecos. Finally the movement reaffirmed its right to claim to speak for the "genuineness of the popular struggle," and sought to embody the values for which Olmeda died and for which three of their members were still in prison. While all three sides, therefore, were willing to make some sort of compromise toward the normalization of everyday life, they all still claimed to be true to themselves. In these claims to represent the genuine Tepoztecos, they also clearly defined the limits to which they were going to carry the struggle and what they were and were not willing to cede. The state, for instance, needed to find the mechanism to reconstitute political control over Tepoztlán in order to keep it from becoming a more widespread social crisis, but it could not simply cede the municipal government to the people. To this end, the governor began negotiating more seriously with the movement, as a means to reinsert at least some form of state control, but would insist on a formula that would guarantee him influence over the council's membership. KS, while lamenting its inability to bring progress to Tepoztlán, also reaffirmed its commitment to safeguarding the investments of its financial supporters, opting to cut its losses given the social instability in the region. Finally, the CUT/*Ayuntamiento Libre* acknowledged its "tiredness" and showed its willingness to work out a solution that did not betray their basic demands.

From this point on, the various sides began working toward the reintegration of the town into the larger state system. While the golf club was the initial spark that caused the breach in everyday life, the conflict had been accumulating a number of other issues as it unfolded. Now, besides the cancellation of the golf club (its "suspension" was not acceptable), the CUT/*Ayuntamiento Libre* was also negotiating the issues of punishing those responsible for Olmeda's death, release of the three political prisoners, cancellation of the arrest warrants and recognition of their municipal authorities.

Process of Reconciliation, April 1996–July 1997

The process of reintegration was long and complicated for many reasons, not least of which was the community's generalized distrust of political parties. By refusing to work through the parties, which are the usual mechanisms of mediation between social groups and the state, the Tepoztecos made dealing with the state very difficult. Also, the unity that the CUT and the *Ayuntamiento Libre* had worked so hard to achieve at the beginning of the conflict, began to disintegrate after the main demand, the suspension of the golf club, was met. The internal divisions, which in some ways were an indication that life within the town was returning to normal, also, however, impeded the process of reintegrating the town with the state system. Decisions became harder to make, as there were multiple perspectives on the best way to end the crisis, and differing opinions about the fundamental nature of the crisis itself. Once decisions were reached, they were difficult to carry out, because people had less time and energy to work on them than they did during the height of the crisis.

The process of reintegration can be delineated temporally as beginning in April 1996 with the suspension of the golf course and ending March 1997 with the election of duly recognized authorities who would oversee the resolution of outstanding issues with state officials. This process would involve extensive negotiations with the state government, an attempted resignation of the *Ayuntamiento Libre*, new officially sanctioned elections, the deposing of the governor, the release of the political prisoners, and the suspension of arrest warrants. The reintegration phase, in other words, lasted longer than the actual "crisis," and suggested that even though normal everyday life had returned, it also had been altered.

By April 1996, several months of constant conflict and no funds had taken their toll on town residents. Municipal employees had gone unpaid for months. While many of them "endured it for the benefit of the town," it was still a hardship (Interview, former municipal employee, 1999). Throughout 1996, elected officials were looking for a way to step down and return to their private lives, so that they could remove one of the main obstacles to normalizing relations with the state government, namely their continued existence as a municipal government. Besides not being paid, the demands on their time meant they could not go to their regular jobs or spend much time with friends and family. Resolving the issues around which the crisis broke out and which had accumulated during the crisis became the focus of nearly three years of negotiations. After Marcos Olmeda's murder, the governor sent Ana Laura Ortega, a high-ranking state official to negotiate with the CUT and *Ayuntamiento*. Unlike Carrillo,

Ortega had a more personable manner of doing politics and held a series of meetings with local leaders to define the issues and to solicit possible solutions. She collected testimonies about the events of 10 April and arranged for compensation for those who were injured. She also insisted on an informal tone to her negotiations, as a way to build trust and so as not to raise expectations that anything to which she agreed could be construed as being accepted by Governor Carrillo (Rosas 1997, 121–123).

In part because of the negotiating skills of Ortega and in part because of the obstacles and lack of political experience facing them, the Municipal Council made a surprising announcement in July 1996. In a public assembly they declared:

> The *Ayuntamiento Libre* has finished its duty. You elected us to head the struggle against the Club; well, that struggle was won. They're not going to build the Club. The current *Ayuntamiento* is tired of so much pressure, and it has also become an obstacle in resolving the conflict. It will help more by resigning, because then they will let the prisoners go. The people of Tepoztlán didn't organize to defend an *Ayuntamiento*, but for the Club business. It doesn't make any sense to continue this movement. The state government has promised to release the prisoners if we show our good will. We are in agreement to name new officials and we have let the government know that. There is already a commitment from the government and from us as well. We keep our word [Rosas 1997, 129].

This statement shocked many people, and it reinforced rumors circulating around town that the *Ayuntamiento Libre* was secretly negotiating with the state government. This surprise, however, turned to anger when the *Ayuntamiento Libre* divulged that the formula for the new elections was that the state agreed to allow the town to name four of the seven council members, while the state would name the other three. The Tepoztecos would be allowed to keep the presidency and with that a majority on the council. After some consideration, the assembly roundly rejected the idea and refused to accept the *Ayuntamiento's* resignation. In the end, the government's formula for democracy was rejected, because the people in the town had made too many sacrifices not only to stop the golf course, but also to exercise their rights to name their own officials. The state's urgency in calling new elections was greeted with suspicion, and graffiti appeared on various walls in town urging "No to elections! Yes to democracy!" Striking a deal with Olmeda's assassin was, in the end, too much for most people, as the conflict had evolved from one over a golf course to one about democracy, human rights and autonomy. The Council, although worn out, was forced to complete its term in office.

This incident shows not only the relative weakness and inexperience of the *Ayuntamiento Libre*, but also suggests that after 10 April the movement itself was seriously divided. While movement leaders were able to construct a good amount of unity around the issue of stopping the golf course, maintaining that unity once the golf course ceased being an issue proved to be very difficult. The movement split into three broad tendencies throughout 1996. The more conservative of the tendencies, made up primarily of PRI sympathizers saw that with the suspension of the Golf Club, there was no need to continue the struggle. The continued standoff with the state was unnecessary, and detrimental to the continued progress of Tepoztlán. A second more moderate tendency saw the suspension of the golf course as a major victory, but insisted on a formal, written and definitive cancellation as well as the state resolving the collateral issues such as prosecuting those responsible for the attack, releasing political prisoners and canceling the arrest warrants against movement activists. For them, the issue of the municipal council was secondary. They tended to see themselves as pragmatic and were willing to make some concessions in order to secure their primary goals. Finally, a more radical tendency, while agreeing with the moderates on most of the above issues, insisted that the state recognize their "uses and customs" in selecting their officials and that Carrillo Olea be impeached and tried for his involvement in the violence committed against them.

Most of the leadership of the CUT and the *Ayuntamiento Libre* sided with the moderates. Throughout the struggle, they had been looking for a way to return to normal. From their perspective, the institutional problem was a serious one, as they encountered roadblock after roadblock to normal governance. What is more, they fully understood that their lack of political experience was a hindrance in dealing with the state government. When they were offered, therefore, the definitive resolution of the Golf Club, the release of the prisoners and a promise to fully investigate the attack, they saw their opportunity to end the crisis. They were unable to convince a majority of the population to go along with their pragmatic proposal, however, as the more radical faction was able to sway opinion in assemblies by framing the issue as not being just about normalizing relations, but also about remembering the sacrifices made to defend what they had won. Between the summers of 1996 and 1997, therefore, the town remained in a kind of institutional limbo, while these three political tendencies worked out a formula among themselves and the state for the 1997 general elections.

The process of electing the new council is also very illustrative of how the movement was attempting to reintegrate itself into the state system.

It became clear from the town's rejection of the *Ayuntamiento Libre's* resignation in July that the *process* that the movement had unleashed was very important. The *Ayuntamiento Libre* had been selected through a series of public meetings involving the *barrio* system. This system, which has historically been used to select church and neighborhood leaders responsible for local festivals and rituals, became the most logical channel to use in mobilizing support against the golf club and then for selecting new public officials. Also, the *Ayuntamiento Libre* had been chosen in a process that was free from the intervention of political parties. Townspeople, in rejecting the State-*Ayuntamiento Libre* formula in July 1996, were clearly indicating their desire to continue with the practice of selecting their own leadership. The question, however, was *how* to participate in a semi-democratic Mexican political system, without losing control over the criteria for selecting local leaders. The discussion of how to participate, then, returned to the local level. Neighborhood committees began to meet and to hold assemblies to discuss how to participate. The major problem was that none of the political parties was particularly trusted in Tepoztlán, yet the rules established by the Federal Electoral Institute (IFE) required that all candidates on a ballot represent a nationally accredited political party. For many people in the town, this would be a big risk, because they feared losing control of their political leadership to one of the national parties. By the end of 1996, however, a solution emerged. The town would "borrow" the registry of one of the political parties, but would select its slate of candidates through the *barrio* system as they had for the 1995 elections. After further discussion, the PRD was approached and agreed to lend its registry to the "People's Slate" for the March 1997 elections, promising not to interfere with the local selection process.

Through a similar procedure used in 1995, neighborhoods and villages held assemblies in which candidates were openly proposed and discussed. In the end, a slate of candidates was chosen in which the different geographical regions were represented. None of the candidates for local office, headed by Fermín Bello for Municipal President, had been leaders of the CUT (although they had all been vocal and visible opponents of the Golf Club), nor members of the *Ayuntamiento Libre*. The campaigning was marked by a decided attempt on the part of the Popular Slate to not only hold events in the county seat, but also to visit and listen to people in the outlying areas. It was a campaign marked by a virtual lack of vote buying. On election day, approximately 10,000 of the 14,000 registered voters turned out and over 7,000 of them cast their votes for the Popular Slate. To put that into perspective, the PRI won 3,900 votes to the PRD's 3,500 in the 1994 election (Quero 2003, 157). The election served as a viable

Support for the new municipal government, Tepoztlán, 1997.

compromise to both sides in the conflict. The state could now recognize the government in Tepoztlán as the elections were duly convoked and administered. The majority of Tepoztecos, particularly those of the moderate to radical factions, could live with the alliance with the PRD, because the process followed their "uses and customs" and because the municipal council had been won with such an overwhelming majority.

The election of the new *Ayuntamiento* in the 1997 elections allowed for the *Ayuntamiento Libre* to step down and cleared the way for more normal relationships with the state government. Funds returned to the municipality and the local government could begin elaborating a public works plan. Employees and officials were paid again on a regular basis, so that they did not have to worry about finding outside employment to support themselves while they were serving the public. Although there were still a number of outstanding issues that the seating of the new municipality in and of itself did not resolve, such as the outstanding human rights violations, the functioning of everyday life moved closer to normal.

New Formations: 1997–2003

With the seating of the new Municipal Council, the Tepozteco community could begin to work out how it would operate, politically and culturally, within the parameters set by its compromises with the state government. They were now subject to institutional rules, but also had access to the goods and services that institutionality implies. They also had the luxuries and difficulties that normal life brings to the construction of political projects. Gone was the urgency that had forged their unity, but they could also operate without the imminent threat of repression. Nationally, the 1997 municipal government took office as the PRI's rule was coming to an end, so local cultural politics were also developing alongside rapidly changing national ones. In order to cement their return into normalness, the Tepozteco leadership had to resolve remaining issues with the state as well as construct a viable model of inclusion and participation that had been raised through the months of social conflict.

One of the last remaining demands of the movement was met in May 1998, when Governor Carrillo was forced to seek an indefinite leave of absence from office. Faced with increasing evidence of human rights violations and criminal activity in his administration, the state congress forced him to step down under threats of impeachment.[22] Not only did they remove him from office, but they also refused to name his designated successor as interim, opting instead for a moderate, Jorge Morales Barud, who was acceptable to the three parties represented in the Congress. Carrillo's removal from office was due not only to events in Tepoztlán, but also to a general sense of insecurity in the state and a quickly deteriorating human rights situation demonstrated by a kidnapping ring allegedly being run by the state police hierarchy as well as the assassination of a political opponent of the governor.[23] The climate of criminality and official impunity had reached unacceptable limits state wide, and as a result, one of the Tepozteco's demands was met. The new governor, Morales Barud, showed a more conciliatory attitude toward Tepoztlán, and his very first official meeting was with their municipal council in order to resolve once and for all the impasse (Bocanegra Quiroz 1999; Flores Pérez 1999). The new council and state governor started off with and continued to enjoy cordial relations, even though the governor would not be allowed to visit the town in any official capacity until all of the other issues were formally resolved (Martínez Zúñiga 1999).

Those other unresolved issues were the unsolved human rights cases and the written, definitive cancellation of the Golf Club. Two of the political prisoners, Fortino Mendoza and José Carrillo had been released in December 1996, for lack of evidence. Gerardo Demesa would remain in prison until after Governor Carrillo's resignation in May 1998, despite pressures from Amnesty International, the National Human Rights Commission, the U.S. Congress and the Morelos State Congress. Although there was no legal basis to continue holding him, he contended in an interview that he was held so long as a form of revenge for his long and visible history of activism and as a means to keep pressuring Tepoztlán (1999). The hundreds of arrest warrants issued for Tepozteco activists were held active but unexecuted until January 1999, when the State Attorney General's office dismissed all charges against everyone involved in activities stemming from the movement against the golf course (Gómez Guerra 1998). With these developments, those involved could consider themselves fully reintegrated into normal life. No longer in prison or with the latent threat of arrest hanging over their heads, they could go about their daily business. Likewise, by resolving these human rights issues, the state could reclaim some of its lost legitimacy to be an arbiter of justice, which is essential for the reintegration of the state into the daily relations of society. The case of Olmeda's murder, however, continues to go unsolved, and given the implication of high government officials, including the former Governor and State Attorney General, will probably never be resolved (Bocanegra Quiroz 1999).

The definitive cancellation of the Golf Club would finally come in March 1999; four years almost to the day after the President and *Ayuntamiento* falsely swore not to approve it. Activists and municipal authorities pointed to the need to have *written* proof not only from the company but also from state and federal agencies indicating that the Club would never be built. They did not trust that KS or some successor would not attempt another project on land that the municipality claimed as communal. That assurance came when governor Morales Barud ordered the corresponding government agencies to rescind any and all approvals made for the golf club. In comments made to the press and to municipal political leaders, the Governor noted that while he was not opposed to the development of the tourist industry, these projects "have to be carried out in viable areas and with the acceptance of the population and of the communal, ejidal and municipal authorities, as it is fundamental to respect the uses and customs of all of the localities" (*El Mexicano*). In this statement he was repeating the often-expressed position in Tepoztlán that people were not against development but that it had to be on terms acceptable to the town. Furthermore, the Governor explained that "these resolutions respond to the formal petitions of several social groups in the town of Tepoztlán, with the purpose being to return to the rule of law and also to guarantee the preservation of the ecological reserves, the aquifers and the cultivable land of the municipality ... in an atmosphere of respect, it is possible to reconcile the very legitimate aspirations of the population and to generate with it economic growth" (*El Mexicano*). With these two statements, and through the actions of releasing the political prisoners, canceling the arrest warrants and delivering written, definitive orders revoking the permits of KS, the governor was making the last necessary gestures toward completing the reintegration of normal relations between Tepoztlán and the state. He implicitly recognized the legitimacy of the town's actions and hoped that with a "return to the rule of law," life could finally return to normal.

In many ways, the return to the rule of law did bring about a return to more normal political practices in the town. The 1997–2000 council worked toward creating a more transparent government that responded quickly and effectively to citizen needs. It also faced criticism from numerous community members for either not going far enough or returning too quickly to old political practices like patronage and favoritism. Some community members were disappointed that the municipal government was too cooperative with the state, and that its members were acting like politicians and promoting the PRD. Other community members did not understand the new rules for influencing politicians and continued to solicit favors from them or sought to carry out business, like obtaining permits, through unofficial channels. Some officials were perplexed by old attitudes, arguing that changing culture is difficult, while others seemed to be open to working in the "old ways, since that is what people expect of us" (Interview, Municipal Employees, April 1999). An unexpected part of the job for these activists-turned-politicians was the amount of paperwork required by central bureaucracies. Many complained that it took almost two full years of their non-repeatable three-year terms just to learn how to fill out and file forms.

The July 2000 elections saw even greater diversity in the electoral process. Four parties competed: the PRD, the PARM/People's Slate, the PAN and the PRI. Both the PRD and the PARM followed the neighborhood selection process for candidates for their slate, while the PAN and PRI followed internal procedures for the naming of candidates. After a close election, in which the PAN made a startling debut as a political force in town, the PRD narrowly won the election, returning the *Ayuntamiento Libre's* leader, Lázaro Rodríguez, to the municipal presidency. Both the PRD and PARM slates consisted of visible leaders from the anti-golf movement, but they had split politically over differences about the involvement of parties in the local process, with the PARM slate representing the more radical faction advocating autonomy and distrust of parties. One PRD-allied activist compared it to "a family squabble. We have our differences, but we basically believe the same things" (Interview 2001). Despite their differences, they quickly formed an alliance within the Municipal Council, in an attempt to ensure a majority of votes on issues of substance.[24] Although the leaders of the PRD/PARM factions maintained a great deal of prestige because of their association with the anti-golf movement, the PAN slate seemed to benefit from the national momentum garnered by Vicente Fox's campaign for change.

Local politics, however, was in many ways disconnected from national partisan ideologies. Although the PAN came within one hundred votes (of over 3000 cast) of winning the elections in 2000, many PAN supporters in town had only a vague sense of what they were supporting at a national level, and were promised classes in the near future to learn about the PAN's ideology and program (Interview, July 2001). Even the PAN official serving on the Municipal Council, although an ardent supporter of Fox and his party, believed that its neoliberal economics were misguided and hurt the poor agricultural and small manufacturing sector (Robles Bladeras 2001). PAN activists supported the party because they wanted change and did not like the way that the previous, and nominally PRD, government had handled itself. They attributed conflicts in town politics to family divisions and divisive tactics of activists-turned-politicians. Likewise, PRD activists gave local matters primary importance, stressing the town's experience with the golf course protest, attempts at participatory politics and concern over maintaining the environmental and cultural integrity of the town as keys to their continued success. PRD Municipal President Lázaro Rodríguez criticized the national party, asserting that, "none of the parties, including my party, has the vision or ability to make structural changes at the national level" (2001).

The 2003 elections saw the surprising return of the PRI to the municipal presidency, underscoring two important themes in local politics. The first is that given the absence of a unifying cause, the electorate tends to be more personality driven. The impression among townspeople was that the PRI won this election because its candidate made a strong personal connection to people, and that as a party it was able to distance itself from its previous support of the golf course. It may also be an indication of the democratic initiative taking root, in which a party could be turned out of office for not meeting the expectations of its citizens, despite wide spread recognition of its past efforts in defeating the golf course project.

Permanent Changes?

The final question in this phase of reintegration is what has changed and what has stayed the same? In Tepoztlán, the normal to which life returned as a result of this process of reconciliation was clearly not the same normal that existed before September 1995. Changes could be observed in both the practices of social and political relations as well as in the inscription of meaning onto commonly held symbols. Although in many ways it would seem that the social movement had simply burned itself out and disbanded, the changes in people's understanding of social relations remain an important element of their embedded cultural and collective experience. Certainly the rebellion did not, and could not have, drastically altered the large-scale economic and political structures under which Tepozteco society is constructed, as it had neither the physical nor ideological resources to do so. It did, however, add to the experiences of resistance and raised important questions about the meanings of democracy and control of natural resources, and proved that the state could be successfully confronted on those issues. Its challenge, built on specific social practices, was to create broader webs of citizens interested in creating a society with more opportunities for themselves and their community. In that process, they left a transformed local environment.

The alterations to local social life can be concretely allegorized through the appearance of the *Ayuntamiento*, as the central stage of this long social drama. At the height of the crisis, it was covered with pro–movement, and anti–KS and anti-state slogans. Effigies of the "traitors" were notable presences. As daily life began to return to normal (and as state funds returned which allowed for it), the building was gradually repainted. In many ways this symbolized the town's return to normalcy in terms both of their reconciled relationship with the state government and with the toning down of the militancy of political rhetoric. The duly elected and recognized municipal government operated inside of the building and popular assemblies decreased significantly in frequency and in attendance. Nevertheless, the building and the collective life that it represents had been somewhat, and perhaps subtly, altered. The slogans were not completely scraped off and some continue to exist beneath the newly painted surface. The two murals deprecating KS and the state government remained. Two plaques were added to the front of the building as well. One thanks the *Ayuntamiento Libre*, naming all of its members, for their service to the community and the second one is a commemoration to Marcos Olmeda, the movement's martyr. Olmeda's plaque characterizes him as "an example for our generations as a great fighter for social causes and for natural resources. Tepoztlán remembers you! No to the golf club!" Clearly, then, even though the building has been returned to its legal functions and appears to have been restored to its normal order, it has been altered from what it was before the conflict. Here, the memory of the movement and what the people involved in it stood for has been quite literally and visibly inscribed as an integral part of this most important public space.

Despite the return to normal, change could be observed in various kinds of public relations in the town. Besides the occasional *"No al club de golf"* T-shirt, people continued to be affected by the events of the conflict. In terms of politics, there was a legal municipal council that functioned within the limits set up by state policies, such as elections under a political party, dependence on state funds and the return of the police. The municipal government began functioning, more or less, as it should. Most people backed away from their earlier militancy, expecting the municipal government to take care of political matters for them. The unity shown during the height of the crisis also diminished as old conflicts and politics as usual returned to the town. Politics as usual, however, had changed.

Institutionally, the official party in town between 1997 and 2003 was the PRD. People came to the PRD office to get issues resolved, rather than soliciting the PRI as had previously occurred. The *Ayuntamiento* was now occupied by new political actors, most of whom had little or no previous political or administrative experience. In 1995 Ricardo Martínez, for instance, was a retired teacher who had never contemplated involvement in politics. He gradually became involved in the anti-golf struggle and was eventually drafted by his neighbors during an assembly to be their candidate for office in 1997, because they saw him as a person of integrity, and because "people thought what I said was correct." He was elected to the prestigious post of the Secretary General in the 1997–2000 Municipal Council, and found that he enjoyed this opportunity for public service (1999). He is just one example, therefore, of how new political actors have come into being as a result of the changing political culture motivated by the movement.

Outside of the formal structures of power, there was a changed attitude toward politics. According to many residents, whereas before the movement, people would generally either accept or just complain about the imposition of proposals, they now discussed them and argued about them. The barrio system of representation made officials more accountable to townspeople, and occasional assemblies would be held to voice complaints about the conduct of officials and even to decide whether or not to replace them. In previous elections, the political parties imposed candidates from within party structures rather than through popular consultation.[25] As a result, politicians owed their success to the party hierarchy and not to the population. Under the system of neighborhood assemblies employed by the PRD and the PARM, candidates were clearly dependent on their relationships with their neighbors to win nomination

Municipal palace, Tepoztlán, April 1999.

and, therefore, were more accountable to them once in office. This attitude of local accountability could be seen in the protests of several of the elected officials whom I interviewed in 1999, who vehemently denied belonging to the PRD (even though they were elected on a PRD slate), insisting instead that they were the "people's" selection, and did not follow or even approve of party ambitions or platforms. By 2001, elected officials were more comfortable with their party affiliations, but maintained a clear focus on the local nature of their ambitions and programs. In a similar vein, people reported feeling more assertive toward authorities, and claimed that they would not accept projects simply imposed from above, but rather would need to approve them first. The corruption generally associated with Mexican political institutions seemed to have been minimized, which, in some ways, made it difficult for some citizens to get their business accomplished, as the new rules about influencing municipal authorities were not always clear.

At the same time, however, we should be careful not to oversimplify the political process in Tepoztlán and see it as a utopian communal democracy. There are deep divisions and sources of conflict. Within the two post-conflict governments, for instance, there were great arguments about how close to be to the PRD, with some favoring a more formal relationship with the national party, and others seeing that stance as a betrayal of the community. There were problems associated with a lack of experience of the municipal administrators, who although they may have been doing the best they could, in the words of one middle aged woman, "were just people from the town, and not really politicians" (Interview, 1999). Officials complained of a very long learning curve on mastering all of their bureaucratic responsibilities. Furthermore, while the fight against the golf course seemed to have raised some very important ecological issues, the return to everyday life witnessed a rapid increase in environmental problems, from the nearly unmanageable amount of solid waste to the continued illegal incursion into environmentally sensitive areas (Ortiz Rivera 1999). Despite the imperfections in political and social transformation, the cultural importance and legacy of the movement lay in its contribution to the ongoing process of meaning production within the town's population.

2

Uses and Customs

Local Construction of Political Actors

Uses and customs are customs that you can use.
— Ricardo Martínez, Secretary General,
H. Ayuntamiento Constitucional de Tepoztlán 1997–2000

At the beginning of my fieldwork in Tepoztlán, I was interested in talking to people about the effects that the movement had on their lives, about the realignment of political forces within the town and about their perceptions of the future in light of their long struggle against the state government. In particular, I was trying to figure out why this movement was successful here, and why other similar types of imposed development projects did not elicit the resistance that the one in Tepoztlán had. Despite, however, my interest in understanding the present and guessing at the future, people continually answered me by referring to the past. Sometimes this was in reference to relatively recent struggles against other projects, or about organizing the democratic tendency of the national teachers' union, or opposing the restructuring of the water system. Sometimes, however, that past, which seemed so important to the present situation had to do with an inheritance from the Mexican Revolution or from even seemingly more remote times of protracted indigenous resistance to Colonial rule. In the context of discussions about the golf course, there seemed to be awareness that being "Tepozteco," while that meant very much being Mexican also meant being "different than other Mexicans."

Part of the success of the anti-golf movement in Tepoztlán was due, at least in part, to the ability of movement leaders to produce a great deal of internal cohesion within townspeople by constructing a Tepozteco identity based on local and historical differences with the rest of Mexico. This process involved forging a broad alliance out of an internally heterogeneous

Mural depicting Quetzalcoatl, and invoking Zapata to urge unity and resistance, entrance to Tepoztlán, 1996.

population. Following a strategy employed my many anti-colonial movements, in the course of their struggle against outside forces represented here by the state and KS, activists sought to define an authentic Tepozteco identity based on a number of fundamental local myths and social practices as a means to distinguish themselves from their opponents and to articulate an affirmative agenda in their on going struggles against imposed development projects.

Local historic specificity played an important role in the ideological and organizational frames created by the movement, as it developed a rhetoric that would bring about unity within the town and temporarily downplay internal differences. The cultural production of the movement revolved around the specificity of concrete practices and beliefs. Tepozteco activists, borrowing from Mexican legal jargon, employed the concept of "uses and customs" to define their rights to follow what they defined as traditional means of organizing and of self-recognition. In that process, they built on what Guillermo Bonfil Batalla has popularized as the concept of "deep Mexico," the often times submerged but living Mesoamerican practices observable in every day life. It is from this position within "deep Mexico," that activists began to draw upon those discourses, practices and beliefs that, while not excluding them from the Mexican nation, nevertheless made them distinct from it, and in particular, distinct from the current national project being carried out under the banner of neoliberalism, with which the golf course project was intimately identified.

In this chapter, I examine some of the raw materials that Tepozteco activists used in creating part of their public persona, based on the understanding that activists were very much aware of the political capital that "deep Mexico" held in contemporary political discourse. That is, in their construction of an oppositional identity, activists were drawing upon the idea that part of their culture was not subsumable to, nor representable by, dominant, neoliberal Mexican state ideology. It provided a direct challenge to the hegemonic notion of an inclusive national-popular identity promoted by decades of state policy and political discourse. This alternative proposal for being a nation, inherent in their movement, suggests that the exercise of power ought not lie in a centralized, Europeanized state, because it originates ultimately in, and therefore ought to be expressed through, local dynamics and in terms of local needs and desires. While there are a number of different types of discourses and practices that I could discuss that would encompass this notion of a deep Mexico from which activists were building an oppositional stance, there are three in particular that I will examine here, because they seemed to play a disproportionately large role in the public symbolism invoked by the movement. The first is the town's foundational myth, the story of *Tepoztécatl* (or Tepozteco); the second, is the figure of Emiliano Zapata; and, the third is the organization of the town's *barrio* system around a series of religious/civic festivals. The meanings of these symbols and practices are actually quite complex and internally contradictory. Nevertheless, through the movement, a seemingly unified meaning could be attributed to them, which aided activists in not only securing internal cohesion, but also in projecting an image of a single, distinct community to the public at large.

The Myth of the Tepozteco King

The story of the Tepozteco King is one that widely circulates through the town, and has been collected recently in writing in several different forms (Gallo Sarlat 1988; Zúñiga Navarrete 1995; Tostada Gutiérrez 1998; Lomnitz 2001). While the myth itself is important, it is also important to note that it is reenacted by the town's population every year, and is considered one of the most important cultural events on the very busy festival schedule.[1] Although versions of the story vary from teller to teller, with some versions leaving parts out, and others contradicting important details, the essence of the story seems to have been authoritatively captured by Ángel Zúñiga Navarrete, a local historian, educator and promoter of the Nahuatl language (Tostada Gutiérrez 1998, 235).

According to the legend, as recounted by Zúñiga (1995),[2] Tepozteco was the son of the wind god, Ehecatepetl, and the beautiful daughter of a prominent family in town. The woman became pregnant one day while bathing in her usual spot on the Atongo River, not far from her house. She was always accompanied by one of the family's servants, and on this particular day a beautiful red bird and a gentle breeze enchanted her. When her pregnancy began to show, it came as a great surprise to her, since she had never been with a man, and as a great shame to her family, who did not understand how she had become pregnant. She was kept secluded in the family's residence, so that her condition would not be known by anyone outside of the family.

When the child was born, the woman's father decided to kill him, so as not to cause any dishonor to his name. While the mother was sleeping, the baby's grandfather, accompanied reluctantly by the mother's servant, took the baby from her sleeping arms and brought it to an anthill. They left him there to be devoured by these particularly vicious ants. When the grandfather returned the next day to make sure the baby was dead, he discovered that instead of eating him, the ants were feeding him. He snatched the child from the anthill and brought it to a maguey plant. He left the baby in the middle of the thorny branches to be killed by the hot sun. When he returned three days later, however, he discovered that instead of being dead in the sun, the baby was cooing happily. The maguey plant had turned its leaves to provide shade, and mysterious cuts on the end of its leaves had appeared and were dripping sweet nectar into the boy's mouth.

Infuriated by his failures, the grandfather took the baby once again. This time, he built a box, put the baby in it, and sealed the cover tightly. He then placed the box in the river, assuming that it would carry him downstream, slowly fill with water and sink, killing the child once and for all. He did not account for the lightness of the baby, however, and the box floated down stream, but did not sink. It traveled out of sight, and the grandfather returned home, assuming that he had been rid of this dishonorable child once and for all. Upon learning of her father's deeds, the mother was, of course, distraught, yet through all of her tears, she sensed that her baby was still alive.

The box carrying the baby eventually got caught up on some rocks. An old couple, who having already raised their own children, was passing by the river on their way up into the mountains to collect firewood, when they noticed the box in the river. Being curious as to what might be inside such a rare looking find, they carefully fished it out of the water. Needless to say, they were shocked to find a baby playing happily inside. They decided to take the child home, hiding him under their clothes, so nobody would see them, and then claimed that the child was theirs. Although people were surprised that they could have another child at their age, he was happily accepted as theirs. "And so, time passed; the light of happiness shown from that humble hut, because, since finding the child, everything was blessed for these humble old people" (53).

As the boy grew up, he became aware that he had special powers, such as being able to kill any game simply by shooting an arrow in its general direction, or the ability to walk all day and not tire. He used his abilities to care for his loving adoptive parents, by providing them with ample food and protection. He loved his adoptive parents dearly, and referred to them as *coli*, which is an affectionate term for grandparent in Nahuatl.

At this time, in the town of Xochicalco, to the south of Tepoztlán, there lived a giant monster named Xochicalatl. He was feared by all of the inhabitants of the region, because of his strength and because his only food was human flesh. "All of the peoples that were considered to be under his domain had to offer him his weekly meal. This was done through his emissaries who would visit every village looking among their inhabitants for the oldest person, which was his favorite dish. Nobody protested because they knew that if someone put an obstacle in the way of his messengers, their entire family would be wiped out, and because they considered him a supreme being who had been sent by the gods" (55).

One week the guards came to Tepoztlán and it was the *coli*'s turn to be taken. The head of the town came sadly accompanied by the guards, to look for grandfather, and since "the destiny of all old people was to serve as food for the giant," he was prepared to go with them (57). Tepozteco, by this time a young man, had come to know through dreams that Ehecatepetl was his true father and that he could use the special powers given to him by his father to defeat his enemies. He freed his grandfather from the guards and insisted that they take him instead. When they protested, noting that Xochicalatl only liked old people, Tepozteco turned one of them into stone. (This stone has since been broken up and used in the construction of many houses in Tepoztlán). Fearing a similar fate, the emissaries agreed to take Tepozteco instead.

Along the road to Xochicalco, Tepozteco marked many important spots along the way, and gave them names that are still used by inhabitants today. He also picked up as many sharp rocks and pieces of obsidian as he could, and put them into his bag. As he left Tepoztlán, he looked back at the mountains of his native land, remembering all of them by name. He also remembered that those mountains were where his father lived and invoked them "to help him in the enterprise that he had begun, that was the destruction of the also powerful Xochicalcatl and thereby free all of the peoples from the tyranny of this cannibal" (58).

After a long journey, Tepozteco and his captors arrived at the palace of Xochicalcatl. When he was confronted with the monster, he was initially afraid and began to rethink his plan, but "an invisible and powerful force pushed him forward, toward him, toward the tyrant to end with the scourge, to break his strength in the name of his father, the powerful god of wind" (60). Although Xochicalcatl was angry that they had brought him a young man, he could not stand his hunger anymore, and he ordered that Tepozteco be cooked and served to him immediately.

The cooks placed him in the oven, but when the time came that he should be done, they opened the oven and discovered a live rooster in there instead of Tepozteco. Surprised, they opened the oven again and were almost bitten by a tiger. They slammed the door shut and noticed Tepozteco standing next to them laughing. They grabbed him, and threw him in a pot of boiling water. When they opened the pot, he was playfully swimming in it. Realizing that they would be unable to cook him, they brought him to their master, who then decided to eat him raw. Tepozteco recommended that he swallow him whole, so as not to get any of him stuck in his teeth. The monster agreed that this was a good idea, and since Tepozteco was not too big, opened his mouth wide, and let him jump in. Tepozteco slid whole into the giant's stomach. At first, Xochicalcatl was very pleased with his meal, but his look of content gradually turned to pain.

Inside his stomach, Tepozteco quickly removed the sharp rocks and blades that he had collected on the journey there and began to cut away at the monster's stomach and intestines from the inside. He made quick work of his task, killing Xochicalcatl before any of his servants could help him. He tried to cut his way out of the belly, but since the monster was no longer breathing, his air was quickly running out. His father came to his rescue, turning him into a breeze, and letting him escape from Xochicalco. Tepozteco found a high hill, and sent up a white cloud, as he had promised, to let his parents know that he had killed the tyrant and survived. The people in Tepoztlán were so relieved and happy that they immediately decided to name him king.

Although he was anxious to return home, to prove to everyone that he was still alive, he decided to visit other towns along the way, in order to get to know them better. As he approached Cuernavaca, he heard the beating of the Tlalpanhuehuetl, the drum that is known as Tepoaztle in

Tepoztlán. The music indicated that there was an important festival going on, and he decided to participate. When he arrived at the city gates, however, guards stopped him and refused to let him enter because he was dirty and dressed in rags (as a result of his long journey and battle with Xochicalcatl). A few moments later, he reappeared to the same guards, only now magically dressed as a great prince. They allowed him to pass, and he announced to the lord of Cuernavaca that he was the lord of Tepoztlán. He was seated in a place of honor next to the host. When the meal of turkey[3] was served, instead of eating it, Tepozteco smeared it on his clothes. The other guests were surprised by his actions, and the host asked if he did not like turkey and if they should serve him something else instead. To which Tepozteco replied "a short while ago, I presented myself to your servants, but because of my humble dress, they ran me off. A moment later, I came dressed as I am and now, they let me pass and that is why I am at your side; I see that you do not pay attention to the person only the clothes and therefore, it is only fair that my clothes enjoy the meal" (63).

Although they did not understand the strange behavior nor the equally strange explanation, the nobles at the feast allowed him to stay. As the other guests all became engaged in conversation with each other, Tepozteco asked if he could play the Tepoaztle that he heard when he was arriving. The more he played it, the more he enjoyed it, and he decided that he should give it to his people as a reward for his having destroyed the monster. To put his plan into action, Tepozteco conjured a strong wind, which blew dust into everyone's eyes making them temporarily blind. He used this moment of confusion to put the drum under his arm and get away. As he left the building, several guards spotted him and began to chase him. He eluded them for a while, but realizing that his escape was about to be cut off, spun himself so fast that he cut a ravine into the hard rock, slowing down his pursuers, and headed quickly to the safety of the mountains around Tepoztlán. They eventually caught up to him, and attempted to capture him, but in the blink of an eye he disappeared, only to be sitting on another peak, joyfully playing the Tepoaztle. In the end, however, he was too fast and too clever for them, and used his mountains to elude them. The Lord of Cuernavaca was furious over this deception and began to put together an alliance of all of the other lords in the region, to capture Tepozteco and to return the drum to its rightful owner.

After his would-be captors returned with their disappointing news to Cuernavaca, Tepozteco came down from the mountains to be reunited with his loving family. The townspeople were so happy to have him safely returned, that they officially crowned him king. Realizing that he now had many enemies, Tepozteco ordered that his temple (*teocalli*) be built precisely between the two highest peaks in the range in order to protect the town from military attack. The temple was a copy of the temple in the main plaza, which received pilgrims from as far away as Central America, and was dedicated to *Ometochtli* (Two Rabbits). The main temple was destroyed by the Dominican Friars and used to build the town's church.

At about this same time, the Dominican Friars were in the region and were dedicating themselves to the conversion of the Indians. The inhabitants of Tepoztlán, however, did not believe in a new religion, as they were very attached to the gods that their ancestors had left them. The friars noticed that the people of Tepoztlán completely obeyed their king and sought an audience with him in order to convert him. They explained to him, clearly, how their god was the true god and would lead to salvation. Tepozteco decided that to prove their case they should climb up to the *teocalli* and throw his god down the side of the mountain. If it broke, it would prove that they were right, and if it did not, it would prove that his gods were more powerful. Although they were a bit reluctant at first, the friars agreed, seeing how far a fall the idol would have, and being sure that it would break upon impact.

People gathered below to see how powerful their gods were, and as the idol fell, a great wind rose up and settled the idol gently on the soft earth and debris, which had accumulated below the mountain. The people in town were all pleased to see how powerful their gods were, and the friars were dismayed that the stone idol had not broken. Being men of great learning, however, the friars convinced Tepozteco to throw the idol off the mountain the next day as well. Before throwing it, however, the friars had all of the earth and debris removed from the ravine, so that when the idol fell this time it smashed upon the hard rock below and fractured into a thousand small pieces. Keeping his word as king, and seeing that his god had been destroyed, Tepozteco accepted his conversion and was baptized by Fray Domingo de la Anunciación. Most of the town's population followed the king's example and were soon baptized, but a few resisted and fled into the mountains. From this day forward, the king recognized the Virgin of the Nativity as his mother and protector of the town, and his baptism is celebrated every 8th of September and known as *Altepeihuitl* (town festival).

On one of these festivals, the Tepozteco King, now converted to his new religion, received a message that his enemies were approaching to overthrow him, not so much for the insult of the drum, but now for having betrayed the old gods. He received the lords of Cuernavaca and the other neighboring towns and invited them to come forward. He explained that he had taken the Tlalpanheuhuetl, but that it was fair compensation to his people for his having defeated the feared Xochicalcatl and thus freeing all of the people of the region. Although he was prepared to fight, and his soldiers would have excellent allies in the rugged mountains and deep ravines of Tepoztlán, the king chose to make peace with his enemies in order to avoid their suffering a humiliating defeat. He had the Tlalpan-heuhuetl played, so that all could see that it was in good condition and being taken good care of. Finally, he gave all of his enemies an embrace and urged them to accept the new religion. Each king then went back to his own people to reflect on their experience with Tepozteco.[4]

The Tepozteco king "continued working for his people" (69) and on a certain occasion he was called to help raise the bells on the Cathedral in Mexico City. He made the long trip to the great Tenochtitlán, and found a large crowd standing around the bells, wondering how to get them up into the tower. Calling on his father, the powerful god of wind, he created a huge wind-storm that knocked everyone down and blew dust everywhere. When the wind subsided people heard the Tepozteco king ringing the bells from their appropriate place. When he climbed down, the people asked him what price he needed to be paid for his work, to which he replied, "nothing but the box which is buried here in the plaza. I will show you the exact spot." After eating, they dug up the box and he sent it with some of the elders from Tepoztlán back to his land with the warning that they should not open it until he returned.

Tepozteco spent several days in Mexico City, visiting important places. The elders returned to Tepoztlán, where they told people they could not open the box. Curiosity was too much, however, and after a few days, the elders gave into the pressure from the people and opened the box. Much to their surprise, however, it did not contain any treasure, but out flew five doves. Startled, the doves flew in different directions, each landing in a different nearby town. When the king returned, he sensed immediately what had happened and ordered the elders to leave town for having disobeyed him. He cursed the people, saying that the five doves were to have been buried in the center of town in order to bring prosperity, but now they had flown to their rivals and would bring prosperity to them instead.

After this defeat at the hands of his own people, it is not known what became of Tepozteco. Some say that he died of old age in some unknown place, unable to accept the good luck which his former enemies were enjoying as a result of his people's disobedience. Others say that he was taken prisoner by the Spaniards and thrown into the ocean in chains, where now only mermaids who live in the deep visit him. The most probable, however, is that his mother, the Holy Virgin, took him to her place in Heaven and converted him into a star so that he can visit his beloved town every night, to see if people still remember him. This can be sensed when, after the celebration of September 8th, if he is not pleased with the festival, he sends a strong wind storm from the inside of his father the powerful Ehe-catepetl[5] to punish the inhabitants.

From this myth, the movement extracted and built on important themes as it built local support for opposing the golf course. The first is a sense of rebelliousness from centralized authority. That is, Tepozteco becomes a hero by resisting and killing the tyrant at Xochicalco, in order to save his adoptive parents and the rest of the peoples of the valley. A straightforward interpretation would be the importance of protecting one's own against the demands of outside consumptive forces. Xochicalcatl is a feared, powerful, ravenous beast, referred to throughout the legend as a monster, cannibal, or tyrant. People in Tepoztlán, and throughout the nearby municipalities, were defenseless against this monster, which insisted on taking their elders. Perhaps most frightening of all, is that, although it is a terrible fate, everyone seemed to accept it as natural and inevitable. There was, in other words, nothing that could humanly be done to overcome the monster's logic. Clearly analogies could be and were drawn from this metaphor by movement activists to not only the situation that the Tepoztecos faced in relation to the golf course, but also, more gener-ally to colonial and capitalist development which naturally and inevitably takes without returning.

Secondly, Tepozteco increases his fame by challenging and tricking the more powerful kings in the region by stealing the Cuernavaca king's drum and fleeing to the relative safety of the mountains around Tepoztlán. Tepozteco's anger toward the other nobles is sparked by his initial rejec-tion because of his dirty and torn clothing. Given his humble upbringing with his grandparents, he would logically be sensitive to such a snub. Also, it serves as a metaphor for the ways in which Tepoztecos, as a peripheral community within the regional, national and global systems are seen and treated by the metropolis, represented here by Cuernavaca. Tepozteco's smearing of his meal represents this rejection of the rules of appearance dictated by centralized and wealthy authorities, suggesting that there is something more important than superficial appearances to understanding people's worth. The challenge to centralized authority, represented by the stealing of the drum, and the importance of the community and natural surroundings to provide protection, again, suggests the values of a com-munitarian identity and the intrinsic worth of the land that they inhabit.

In these two episodes of the narrative, heroism is being defined as both protecting, and receiving protection from, the community and its physical location against more powerful, centralized authorities. On his way to meet the monster, Tepozteco is inspired by looking back at his beloved town and mountains, and then uses these mountains to elude his enemies. One contemporary Tepozteco, Victor Flores, explains the continuing importance of the mountains, not only as a source of beauty and inspiration, but also in that they "...have been and will continue to be resources for the people of the town. They were a refuge for the protection of their lives in several eras. During the Revolution it was a strategic place to protect themselves from the battles. For some people who still have economic needs, the hills continue providing resources for their survival" (70). These protective attitudes were clearly deployed as people in the community confronted powerful adversaries in terms of the state government and KS, and as they braced themselves for the expected consequences of their actions. Time and again, activists expressed that they were motivated by a desire to serve their people and to protect the natural beauty of their land, and that the more risks they took, the more supported and protected they felt by that community. Furthermore, as in the legend, townspeople used the limited access to the town, provided by the mountainous terrain, to successfully seal themselves off from possible police assaults, while launching a series of media attacks against the governor and KS, mirroring Tepozteco's taunting of his enemies from the safety of his mountain refuges. They were, in a sense, invoking Tepozteco's deeds by challenging the insatiable monster of KS and by keeping themselves out of angry "king" Carrillo's grasp.

At the same time, however, the myth does not provide a simple, anticolonial reading. The ceremony in the town is timed to coincide with the anniversary of Tepozteco's conversion to Christianity and celebrates his, and by extension the community's, voluntary and heartfelt cooperation with the Church. Part of the legend that is keenly emphasized in this ceremony is not just his heroism in confronting Xochicalatl and his rival kings, but also his leadership in converting Tepoztecos, as well as the rest of the indigenous leadership of the region, to Christianity. The coercion and co-optation that generally accompanied such conversions is not present in the story, instead, the king converts out of reason and proof. This conversion, nevertheless, continues to be problematic throughout the narrative, because it does not require the absolute disappearance of older gods and beliefs, but rather their subservience to the new Spanish, Catholic order. The legend, for instance, not only never explicitly negates Tepozteco's status as the son of Ehecatepetl, the wind god, but goes so far as to invoke the deity toward the end of the story when Tepozteco calls for his father's help in raising the bells on the cathedral in Mexico City. This reappearance of the seemingly discredited god at the end of the legend, to further the interests of the Catholic Church, no less, must raise some questions as to the depth of the conversion process, and in fact reflects the kind of religious syncretism which is prevalent in many Mesoamerican communities.[6]

It suggests that over time different belief systems were fused into a single, multifaceted one that reflects the diversity of local historic experience. It makes it impossible to point to a single, monolithic belief system that has successfully excluded others, pointing instead to a much more complex one that corresponds to local needs and desires. This contradiction is plainly visible even today, where a mural composed of seeds glued on to the churchyard gate, depicts parts of this legend, as well as the Spanish, and by association, the Church's, violent destruction of much indigenous culture. Notably, the writing is all in Nahuatl and the mural itself is meant as a tribute to pre–Conquest culture and a condemnation of the European invasion, yet it is sponsored by the very Church that had a decisive role in that conquest.

The ambiguity and syncretism in this founding myth and the subsequent practices and representations which have grown up around it, is an indication of complex logics contained in hybrid cultures. The depth of this hybridity cannot be overlooked in understanding the cultural project inherent in the anti-golf movement. Activists built on the communitarian ethics highlighted throughout the story which privilege "working for the community" as a value that survives throughout other kinds of cultural change. Tepozteco is driven by a desire to protect and serve his community both before and after his conversion to Christianity, suggesting that local community is at least as important as the larger cultural discourses that contribute to its social structuring.

The telling of the legend demonstrates the capacity to accept the simultaneous existence of different and contradictory logics that would allow activists not only to build internal cohesion by associating their movement with "inherent" Tepozteco values, but which would also allow them to move between the specificities of local concerns, often times expressed in a non-modern language dominated by spiritual connections to the land and non-economic ties to local community, and the larger concerns of the state and the global economy, expressed in the terms of modernity and the commodification of human relationships. It would appear to confirm García Canclini's assertions that cultural hybridity results not simply from the juxtaposition of cultural codes, but rather through their meaningful consumption. In this case, movement activists were able to extract useful parts of the cultural codes contained within this, and other, myths and rearticulate them around a particular issue. It suggests, therefore, that the notion of cultural hybridity is not necessarily a politically neutral or undifferentiated mixture of all possible cultural content, but rather that social agents can negotiate that hybridity in order to construct an oppositional stance by articulating certain aspects of existing, sedimented cultural artifacts. In fact, they are able to exploit the ambiguities inherent within hybrid formations (i.e. the unresolved tension between a "defeated" millenarian culture and a conquering Christianity) in order to challenge the very success of that dominant project. In this case, for instance, a dominant reading of the legend would certainly be the successful conversion of indigenous culture to European standards and values. The movement, however, is able to rescue the defiant aspects inherent in the legend (i.e. the continued existence and power of the Mesoamerican deities), in order to make Tepozteco a rebel and thus to mark the entire town as rebellious and righteous in its resistance to the modern, capitalist, Europeanized project represented by the golf course.

Zapata and Contesting Hegemony

Emiliano Zapata provides another contradictory and contested symbol that the movement repeatedly utilized at public demonstrations as a means to garner internal cohesion and to challenge the foundations of dominant hegemony. If Tepozteco represents the ongoing struggle between Mesoamerican and European world visions, then Zapata represents the continuing struggle between local and centralized authority. This tension can be traced back to the town's resistance to paying high tributes to Tenochtitlan, through occasional violent uprisings against Spanish colonial authorities to constant friction created by the imposition of unpopular candidates and economic programs by the PRI in more recent times.[7] The most important symbol of this struggle can clearly be found in the chaotic and utopian projects of the Revolution headed in Morelos by Zapata. Like Tepozteco, Zapata, too is celebrated annually at a public ceremony, and holds an important place in the local pantheon of heroes. The contradictions in Zapata, as a symbol, however, lie both within hegemonic struggles with the state over his meaning and the meaning of the revolution more generally in Morelos, as well as the contradiction between Zapata the hero, and accounts by many people who lived through the revolution in which they express very ambiguous, and sometimes explicitly negative, sentiments about their treatment at the hands of Zapatista forces.

Although Emiliano Zapata would rise to the rank of Supreme Chief in the Mexican Revolution and be forever associated as the leader of the politically and socially radical faction of those turbulent times, he began his political career as president of the Anenecuilco village council in 1909. At the age of 30 he was relatively young to hold such a prestigious position, but the village elders who headed the council until 1909 saw troubled times coming, and decided that they needed younger leadership to defend the village's interests against the encroaching hacienda and its allies in the state and federal governments. Because of his family's connections in the village and because he was judged to be of good character and reliable, he easily won election at the village meeting and was entrusted with safeguarding the population's interests. Of particular importance, he was charged with protecting colonial documents that outlined the extent of their land holdings (Womack 1968, 3–9).[8] He proved to be a good pick, and using those colonial documents to which he had been entrusted, began pressing his villagers' claims in courts in Cuernavaca and Mexico City. Although he had some initial and surprising successes, court rulings did not necessarily translate into reality on the ground, and he eventually began urging his compatriots to arm themselves in order to protect their lands, victories and identities against the never satisfied desires of the local hacienda.

From the beginning of this struggle it was obvious to Zapata and to the other villagers in Morelos that the struggle against the rich *hacendados* was not just about the rights to use land and water as a commercial enterprise. While the villagers certainly needed access to them, they were more than just factors of production. The people in Zapata's village had continually occupied that place for more than 700 years and the attempts of the liberal government and the hacienda owners to alienate them from their lands represented a threat to the very fabric of who they were. Their institutions and families had existed for literally centuries tied to the land on which they found themselves, and their struggle, therefore was one aimed at maintaining that *status quo* in the face of powerful interests that were attempting to push them into another way of life. When the chaos, which was about to be unleashed in 1909 came to an end more than a decade later, the *campesinos* of Morelos could claim a very costly victory, notes historian John Womack, "simply in holding on as villagers, not in refuge in the state's cities or huddled into the haciendas, but out where they felt they belonged, in the little town's and pueblos and ranchos" (1968, 370). The papers that had been entrusted to Zapata, and that he risked his life time and again to save and to hide from the authorities were not just "land titles, but (a) record of constancy and uprightness" for which Zapata and his followers were fighting (372). Land, therefore, represented the historical self-construction of these communities, and it was the preservation of that communal life which the Zapatistas were ultimately attempting to preserve.

Seeing that the Díaz era was coming to an end, Zapata opted to join the forces of Francisco Madero in 1910, hoping to secure the social and agrarian reforms that he was espousing. After Madero took power, however, it was obvious to Zapata that he had neither the intention nor the ability to carry out the land reforms that he saw as key to the revolution, and he quickly broke with the new democratic alliance in Mexico City by issuing the Plan de Ayala. In this famous set of political principles, the Zapatista leaders renounced Madero and outlined their plan for national, structural land reform promising to completely expropriate *hacendados* and politicians who did not cooperate. With this plan, then, the Zapatistas transformed themselves from local rebels into a revolutionary organization dedicated to structurally transforming Mexican society (Warman 1988, 110). Indeed, the Plan de Ayala came to be *the* defining instance of the Zapatista initiative, which "the Zapatista chiefs considered ... a veritable catholicon, much more than a program of action, almost a Scripture" (Womack 1968, 393). The Liberating Army of the South would not waver in spirit or letter from the plan from that November of 1911 until 1918, thus defining itself as the radical tendency throughout the multiple negotiations and shifting alliances of the decade. This commitment to radical land reform and social change always put the Zapatistas at odds with the political reformists who were willing to let the land and economic issues stand unresolved in the interests of ending the political conflict.

Widespread fighting broke out again in 1913 after Victoriano Huerta overthrew and assassinated Madero. The Zapatista forces played a key role in Huerta's eventual ouster, with Zapata from the South and Francisco Villa from the North briefly occupying the presidential seat in 1914. But, for Zapata and his troops, such high-powered politics were clearly not to their liking, and they soon, quietly, retreated from Mexico City to rejoin their communities throughout Morelos (Warman 1988, 114). Despite their abdication of national politics, of which they were always suspicious because they feared that such involvement would eventually lead them to betray the principles of the Plan de Ayala, they continued to play an important role in staking out the agrarian question throughout the revolution. Their point was not to capture state power, but to see to the possibility of free and autonomous municipalities at home, where *campesino* families could preserve their way of life. This retreat back to Morelos showed, once again, that Zapata and the forces that he represented cared less about political change and legalities and more about effective change on the ground that would directly benefit the state's *campesinos*.

That following year was, in many ways, the chance for Zapatismo to be put into practice. Although the rest of the country was dragged into another round of fighting as the various forces from the North jockeyed for position at the national level, Morelos enjoyed a relative calm, and the much hoped for reforms outlined in the Plan de Ayala were put into effect. The great haciendas were broken up and land was returned to the *campesino* villagers from whom it had been taken. Land was redistributed either as communal land in which families had a right to work part, or as small land holdings, depending on the desires of the community, with the only restriction being that the land was permanently inalienable from the families to which it was ceded (Warman 1988, 115). As John Womack describes it, "in this social wilderness (the population had been dislocated and almost all vestiges of political authority had been displaced by the fighting of 1911–1915) they moved in a remarkably constant direction toward the establishment of democratic municipalities, country neighborhoods where every family had influence in the disposition of local resources" (224). Since the population had been greatly reduced and the land monopolized by the haciendas returned to village control, there were few territorial disputes. Every village's ancient papers, like those of Anenecuilco that Zapata himself had been hiding, appeared, and villages were able to agree upon limits and boundaries. When there was ambiguity, village elders were summoned and new maps were drawn based upon the consensus at which they arrived, usually marking boundaries by existing crooked fences and other land marks (Gilly 1971, 264–266). In other words, the *campesino* communities themselves became subjects of their own land reform and were vested with the political rights to make and enforce decisions.

Political authority changed dramatically as well. Although technically under the control of Convention Government in Mexico City, authority rested in the Zapatista commanders, who negotiated with the central authorities, but who would not let them impose order where it contradicted the principles of the Plan de Ayala. This represented an important democratic advance, as Zapata and all of his commanders derived their original authority from local councils, and who (for the most part) remained loyal to those councils. They saw themselves as the armed extension of the village, rather than an autonomous military organization. "Zapatismo always understood that its survival depended on this quality and it took care to maintain this nature. It turned over not just land but also political autonomy to the villages and guaranteed its exercise against military bosses" (Warman 1988, 116). They attempted to rule through established uses and customs of local villages, based on kinship and personal relations rather than imposing a vertical organization upon them. When there were local disputes, it was Zapatista commanders who were called in to act as judges and arbitrate a settlement. "When (Zapata) himself took part in settling local troubles, as he did more than once, he limited his involvement to enforcing decisions the villagers reached on their own" (Womack 1968, 227). The Zapatista armed forces, in other words, did not create the mechanisms of political order, instead they attempted to act as the protectors of long standing democratic processes.

The Zapatista "communes" were of short duration, however, as the war returned by the end of the year disrupting the nascent social structures being nurtured in the villages of Morelos (Gilly 1971, 261). Having defeated Francisco Villa in the North, Venustiano Carranza was attempting to consolidate his hold on the Revolution from Mexico City by the end of 1915. Zapata's independence from centralized authorities clearly presented him with a challenge, and the radical reforms being successfully carried out throughout the state represented a serious threat to the bourgeois order that Carranza envisioned as being the outcome of the Revolution. Troops were dispatched to the South, and violence, chaos and hunger quickly returned as communal farms were attacked and burned, and villages were plundered. As the social bases of the Zapatista army came under increasing pressure from federal troops, they were unable to sustain the fighting forces, which became effectively disarticulated by the beginning of 1919.

Under the guise of cementing a new alliance with a break away federal general, Jesús Guajardo, Zapata was lured to the former hacienda at Chinameca. Guajardo, however, was still very much loyal to Carranza's forces, and when an honor guard raised their weapons to salute the Supreme Commander of the Liberating Army of the South, instead of firing in the air, they fired at him and his entourage. With his death on 10 April 1919, the Zapatista forces gradually disbanded and returned to their homes to attempt to rebuild their lives. They would be called into service one last time the following year, as Alvaro Obregón promised the country people of Morelos substantial and meaningful land reform in exchange for their support as he consolidated his regime against the discredited Carrancista forces. Keeping his word, Obregón made Morelos the first state to benefit from a relatively radical land reform, although now the politicians and bureaucrats in Mexico City rather than the communities controlled the administration and distribution of lands (Gilly 1971; de la Peña 1980; Warman 1988). Nevertheless, the *campesinos* of Morelos could count theirs as at least a partial victory as they were able to maintain (for the time being, anyway) the historic cultural ties that defined their communities.

This pride in defending local continuities and sovereignties finds itself into the ways in which Tepoztecos today tell the story of Zapata.[9] In fact many in Tepoztlán, and other rural areas of Morelos, believe that Zapata (both the man and his ideals) lived well beyond April 1919.[10] As Benito Peñaloza explains,

> ...for we Morelenses, the southern leader did not die, because his ideas continue to be valid, although there is much that has not been fulfilled and only taken advantage of by the politicians. Officially, they have made us believe that Zapata died, assassinated in Chinameca, betrayed by the enemy of the *campesino*: the government. We have testimonies from some of the people from that era, that were present when the supposed body of Zapata was exhibited by the government of the city of Cuautla.... After the Revolution they would visit us in our house and they always repeated the same thing that the body displayed was not that of general Zapata [Peñaloza Rojas 1998, 129–130].

When people were asked if the body was his, those who said no were beaten and taken away. Some noted that Zapata was missing a finger from an accident in his youth, but the corpse was complete. Likewise, Zapata had a prominent mole on his cheek, but the corpse had none. "What is certain," however, according to Peñaloza and other Tepoztecos, is that on his way to Chinameca, Zapata sensed that something was wrong. He was accompanied by a Tepozteco named Agustín Cortés, who bore a remarkable resemblance to the general. Zapata and Cortés briefly left the entourage on its way to the hacienda, and a few minutes later, only one of them returned. He kept his hat low and continued on to Chinameca without saying a word. Cortés never returned from the Revolution, and many Tepoztecos are convinced that their compatriot took the bullet for Zapata, who then quietly disappeared. This theory is backed up by the numerous sightings, well into the end of the century, of Zapata, or of letters sent in his hand years after the Revolution. He was, however, never officially seen in public again.

This Tepoztlán connection to Zapata is deeper than simply this legend of Agustín Cortés, however. Many Tepoztecos did join the Liberating Army of the South, and several rose to prominence as important generals in that army. Furthermore, because of Tepoztlán's strategic location, near the rail line, and within striking distance of Cuernavaca and Mexico City, as well as its protective mountains, it was used frequently as a headquarters and staging ground for Zapata's troops. There are rumors that Zapata had a Tepozteca lover and a child by her, who died during the Revolution. What is more, the sense that the Zapatista revolution was never completely fulfilled, continues to weigh on the consciousness of many Tepoztecos when remembering Zapata. In discussing the revolution, Victor Flores, for example, writes, "The fate of the struggle for the lands was and is a tragedy. We have spent several centuries fighting for them and we still have not been able to enjoy them. In another epoch it was the *hacendados* from the huge estates; now it is the rich and the politicians who ... believe they have the right to occupy the lands of the villages" (1998, 73). In other words, the very essence of the Zapatista struggle continues on in contemporary discourse about the importance of land tenure to the every day experiences of people.

The qualities that townspeople ascribe to Zapata play an important role in reinforcing desired values and were exploited by activists in the movement. As noted in the historic accounts, Zapata, despite his being a powerful and cunning military and political leader, never lost track of the fact that his true power came from his community, and that he maintained a humble and respective attitude toward regular people. He never became detached from the problems of everyday life, because he chose not to pursue the individual glories and riches which power would offer him. Womack notes that his associates never referred to him as "General" or "don," but simply as "'Meliano." This humble connection to everyday life and, subsequently, to its problems, comes out in several accounts of the end of Zapata's life. Benito Peñaloza, again, describes very eloquently this human side of the myth. "In reality (by the end), very few people were following the general. It became more and more difficult to sustain his movement and to support the expenses" (132). He may have had Cortés substitute for him, so that he could carry on his struggle in another way, "or perhaps he thought that to continue with the movement was now a sacrifice for his soldiers and their families that had suffered throughout those nine years of fighting. So, it had now come to an end for which he fulfilled his duty and did not reappear in public, even though he did continue to be in these lands (for some time)" (132). Peñaloza further speculates that Zapata had grown somewhat disillusioned with the struggle,

> It was commented that Guajardo's plan was to end with general Emiliano Zapata, and perhaps it was that general Zapata accepted this. There was peace, already, and the Zapatistas were dedicating themselves to organizing rodeos and fights in the cantinas. After a few drinks, spirits were raised leading to scuffles in which someone would say they had been braver and others more cowardly and would end up killing each other. General Zapata seemed depressed when Eufemio Zapata, his brother, was murdered in a cantina. He was beating a Zapatista boss, who was then rather old, for being drunk. At that moment,

the man's son arrived, who at seeing that they were beating his father, took out his pistol and killed general Eufemio Zapata — at least that is what they said. Reality was difficult for general Emiliano Zapata, and we think that he took advantage of this situation to retire with honor... [134].

The telling of this tale of Zapata reveals the importance not only of seeing Zapata as a great man, but more importantly as a regular man as well. He is depressed about his brother's death, and concerned about the disintegration of his movement. He is tired and is looking for a way out of his troubles. He is also greatly concerned that his struggle has now become too costly not only for him, but, importantly, for the soldiers and families that it is supposed to benefit. This quality of being all too human and always concerned for the benefit of the community can be seen inscribed in the ways in which people talk about and evaluate politicians. There continues to exist a residual *campesino* ideology about politics in general within Tepoztlán, in which for a political action to have success, it must be supported by *campesino* organizations.[11] The prevailing logic is that professional politicians are inherently, and almost by definition, corrupt and parasitic. *Campesinos*, on the other hand, are honest and hardworking people who know better than to get dragged into superficial political conflicts. When they do get involved, therefore, the cause must be just. Politicians are hampered by their needs and abilities to use fancy language and their pretensions of power. What is more valuable in terms of winning respect, however, is the ability to appear, and to actually be, a regular person from the community, whose true interests are the betterment of the community. It is, in other words, necessary to follow Zapata's example. In discussions that I had with Tepoztecos, the highest complement that could be paid to any politician was that "he is a man of the people," or a "real Tepozteco," or (in the case of the new governor) "a real, but real, Morelense." This distinction was made to me on several occasions when I solicited advice on who to talk to about political issues in the town. The split in the movement over whether or not to work with political parties, for instance, was along the lines of "people's" politicians and regular "politicians," with the non-professionals (i.e. those who continue to maintain their distance from the PRD establishment) singled out as being true to the cause and to democracy, and those working too closely with the PRD viewed as suspect. These values can clearly be seen in the ways in which Zapata has been created as a "real" person, with emotions and troubles, as well as someone who eschews politics in favor of self-sacrificing service to his community.

The figure of Zapata is also important to the construction of the movement in that he represents not only rebellion and service to the community, but also a consciousness of the importance of the historic continuity of that community. The struggle for land in which the communities of Morelos have been involved since before the arrival of the Spanish, runs necessarily through Zapata. He is the key to connecting contemporary struggles with the more remote colonial and older struggles about maintaining control over the natural resources of the lands that people inhabit. Ángel Zúñiga (1998) writes,

> Since ancestral times these lands have belonged to the inhabitants, as a gift that the Creator gave to his children. The extension of the municipality of Tepoztlán has always been recognized, because one of the viceroys of New Spain gave to its inhabitants the Primordial Titles that date back to the seventeenth century. These mark, in the Nahuatl language in a very clear form the limits of the municipality by the four cardinal points [236].

Land tenure even today in Tepoztlán is related to these colonial documents, like the ones that Zapata protected. Likewise, Zúñiga goes on to explain that, "the lands of Tepoztlán have always belonged to the community. The land belongs to those who work it with their hands, as the agrarian general don Emiliano Zapata declared" (236). Indeed in Tepoztlán the land has maintained a particularly close tie to the population. Because it was not suited to the needs of the sugar producing haciendas in the south, almost none of the land was lost to them in the nineteenth century. As a result, most of the land within the municipality continues to be communal, having never been alienated from the community.[12] Zapata is the most visible and important symbol, then, not only of the protection of the land, but also of the historic continuity of the community associated with it.

In addition to using the figure of Zapata as a means to tie this particular conflict to a longer history of land struggle, the movement very consciously used him to attempt to work out a political solution to the crisis. One of the leaders of the CUT explained that the elections they held in 1995 (and subsequently in 1997) were

> *Zapatista* elections, because it was based on a system defined by personal trust. Zapata was a *calpulec*, that is, a village leader, who was charged with safekeeping the documents that defended the land. He was elected because he was a person of confidence and honesty. In the elections in town, people were selected in the same way by their neighbors and were also entrusted with protecting the land and the community [Interview 1999].

By using the example of Zapata, who was chosen by (the men, at least, of) his village to protect not just the land but also the concept of community, the Tepozteco activists were invoking a similar claim on their attempts to establish a new local political order. Zapata, therefore, accompanied the Tepozteco activists not only as a symbol carried in protests, but also represented the ideals and values that were woven into the movement itself. He sets the example whereby political decisions were organized, and symbolizes the importance for politicians to be addressed as *compadre* (close friend) rather than *licenciado* (a formal title for someone who has graduated from college).

Zapata was such a crucial figure to the Tepozteco movement, however, not just because he is a local hero, but also because he is an integral part of the pantheon of official nationalist symbols as well. By invoking Zapata, movement activists were engaging the state in the contestatory process under which the meaning of Zapata is continuously revised through often bitter negotiation with centralizing authorities. Throughout most of the twentieth century, much of the Mexican state's claim to legitimacy lay in its ability to produce a public history in which it was the obvious and only heir to the revolution. In order to carry out this process of legitimization, it changed official representations of Zapata in textbooks, speeches and public art from that of a bandit, to a fiery revolutionary, to a paternalistic protector of the *campesino*, to, more recently, a fairly ambiguous character. To give a concrete example, for instance, when President Carlos Salinas signed into law changes altering the special protection of *ejidos* and declaring land reform finally complete in 1992, he did so under a mural of Zapata, and claimed that this was the final step in the liberation of rural people, as now they would be freed of the paternalistic protection of the state and able to reap the benefits that unfettered integration into global capitalist markets offered them. Clearly, such action went against every principle for which Zapata stood, but historically, the Mexican state has been adept at overcoming such contradictions, exemplified by its incorporation of Zapata as a national hero, despite its assassination of him for being too dangerous to its project. By glorifying people such as Zapata, the state hoped to cement its legitimacy to the very people who fought against it.

In her study of a land dispute in another town in Morelos in the 1980s, JoAnn Martin, noted however that, "many Morelos peasants view this exploitation of history in the construction of national ideology as a violation of their local heroes" (1993, 450). In other words, the state, despite its proficiency at appropriating local histories for its own end, could never completely establish hegemony, because local memory and agents were also reworking the myths and reappropriating them from the state as well. Rather than creating entirely new symbolic and organizational systems, local activists do not have a relationship "of simple opposition in which (the movement) becomes the opposite of the state. Indeed, its tactic of mass organization and ... discourse of peasant rights and power echoes the populist strategies of the PRI. Instead of deploying an entirely new discourse and new strategies, the (movement) reappropriates the mechanisms of state power established after the Mexican Revolution and uses them to new ends" (Martin 1993, 448). By invoking Zapata, the activists in Tepoztlán, therefore, were participating in this ongoing struggle between the state and local communities over his meaning, which implies that they were laying claims to meanings produced both by the state and those local communities. Zapata, in other words, does not exist purely as an official nationalist icon, nor does he exist purely as a local oppositional symbol. He has become a hybridized symbol, whose meaning is worked out through social conflict. In this conflict, Martin argues, "the central dilemma for the state is how to exploit images of the power of peasants in the revolutionary struggle without reminding contemporary peasants of their power and their historic duty to oppose injustice. For the peasants of Morelos, the problem is how to retain control over the representations of history in a setting in which the state attempts to use history for its own ends" (443).

One can see this conflict clearly at play, for instance, in the textbook used in schools in Tepoztlán (and throughout Mexico) until the early 1990's.[13] In these texts, which would certainly have influenced many Tepozteco's perceptions and beliefs about Zapata and their (as Morelenses) particular role in social change, the revolution in the south is portrayed as noble and necessary. The history textbook declares, for instance, "The dispossessed class had to resort to insurrection in order to survive" (*Monografía* 1990, 156). Zapata is introduced by explaining "we can not understand the figure of Emiliano Zapata Salazar, one of the most illustrious characters from the Mexican Revolution, if we do not remember that for generations the *campesinos* of Morelos have embodied the secular struggle for land" (161). The reader is told that in Zapata's "veins ran the blood of the three upright races of the Morelos people: the indigenous, the Spanish and the African" (165). Zapata is moved to participate in politics out of a desire to protect his community and his family and that "men and women, carriers of a traditional culture, who lived in the rural communities participated massively in the movement. By any means possible, they wished to defend their culture: their beliefs, their customs, their communal institutions" (178). This glorification of the revolution and of the use of force to create social change, however, is tempered by observations that "many Zapatistas were prepared to suffer the existence of the *hacendado* as long as he did not invade the village's lands" (178), and of further portrayals of the state as the ultimate benefactor providing land reform. This is perhaps most thoroughly symbolized in an image produced by the Mexican State in the 1930s and circulated widely since then, showing Zapata on a white horse looking down upon a peasant, with his hand resting lightly on his shoulder, with the peasant looking up admiringly at his liberator (Martin 457). These and other similar representations of Zapata and the Revolution amounted to the state's attempt to simultaneously recognize and control the rebellious power of *campesinos*. By acknowledging people's rights to and traditions of rebelling, the state hoped to posit itself as the institutionalization of that revolutionary impulse by portraying itself as the last instance of that rebellion.

Pure, preferred readings of messages, however, are very rare. The case of Zapata is certainly no different, particularly given the glaring contradictions between a supposedly benefactor state and the continuing exploitation that the people, whom it was supposed to be protecting, continue to experience as part of their every day existence. "In contrast to the state's view of history, which emphasizes that revolutionary leaders have bestowed agrarian reform on the population, the view of history that emerges in local narratives stresses ordinary people who take charge of situations to resolve their problems" (Martin 458). As noted above, many of the Tepozteco narratives about Zapata focus on the issues surrounding his humanness: lovers, despair, frustration, and loyalty to community. Zapata is a representation of an ordinary person forced to act under extraordinary circumstances. A member of the "radical" faction of the anti-golf movement described the movement as,

> ...an excellent experience in self-organizing. People were involved because they had *power*. The realized that they needed to take power to keep the golf course from being built. They took the Ayuntamiento; they blocked the town's entrances; they threw out the police; they took responsibility for themselves. Some people tried to take advantage of the lack of recognized authorities, but people made them stop what they were doing. It was a true experience of being an autonomous municipality [Interview 1999].

The same criteria of taking responsibility for change are often used to describe Zapata and the revolution. Municipal Council member Malaquías Flores noted that, "With the golf course, everyone started getting together with their neighbors to talk about it. From there, different committees were formed who talked to other committees. When we took the town hall on 24 August, all of the committees came, so that everyone was responsible" (1999).

Activists built on the radical aspect of the Zapatista heritage, which emphasizes the rights and abilities of every day people to take power into their own hands, while ignoring the more compliant sides stressed by the state. The importance of the Zapata myth, built on the decades long struggle between communities and the state, in this instance, lay in Zapata's role as a regular person, and the power, therefore, that regular people have when they "get together" and begin talking, planning and acting cooperatively on a particular problem. They took seriously, in other words, the state's glorification of Zapata and the right to use whatever means necessary to defend their land, community and culture, together with their own local interpretations of collective power in order to fashion a Zapata which would aid them. They could believe they were being loyal Morelenses and Mexicans despite, or perhaps more accurately because of, their rebelliousness, by acting on their "special role in defending the principles and morals of the revolution against present day government" (Martin 459).

To further complicate matters, however, we should not assume that the construction of a suitably radical and benevolent Zapata is simply a struggle over meaning between the state and the community. Just as the state has multiple and changing images of Zapata, so does the community. While Zapata is often projected as being the great hero, liberator and ideal of community activism, the actual tales that people tell of Zapata and of their experiences of the Revolution often deviate from that script. Martin, for instance notes, "tales abound in the literature on Zapata of women who, having been kidnapped and raped, proudly accept their fate" (457). This is hardly the image of a great liberating army. From their interviews of participants in the Revolution, anthropologists Redfield and Lewis (who conducted research in Tepoztlán in the 1920s and 1940s–1960s respectively) suggest that there were multiple divisions within the Zapatista movement, and that there was not always a clear idea of what people were fighting for. Accounts of the Revolution are often rich in detail about battles and heroes, but short on an analysis of the political underpinnings of the fighting or even the personal motivations for joining the Zapatista movement (Warman 1988; Tostada Gutiérrez 1998). Even the stories about Agustín Cortés substituting for Zapata in Chinameca, while perhaps told to stress the importance of Tepoztlán in the struggle, leave rather troubling questions about Zapata's character. What kind of hero orders somebody else to die for him, and then quietly disappears?

In the preface to her collection of contemporary Tepozteco narratives, Marcela Tostada notes that the Revolution harbors

> ...bitter memories ... it is mentioned as a "time of hunger," of loneliness, of forced migration, of refuge in caves. The testimonies narrate the abuses and cruelties of both the Carrancistas and the Zapatistas, and even if the town was associated with the latter, certain anecdotes allow for doubt about the conviction or commitment of the population in those times with the Zapatista ideal, even if they now declare themselves Zapatistas [14].

One man, Domingo Peñaloza, who was born in 1907, recalls his childhood being filled with fear and constant moving. He recalls two exiles to Cuernavaca and a long period hiding in the mountains. When he talks of attacks on the community, including the murder of his father in front of his eyes, he makes no distinctions between the belligerent forces. He often times refers to perpetrators of crimes by name and gives many other details, but never clearly identifies which side they were on. He details abuses by both sides, and notes that "in that time, the Zapatistas took the girls away or simply abused them," as an introduction to the story of the kidnapping and rape of his young cousins (1998, 145). Apparently, despite the label of "Zapatista" often used now to describe their past, both in relation to the golf course and previous to it as well, many Tepoztecos of that time were *pacíficos*. They chose not to fight and fled to the mountains or nearby cities to avoid the conflict and returned when it appeared safe to do so (Lomnitz 1982, 156). While that does not mean that many were probably not sympathetic to the demands of the Zapatistas for land reform, from which many would certainly benefit, it does imply that their actual Zapatista heritage is more of a construction from later times than an actual reflection of the majority of people's experiences.

These ambiguities in part relate to the contradictions between official nationalist reconstructions of Zapata, and continual efforts by local people to maintain authentic and politically useful memories of him. Inevitably, the two divergent cultural projects end up influencing each other, producing a hybrid image of Zapata that is continually evolving. The task of the movement leadership, therefore, was to extract, recycle and consume those aspects of Zapata, drawn from the continuous negotiation between centralized state and local community, which helped to produce internal cohesion around an identity marked by the responsibility to rebel against injustice. In order to successfully do this, they needed to repress or otherwise ignore those aspects of the legend that were counterproductive. In other words Zapata as the paternalistic benefactor was banished and replaced by Zapata the common man who rose up and successfully confronted the powers that be. The Zapatista forces that were responsible for rape, murder and pillage were ignored and those that were true, respectful and honest were glorified. This malleability of Zapata is due in no small part to the maneuverings of the PRI-State which had manipulated the image for the past seven decades, and which now found itself the target of similar manipulations, with the images that it created turned back on itself. This was an effective strategy on the part of the movement leadership, as it allowed people not only to have the courage to stand up to the project, but to portray it even as a responsibility. It also created, in part, the kinds of strength that would allow a Tepozteco leader to later brag that "we get what we want from the state government now, because they know what we can do, and they are afraid of us" (Cedillo Méndez 1999). Zapata, after all, was a strong, and at times ruthless, warrior, and while he may very well deserve the reputation as a protector of the poor, was not called the "Atilla of the South" by his enemies for no reason.

Of Mayordomos, Calpulli, Barrios, and Coatéquitl

The symbols discussed here do not simply take on meaning by themselves, nor are they simply manifestations of ideas, but rather they are rooted in the communicative networks through which people actively construct their community. In Tepoztlán, these networks can be traced through the functioning of active associations built around the neighborhood *mayordomo*, who organizes neighborhood religious festivals, communal work and in general is the focal point of organized community life. The symbols that the movement was using in order to build internal cohesion, in other words, were also manifest in concrete practices.

The question of community and continuity was ever present in discussions with people in Tepoztlán, around both the struggle against the golf course and about everyday life as well. People repeatedly insisted on "authenticity" as a means of measuring the value of a particular story or the right of a person or family to have input on collective decisions. Many interviewees believed, however that the integrity of the community, nevertheless, is continually under attack from non–Tepozteco influences, as outsiders move in, as young people leave to search for work or educational opportunity, and as television and movies "corrupt" the values of local youth. One group of Tepoztecos that I interviewed during a neighborhood festival bemoaned the alienation of many young people in town, expressing their displeasure at "the groups of youth that go around drinking and causing trouble. Many of them wear earrings. The girls even have them in their belly buttons. They have no shame anymore" (Interview, July 2001). José Salazar (1998) writes that, "Tepoztlán has been characterized as being a great conserver of its traditions and customs. These traditions are very beautiful but are nevertheless being spoiled through time, as everyday life becomes undone under the influence of outside forces in our region" (199). Malaquías Flores (1998) also laments the gradual deterioration of customs due to the influence of the modern world: "Soon came the battery powered radio, then came electricity and more radios and television, and here we can see the results: our beautiful culture is on its way to extinction" (83). Nevertheless, there is a strong desire and effort to maintain social relations and identities based around local customs and traditions. These ongoing practices, centered on very local, neighborhood level organizations and rituals, tend to a certain degree to counterbalance the centrifugal forces of modernity. Marcela Tostada observes, "even today, the Tepozteco community, which formerly spoke Nahuatl, maintains a strong identity and cohesion within its people and its neighborhoods through a rich calendar of religious festivals and other celebrations of pre–Hispanic rituals" (1998, 17). Although these rituals are constantly changing, they nevertheless draw people together in a common effort and maintain a very visible continuity to a unique past. In describing his town's efforts to preserve traditions, Victor Flores (1998) argues that, "the essence of the correct life is to maintain in effect all of the traditional rites, since good customs and traditions are what maintains the equilibrium of our town" (58). The preservation, and transformation, of these traditional rituals lies primarily in the various neighborhood organizations that form the backbone of town-wide structures as well.

Tepoztlán is divided into eight neighborhoods. Each neighborhood has a colonial era chapel and holds at least one major and one minor annual festival to honor its patron saint. The neighborhoods themselves have an important, although not always very clear, history. Many residents argue that each neighborhood is actually the direct descendent of a Tlalhuica/Mexica era *calpulli*. The *calpulli* were primarily kin organizations and each neighborhood was defined very strongly in terms of family relations. According to residents, the *calpulli* were generally democratically organized institutions, in which the most trusted and worthy family members would be named as rulers through a process of consensus. These rulers could be removed for failing to carry out their duties. Their primary responsibilities were caring for the temples located in each *calpulli* dedicated to the various gods associated with the family and territory, organizing communal work or *coatéquitl*, and seeing to the community's general welfare. They point to a very direct continuity between this pre–Christian system and the contemporary *mayordomo* system in which the most trustworthy and honored residents in the neighborhood are selected to care for the chapel, and to organize and raise funds for the annual festivals. Some scholars are skeptical of these kinds of claims, however, arguing instead that neighborhoods and some villages were actually a creation of the Spanish colonial system (de la Peña 1980; Lomnitz 1982). In order to maintain control over a very dispersed and potentially rebellious population, colonial administrators forced indigenous communities to congregate in areas that they could more easily surveil and control (Salazar Peralta 228). Nevertheless, they were institutions created for and run by indigenous peoples.[14] According to Lomnitz (1982, 233), families were grouped according to paternal lines and each *barrio* did the same kind of work in order to avoid internal competition and differentiation. It was in the interest of the colonial powers to keep these neighborhoods weak and at odds with each other by promoting rivalries associated with religious rituals.

Observers in Tepoztlán through the 1970s noted the continuing legacy of these neighborhood rivalries and divisions. Redfield and Lewis, for instance, both comment on the internal homogeneity of the neighborhoods, with each neighborhood fairly easily identifiable by the kinds of work performed by its inhabitants. While marriages did occur frequently outside of the neighborhood, they were almost always lateral marriages (i.e. people from the poorer *barrios* up in the hills married each other, and people from the richer *barrios* in the center of town married each other.) These differences were further highlighted by the intensity of competition around neighborhood and town-wide festivals. Each neighborhood would attempt to hold a more elaborate celebration than the others, or have the best Chinelo dancers as a means to secure its place of prestige and honor (Lomnitz 1982, 255). While the internal homogeneity has changed greatly in the past thirty years, and the neighborhood rivalries have become a bit more friendly, they nevertheless continue to be a means through which people develop and cement important bonds to their immediate neighbors. This is particularly important given the changing nature of family relationships within the town. Since neighborhoods are no longer easily identifiable with particular families, neighborhood ties are not as automatic as they perhaps were in past years. Religious festivals, therefore, become a common project to which people are regularly dedicated.

Because these festivals are one of the means through which the town becomes "a single community," the *mayordomo*, or *in calpixqui*, is an extremely important figure in local social life (Flores Ayala 1998, 54).

Mayordomos are usually men, but increasingly women as well, who are selected in a public assembly to oversee the well being of the neighborhood chapel and the festival. These leaders are selected because of their honesty and are held in high regard by their peers. It is a great honor as well as a great deal of responsibility. Salazar Peralta notes that in addition to their financial and organizational duties, they are also a "bit of a spiritual guide for the community," providing people with assistance and advice (234). In Tepoztlán *mayordomos* have often been called upon to use their "convocatory power" for other projects as well such as organizing collective work, which is often used for such mundane projects as caring for the saint's field, paving streets, improving potable water systems or installing street lights.[15]

In addition to their abilities to raise funds from neighbors, organize various projects and maintain lines of communication, the process through which the *mayordomías* are reproduced as institutions make them important agents in creating a sense of a living and mutually committed neighborhood. People who serve as *mayordomos* are openly selected at the end of the annual festival to serve for a one-year term. This is done in a public assembly where candidates' qualifications are openly discussed. "Everything is spontaneous and of good will, with the only desire being that this local tradition is not lost" (Salazar Garrido 1998, 206). Local residents, therefore, have a very visible stake in the selection process and feel that they are an important part of that system. Many people report having greater faith in these leaders than they do in their civically elected officials, because candidates are not imposed and because people serve out of a genuine interest in helping the community and not just personal gain, although it is certainly an honor to hold this position (Echeverría 1994, 8). People generally are disengaged from regular politics and believe that politicians are out to enrich themselves, but the office of *mayordomo* holds little chance for personal enrichment as all financial transactions are strictly transparent, and in fact, many *mayordomos* end up losing a good bit of their own money in order to ensure the successful fulfillment of their duties.

The legitimacy of this system, however, ultimately rests on its ability to reproduce local religious festivals that meet the expectations of inhabitants. The importance of these festivals cannot be underestimated in understanding how local identities and loyalties are reproduced. Eduardo Hernández, Director of Popular Cultures with the INAH — Morelos has noted for instance that, "popular festivals condense and assume communitarian forms of organization and mechanisms of cultural resistance that remain viable, despite the pounding of modernity and economic materialism" (1994, 1). Similarly, in their study of Tepoztlán, Corona and Perez y Zavala (1999), insist that the ritual reproduction in Tepoztlán of important myths and historical events, such as the legend of Tepozteco and his conversion to Christianity, serve to cement a collective identity that helps Tepoztecos maintain a sense of difference from the rest of the world, even as they engage the social, cultural and economic pressures of modernity. To begin with, simply the mechanics of producing these festivals require a collective effort. While some are more involved than others, everyone (including foreign researchers temporarily residing in the neighborhood) is expected to contribute financially to defray the costs of the celebration. There are commissions that come around and collect for the band(s) that play day and night, the decorations, the fireworks and the rockets. On festival days almost everyone attends the various public displays, dances and music and thereby interacts with their neighbors. Furthermore, on the actual saint's day (the festival usually occurs on the days before and after, as well), there is a mass which most families attend, and families open their houses and courtyards to visitors and neighbors alike, inviting them in to share in the traditional meal of *mole*, rice, beans and tortillas (and Coca-Cola, of course). Besides this sort of face-to-face interaction and sharing that the festivals encourage, they also form a strong living connection with the past as well. Although they are dedicated to Catholic saints and held in the churches, many of the rituals continue to maintain pre–Columbian elements, and are usually timed to coincide with festival days honoring more ancient deities. This historic remembrance deepens participants' sense of belonging to a long, well established and unique community.

Since the festival calendar in Tepoztlán is quite full, with there being over fifty major and minor ones being carried out in the course of a year, I will examine one of the two municipal-wide festivals, because it illustrates the depth to which all of the festivals contribute to a sense of rooted identity and democratic participation in community life. Carnival, held over the four days prior to Ash Wednesday, is the highlight of the year. In preparation for the event, market vendors are relocated from the central plaza, making way for a large gathering area. Mechanical rides are brought in and set up in front of the *Ayuntamiento*. A lottery is held to award locations along the town's main streets for vendors— this is a prime money making time for many residents, who sell food, beer, and souvenirs. It attracts thousands of people from all over the region who come to observe and participate with the Chinelo dancers, nighttime light and sound shows and other non-stop festivities.

Although the exact origins of Carnival are not entirely clear, the

Top and bottom: Community members at a neighborhood festival in Santa Cruz, May 1999.

consensus among town residents seems to be that it began being celebrated in Tepoztlán in the mid-nineteenth century with the first competitions of neighborhood Chinelo groups. People often point to the mixed cultural inheritance of Carnival in order to more fully explain its origins. From the Spanish side, the days leading up to Lent were seen as times of excess and celebration in preparation for fasting and penance. From the indigenous side, Tepoztlán was the place in which people throughout Mesoamerica worshipped the god Ometochtli-Tepoztecatl. He is credited with inventing the alcoholic beverage *pulque,* and celebrations to him were characterized by drunkenness and excess. The two celebrations seemed well suited to each other.

The highlight of Carnival, however, is the Chinelo dancers. It is an honor for men to participate in Carnival as Chinelos, and families spend a great deal of time and money developing their elaborate costumes. Although each Chinelo designs the specifics of his costume, in general they are dressed in long black velvet robes and large ornate hats adorned with feathers, mirrors and various images painted or beaded on to them. On the back of each Chinelo is usually an image derived from nationalist icons such as a very stylized Aztec warrior, a stereotypical "maiden" in skin tight clothing, animal imagery (particularly jaguars, eagles and serpents) or a *campesino.* Recent costumes have also begun to show the influence of other sources as well, with cartoon characters appearing along with images of Zapatista guerrillas from Chiapas. According to the regional history museum in Cuernavaca, the dress of the Chinelos is a stylized parody of Belgian soldiers who accompanied the French in their invasion in the nineteenth century. Others believe that the dress represents an Arab influence on Spanish dress that the early colonists brought with them. The dance itself, called the *brinco* (literally "jumping") is believed to be a modification of dances carried out in pre–Columbian rites. Enrique Villamil (1998) argues, for instance, that the survival of the dance is a remembrance of the importance that dance played in the everyday and the spiritual lives of his ancestors (231). Neighborhood bands using European instruments accompany the dance. Although they attempt to preserve the essence of the older music, they have necessarily changed the tunes over time (Villamil Tapia 1961). Despite, in other words, the emphasis on tradition, the practice of that tradition is clearly marked by interaction with non-traditional influences.

The dancers themselves are divided into four companies, with each company corresponding to two of the eight neighborhoods. At the appointed hour, the companies march into the central plaza accompanied by their neighborhood flag and band, where they will play and dance for hours trying to show everyone who has the best band and the best dancers.

> Each company generally is composed of neighbors from that *barrio,* although there are many exceptions. It is not necessary to sign up, be voted in, make a promise, or complete some initiation to belong to a company, as often happens with other dance groups that belong to a religious association or brotherhood. Every dancer is free to *brincar* with the company that is most to his liking, just as every visitor or

spectator, of whatever age or sex can join in as a spontaneous dancer to the usual *brinco*, with preference going to the band that best plays the sounds of the Chinelo [Salazar Garrido 1998, 206].

For many in Tepoztlán, the Chinelos are an important identifying symbol. Salazar Garrido, continues, for instance, "throughout all of its eras, the *brinco* of the Chinelo has been and is a spectacle full of color; it is an inborn pride of all Tepoztecos" (207). For other community members, the *brinco* is an inherent part of being Tepozteco. Mario Antonio Quiroz (1998) writes that "the *brinco* of the Chinelo is carried in the blood; you are never told anything about rhythm, steps, shoulder movement or cadence: it is something that you simply know since the time that you are able to use reason" (164). He describes the dance as an emotional, physical and mystical experience in which "there is no time, no place, no anything except the music and the *brinco*: you could do it until infinity, tiredness does not exist. When you finally return to reality, it is already night ... the *brinco* is over, you feel full of everything, you have fulfilled your great yearning, nothing else matters" (165).

There is an egalitarian aspect to the dance and festivities that help to expand the sense of community. Although the bands and the companies practice long hours and invest considerable time, effort and money in perfecting their costume and performance, everyone who attends is welcome and encouraged to join in. Since there are no fixed steps or incorrect movements, people move their bodies to the inspiration of the music and the pushing of the crowd. "In their enchantment at entering into the *brinco*, all of those visitors from throughout the country as well as from foreign lands, without limits of age, social position or faith, become confused with the people that dance around the Chinelos" (Salazar Garrido 1998, 207–208). Since virtually all Tepoztecos participate in Carnival and in the *brinco* as either a Chinelo or just join in, they have an important shared experience, repeated ritually, through which they identify each other and are identified by others as being different. Although there is strong competition and rivalries between neighborhoods during the *brinco*, it is also a time in which the entire town "becomes one community," which even includes outsiders who have come to observe and participate in the festival. It is a time in which differences can be put aside and participation is encouraged from everyone despite what at other times are important cleavages, such as gender, class and origin.

Carnival also represents many of the contradictions of social life in

Opposite: Chinelo dancer, Tepoztlán, February 1999.

Tepoztlán. It is seen and considered to be the hallmark of "tradition." People talk about mask making techniques, costume design, dance and music as all being handed down from generation to generation. There are attempts to tie Carnival to long past indigenous rites as a means of further increasing its value as "tradition." The elaboration of Carnival, however, also demonstrates the hybridity inherent even within tradition. The costumes, for instance with their long robes and pale, bearded masks represent European dress. The instruments that play music of indigenous origin are European and the dance itself is a modification of pre–Columbian dance. Tepoztecos talk about Carnival as being one of the defining and quintessentially Tepozteco activities in which they participate, but outsiders are encouraged to visit and participate, both in the dancing, and certainly in the money spending aspects of the festival. This reflects one of the prime contradictions within the town, namely the tension between being "authentically" Tepozteco and being from somewhere else. Despite the fact that outsiders are invited to participate, and that Carnival becomes as much a spectacle for them as it is a meaningful ritual for Tepoztecos, it clearly remains a Tepozteco project. It is defined by neighborhood practices and organizations, and the traditions (such as costume making) are carried on through families and the town as a whole, which periodically holds classes to teach new generations the techniques.

Carnival and the other festivals exemplify one of the ways in which community is defined and cemented through ritual. People are able to put aside differences and get mixed up together dancing, or inviting others to their house to share a meal. The living out of these rituals, while meaningful in and of themselves in terms of creating community, also provides a deeper context for the political signification of the stories of the Tepozteco King, Zapata or indigenous inheritance, by creating historical and cultural continuity within the everyday life from which people interpret those myths that value community, autonomy and difference. Those stories, in a sense, become alive through ritual practices. Those ritual practices, in turn, help to create a sense of interdependency among community members who collaborate to keep stories alive, rework their meaning and produce elaborate festivals. Victor Flores (1998) reflects that, "it is the town which gives us meaning. The people know that their good customs and traditions are the seed that contains the essence of being that has been and that will always have been" (60). These "good customs and traditions" embody a sense of historic continuity in which the community gives meaning to the individual. They provide a way for townspeople to show their

Opposite: Chinelo dancer, Tepoztlán, February 1999.

love and dedication to community and to define the difference that makes them unique from other Mexicans.

The sense of community created by those practices and stories allowed activists to create a very rooted movement when the political opportunity presented itself. Elements of trust and cohesion are constantly being tested and reworked outside of the pressures of a political movement. Since collective efforts are part of people's everyday experiences, and are associated with the sacred, the movement's utilization of the *barrio* system, according to one activist, "became a very effective way to organize. It has always had a religious and social importance; as the movement was developing it became the logical way to keep organizing. People already respected the structure" (Interview 1999). Since that trust and respect existed, neighbors could rely on each other to be responsible during their turn at guarding the town. Just as people pull together for competing in Carnival or for organizing their *barrio*'s patron's festival, so they pulled together to support each other in protecting themselves from repression. The respect that the system commands further allowed it to be used as a legitimating mechanism in the electoral process, by tying political representation with the religious and civil meanings associated with the institutions of the *mayordomías*. Finally, the democratic structuring of the neighborhoods and of the festivals with the explicit importance on trust and face-to-face politics reflects the ideals of Zapatista ideology and provides a means through which democratic politics can be practiced outside of officially recognized state institutions. The stories of Zapata as a local leader tied to village councils is easily believable given the structuring of the *mayordomías*. It is therefore, a credible step to signify those neighborhoods with the rebellious identities associated with Zapatismo.

This is a process carried out with a very deliberate understanding of constructing community. While it may seem to reflect Bonfil Batalla's description of "deep Mexico," it avoids the easy essentialism into which that analysis falls. The traditions that continue under the surface of European domination are the result not of an innate Mesoamerican awareness, but rather the very deliberate cultural work of people attempting to preserve customs and who can put those customs to use. Carnival, for instance, was deliberately reinstated after the Revolution by community leaders and intellectuals who did not want to lose it. The *Challenge to Tepozteco*, which is reenacted every year is not just a memory, but is based on the active work of several people at the turn of the century to investigate the story and compile the various myths into a coherent narrative (Salazar Garrido 1998; Sánchez Ascencio 1998; Corona Caraveo and Pérez y Zavala 1999). In many of the neighborhood festivals today it is often school teachers with certain radical tendencies who work hard to maintain those traditions as a political act as well as a cultural one (Interviews with activists 1999, 2001).

This politicizing of culture should not be underestimated. Although Bonfil Batalla does provide a description of surviving Mesoamerican consciousness and practices, he assumes those beliefs and practices to be *a priori* oppositional. In the case of the anti-golf movement in Tepoztlán, however, we see just the opposite. We see potentially oppressive symbols and practices resignified within the context of social conflict to *become* oppositional. In the story, the Tepozteco King, after all, gives in to his Spanish superiors and renounces his indigenous beliefs in favor of theirs. Clearly, this kind of colonial reading would be detrimental to building an oppositional movement. Instead, however, and certainly building on years of other similar interpretations, the movement emphasizes the rebelliousness of Tepozteco and his loyalty to a unique people. Similarly, Zapata has been used repeatedly by the state to maintain control over rural and radical opposition groups. The movement managed to contest those dominant readings, allying itself instead with the historic revolutionary tendencies of Zapatismo, highlighting Zapata's right to rebel and associating themselves with the new Zapatistas further south. Signs and graffiti often referred to the town as tEpoZtLáN, and letters of support from *Subcommandante* Marcos were always big morale boosters. Finally even the institutions of the *mayordomos* are not inherently democratic. They generally formed a part of Spanish colonial institutions designed for vertical control and are associated in other areas with *cacique* politics. In the case of Tepoztlán, over time, these institutions have come to be seen as the authentic voice of people, and the movement successfully took advantage of that respect, and at the same time resignified those institutions with more explicitly political meanings by making them responsible for security and for civil elections.

Although these practices and institutions exist and form an important part of people's everyday experience, they are not automatically oppositional. The process of signifying them as such requires the political opportunity provided by a particular social conflict, as well as the capabilities of individuals within the community to organize and convince their compatriots of new, or at least more profound and explicit, ways of understanding them. This organizational ability, furthermore, is the result not only of just this one particular conflict, but is, of course, based on the experiences of multiple conflicts and multiple oppositional discourses. Finally, that resignification takes place within a context of dynamic social relations, both within the community and between the community and larger political and economic institutions. Activists, despite their repeated interest in using tradition, do so with a keen understanding that they are not isolated from the rest of the world, and that the very articulation of those traditions is very much related to influences, both positive and negative, with an increasingly close global community as well.

3

Embodying the Global in the Local

Environmentalism and Human Rights

Despite their concern with local matters and the reworking of local signifiers and identities, movement activists were keenly aware of their connectedness and even dependence on social and cultural systems that spilled beyond the borders of the municipality. Although the local uniqueness of Tepoztlán was continually stressed throughout the conflict, the movement also made alliances with numerous national and transnational organizations and adapted global discourses of change to organize their struggle and to communicate their position. Even as they glorified a remote indigenous past, for instance, movement leaders also invited globally oriented institutions such as Greenpeace, Amnesty International and the Anti-Golf Network to support their cause. Letters from the EZLN were read at public meetings in which the rebel leaders commended the Tepoztecos for their spirited and courageous defiance of neoliberalism. This simultaneous invocation of local and global throughout the course of the conflict suggests that rather than local an global being mutually exclusive and competing discourses, they interact with each other and that interaction provides meaning and direction for individuals within the specific context of the community's history and relationships with outside institutions.

The coexistence of local and global dynamics are apparent everywhere in everyday life in Tepoztlán: Nahuatl speaking market vendors selling Nike shoes, taxi drivers recounting their adventures in Arizona, "Xochitipec Pizzas," and the ever present foreigners living in or passing through town, all speak to the infusion of transnational influences in the everyday life of many, if not all, Tepoztecos. At the same time, however, the

A mixture of old and new, Tepoztlán, March 1999.

specificities of local life continue to be the dominant matrix through which people create and reproduce social relations, and consume and make sense of the global goods and ideas that circulate in their lives. That is, despite the importance of global influences, culture is still produced through the rules of local grammar.

These ambiguities between global and local in every day life were apparent in the struggle against the golf course as well. To begin with, the project was proposed by an outside entity. KS, while predominantly a Mexican corporation had significant financial support from international investors. At no time were local sentiments seriously considered. Above all, they employed a neoliberal logic that assumed that all goods and services, including land, were ultimately commodities and should obey the laws of the market. Pitted against this imposition of the project, local activists repeatedly employed a discourse through which local rights and traditions were privileged as a counterbalance to the lack of democratic entrance into neoliberal political and economic practices.

This apparent polarization, however, has to be understood as an ideological position rather than a simple truth. Leaders of the anti-golf movement sought to create political actors by negotiating the dialectics of homogenization and fragmentation of globalization, through the incorporation of transnational discourses and movements into the language and practices of local social relations. Movement activists, for instance, while they did privilege local rights, did so using both networks and discourses of larger national and transnational movements. In particular, they successfully accessed the transnational advocacy networks of the environmental and human rights movements as a means to frame their conflict to a broader audience. This involvement with the universalizing discourses of environmentalism and human rights changed the ways in which movement participants saw themselves and hence acted. It also simultaneously changed the articulation of those discourses, by subordinating them to the logics and specificities of local dynamics. In other words, the Tepozteco activists successfully defended local interests against a neoliberal development project by accessing similarly global discourses of resistance, and in that process, transformed the global discourses as well as local identities and organizational patterns.

The Mutual Constitution of Local and Global

It is undeniable that the world is becoming ever more integrated. Economic, technological, communication and military mechanisms ensure that the peoples of the world continually relate to each other through an increasingly singular system. Many critics of this kind of vertical globalization headed by transnational corporations, multilateral financial institutions and powerful military alliances argue that this creates and enforces economic and social inequalities, endangers human cultural diversity, leads to environmental degradation and erodes democratic institutions. In response, some have turned to extreme nationalism and fundamentalism as a means of countering the loss of local power and to counteract what they perceive as the drawbacks to global integration. Others critics, associated with the anti-globalization, or perhaps better named "other world," movement, which has coalesced transnationally in and around the World Social Forum, would argue that while closer global relations are inevitable, the tools of top-down integration, such as instant global communication, can be used to empower local groups and contribute to the tentative foundations of a transnational civil society through horizontal alliances to articulate a different view of a more just, equitable and free world (Brecher and Costello 1994; Brysk 2000; Guidry, Kennedy et al. 2000).

Inherent in these diverse opinions about globalization, besides political and ideological opinions about the benefits of virtually unregulated capitalism, is that individuals and communities occupy extremely different positions within the historic construction of globalized social relations. Zygmunt Bauman (1998) argues that it is the very logic of what he terms late or post modern global society which produces both homogenizing and diversifying effects, because people have vastly different experiences of globalization. For a relative elite, globalization has created immense wealth as well as a freedom from place, as they travel through the world and move capital as they please across borders. Freed from the restrictions of national cultures and laws, this elite experiences globalization as a kind of unfettered consumerism and cosmopolitanism in which culture truly becomes a global process. At the same time, however, the majority of people also experience globalization as a separation from local spaces, but, highlighting the power differentials inherent in the global system, these people do not choose to be part of that cosmopolitan culture, but rather have it "descend upon them as a cruel fate" (70). It is these vast peripheries of globalization that life experiences are tied up with trying to preserve local places as a means of sustenance and identity. He argues that under postmodern hegemony (in terms of both economics and ideology), localities have been disappeared and that under globalization there is no longer the possibility of locally transmitted knowledge or horizontal justice, because non-elites ultimately fail to preserve that which makes them function as a unique community.

In painting such a universalizing picture of contemporary transnational relations, however, Bauman falls into the same trap for which he criticizes other analysts. Namely, he vacates the possibility of political agency on the part of what Luis Hernandez Navarro (1999) has coined "the globalized." Rather than portraying groups from the peripheries of global processes as incapable of resistance, the other spectrum of the debate notes that a weak central state has led to the rise in local identities and local resource mobilization. As states have been weakened under neoliberal reforms, so has their ability to propose a national imaginary which supersedes other regional, religious or class identities. As Rodolfo Stavenhagen (1998) has argued, "people have stopped identifying themselves with the state in order to identify themselves with neighbors because they speak the same languages, or come from the same village, both of which distinguish them from others" (171). This suggests a failure of modern states to create a national identity based around the state, particularly now, when due to the state's withdrawal from active intervention in the economic sphere, it can no longer function as a benefactor. As a result of this failure, people return to, create, or otherwise place more importance on localized identities, insisting on the importance of cultural specificity and difference in contrast to the unified national image put forth by states. The logic of state-centered nationalist discourse becomes less effective when faced with the multiple demands of pluricultural societies, thus exasperating divisions between different cultural groups. While this breakdown may lead to militant rejections not only of imposed national orders, but also hostility toward and rejection of other groups, the lack of a viable, legitimate, centralizing authority, according to this argument confers, at the very least, increasing importance on local identity demands.

The weakness of the state, however, is only one factor related to the kinds of fragmentation that this era of globalization has witnessed. Stavenhagen further argues that, ironically, the mechanisms of globalization actually encourage diversity, even as it attempts to create homogenous societies. In their never ending search for new, specialized markets, for instance, transnational corporations create and market products to specialized groups both at an international and national level. These niche markets tend to reinforce localized cultural identifications, rather than a monolithic, global consumer culture, even though they are created and strengthened by the forces of the global economy. This specialization of markets coupled with the crisis of states' nation building projects, "contribute to a new strengthening of ethnic and cultural identity which is, of course, a constant of human nature: we all need to feel identified with some group, with our family, our home, our clan, our neighborhood. Very few people identify themselves with universality" (170). Even while incorporated into projects aimed at creating homogenous systems of production and consumption therefore, people still turn to more local beliefs and practices as a way of fundamentally distinguishing themselves from a faceless, mass national and world culture. The idea of belonging to a global village, in other words, is often incongruous with the experiences of living in a local one.

Speaking specifically of Mexico, Luis Villoro (2001) has argued that the project of the nation-state is in serious jeopardy. He contends that the Mexican national project has a built-in contradiction that the forces of globalization have brought to the fore. He sees the state as the mechanism through which authority is administered; that is, it represents the imposition of a single system of management over a multitude of individuals and groups. Nation, on the other hand, is fundamentally a cultural category in which people belonging to it see some sort of connection or shared experience with others.[1] With the orientation away from internal national development projects along with the state's general weakening and lack of legitimacy, people have been searching in places other than official culture for answers to the questions of who they are, and what it means to be Mexican. While this may be a common predicament for people around the world, the case of Mexico is particularly poignant in that an important part of Mexican national culture has been the state's support, since the end of the revolution, for the idea of a *mestizo* nation, thus laying the groundwork for multiple ways of being Mexican. Although the idea of *mestizaje* has racial origins, the idea has been used more recently to incorporate a multitude of other differences into the national make up.[2] The problem for the Mexican state through the transition process is that as the PRI legitimacy has waned, along with its ability to incorporate and control the multiethnic and multicultural makeup of the nation that it so painstakingly developed over the past seventy years, there has been no other viable proposal for nationhood. The neoliberal project endorsed by political and economic elites is not capable of articulating a coherent national identity or project, leading, in part, to the proliferation of locally based and identified social movements.

Gustavo Esteva and Madu Suri Prakash (1998) go even further, arguing that local communities are increasingly opting out of the globalization/modernization paradigm through a politics of saying "no." They note that communities of indigenous peoples, rural workers and marginalized urban dwellers have never been fully incorporated into the modern economic and political system. For them, promises of prosperity, democratic governance, respect for individual choices and other benefits of modernity have never materialized. In fact, modernization for them has meant just the opposite as it has disrupted social networks and communities, while marginalizing them further from the material and cultural benefits of modernity. Rather than trying to catch up to those social sectors that do benefit from contemporary arrangements, they argue that these communities, instead, are forging "a multiplicity of escape routes" from the false promises of globalization. They contend that these types of communities, which they refer to as the "social majorities," have moved beyond the slogan of "thinking globally and acting locally" to think and act locally as the only viable means of creating a sustainable existence for themselves in the world today. They reject the abstract institutions of state and transnational organizations, preferring instead to build politics on a more concrete, human level.

This abandonment of global thinking in favor of local thinking and action, they contend, represents a quantitative step forward in rethinking issues of exploitation and liberation in the world today. They argue against the "...possibility of regaining the experience of human agency and autonomy by supposedly 'thinking' on the global scale to contend with the oppression of 'global forces.' No challenge to the proliferating experiences of people's powerlessness succeeds when conceived and implemented inside the institutional and intellectual framework which produced it" (20). By recognizing the impossibility of understanding much less affecting relations and institutions at the global level, local activists realize that they can only effectively understand a small piece of the earth and interact with a reduced number of people according to the specificity of cultural rules that have been developed through generations of social interaction. To pretend otherwise, as even the best-intentioned globalizers do, means reducing the complexity of the world and sacrificing much of its diversity.

Such an attitude is not a reaction of hopelessness against an implacable opponent. Rather, it is a recognition not only of what is politically and socially feasible. Despite the pretensions of neoliberal economics to homogenize, or reform, markets and political systems, transnational corporations and the policies enacted on their behalf by national states and supranational organizations such as the IMF and the World Bank, take form and become reality only in local spaces. "Global powers can only have material existence and do the harm they are doing, in their local incarnations.... For the very logic of those 'global powers' forces them to leave places where they confront persistent, rooted and fiery local opposition" (Esteva and Prakash 1998, 34). People must attend actual physical markets in order to purchase the global economy's goods, just as they must be physically present somewhere to work or otherwise participate in social relations. It is at the local level, therefore, where the power of the global project can be most logically and effectively resisted or, as Esteva and Prakash suggest, simply ignored.

For these authors, "liberation from the logic of 'global forces' implies rethinking the world. It requires a shift in focus from the goal of living in One World, a *universe*. In its stead, the door is opened for settling in a *pluriverse*.... Communities and their social movements are seeking not so much to join the global village, as they are seeking ways to continue being themselves in the contemporary world" (36–38). They want to negotiate a different kind of relationship with other communities and cultures of the world in which each culture can flourish and find ways of supporting each other, without reducing that diversity to some abstract global citizenry. This is a struggle for true autonomy *vis a vis* the integrationist tendencies of the various aspects of globalized modernity.[3] By rejecting the mono-culturalism of modernity, in favor of the pluriverse of autonomous communities, each of which negotiate their relationship to each other and to global institutions, localized movements offer radically different ways of understanding and resisting the effects of global conditions. This grounded politics replaces the abstractions of transnational space as a position of resistance with the concrete details of specific experience.

Although their assessment does reflect the position and attitude of many socially active groups, particularly with their emphasis on autonomy and horizontal linkages, the distinction between global and local is not as clear-cut as Esteva and Prakash paint it. It is quite arguable, for instance, that local communities do not seek isolation, but seek to be themselves in the modern world; but it is not so clear what "they" are anymore. While local communities do not have to surrender that which makes them unique, their experiences with the rest of the world definitively change them, as they add those ideas, beliefs and practices that they find useful to their own. In a more general sense, groups and individuals, even when not actively resisting globalization, incorporate its discourses and practices into their lives according to their own historic circumstances. The experiences of each community in terms of its historic experience and connection with the global project, however, is so varied that to generalize a position of "local vs. global" loses the richness of that diversity. While recognizing the important interconnections created by the global economy, Carmen Bueno (2000) argues that paying attention to diversity of local adaptation to the global is essential in order to avoid the oversimplification and homogenization not only promoted by global industries, but often repeated by critics of that process. She writes,

> We are facing a civilizational process that has been set up under universal, deterministic, unilinear and homogenizing parameters that support a scientific, rational logic for efficiency, competitiveness and the aggregation of value, which disrupts and distorts local realities by imposing certain forms and rhythms. Nevertheless, this unifying process has been challenged by the local particularities of globalization that assign it multiple meanings, not only giving a foothold to the creation of new social formations, but also promoting the transformation, reinvention and repositioning of already existing processes [8].

She contends that globalization is a highly uneven and discontinuous process, and as such, can only be understood by examining the diversity of ways in which the local negotiates with, appropriates meaning from, and relates to the global.

> Local society responds in very different ways: it appropriates, reconfigures and assigns new meanings to the global model. The local and the global simultaneously and reciprocally constitute each other in a complex tangle of relationships, that imply multiple mediations, develop new realities, construct new identities and put into contact distant social, economic and cultural spaces, in such a way that the fate of local situations appears affected by events that occur in other parts of the earth and vice versa. In this way cultural diversity is inherent to globalization for the simple fact that there is a local referent that maintains a dialectical process of confrontation, rejection or accommodation of global influences. It is such a process of give and take that at times the border between local and global appears to blur in such a way that local conditions go through changes through participation in worldwide processes, while at the same time, the global dimension adopts new meanings when it is put into practice in these particular spaces [23].

For Bueno, the problem of understanding this "interpenetration of the local and global" (Robertson 1992), lies in being able to adequately and accurately describe the specific ways in which local communities enter into, resist and adapt to their increasing interdependence on other places and distantly located social and economic organizations. Global processes need to be seen not just as top down attempts at creating homogenous markets, but also as multiple and particular ways of negotiating those processes.

Social Movements as Negotiators of Global Processes

Because of their ability to interact within both localized political systems as well as transnational networks, contemporary social movements have been an important vehicle through which locally based people project agency from the periphery of the global system. For both practical and ideological reasons, activists navigate the ambiguities of creating collective identities that are simultaneously global and local. Although movements tend to have very specific and local focuses, they face increasing needs to form alliances with broader based organizations in order to counter globally connected adversaries. In addition to strategic motivations, political activists are themselves caught up in the fragmentation of consciousness associated with globalization, and as they have become disillusioned with state-centered notions of nation, they are searching for new identities which incorporate notions of heterogeneous civil societies, which do not conform, necessarily, to internal or external state boundaries. Their general anti-state position, furthermore, predisposes many activists to contemplating new ways of imagining community, which due to the necessities of their struggles may incorporate global discourses into the specificities of local and regional cultural production.

The very restructuring of the state and of geopolitical relations under neoliberalism has made the containment of specific problems to local arenas impossible. Activists and analysts alike have realized that by defining themselves in a narrowly local way, movements are unable to access a wider array of potential allies and fail to confront their opponents on the larger underlying issues. George Yudice (1998), points to the transnational linkages that many grassroots organizations develop, as evidence for what he calls a fundamental reconsideration of how social movements are inserted into the formation of political cultures. He argues that the strictly local and nationalist discourse of much leftist rhetoric through the 1980s has been abandoned

...as an ineffective analytical framework that did not adequately engage a series of new realities, such as the action of international NGOs with agendas that addressed human rights, gender and racial equality, the landless, street children and the environment. This international linkage to certain social movements, as well as the transnational flows of communications, information, gendered identity images and lifestyles, and their relation to the breakdown of formal politics, created a new imaginary that could not be faithfully captured by [an] anti-imperialist framework [357–358].

Left-leaning social movements, in other words, have been moving from a position of complete distrust of outside intervention to a realization that the world is, in fact, very much interrelated and that effective protest and consolidation of victories relies on their engagement with that wider world. As nationalist states lose their central importance in economic, political and cultural life, it becomes more apparent to activists that their opponents are not just national elites but transnational entities as well. Also, as the state retreats from its position of providing economic, social and political support for different social sectors, civil society, particularly with connections to transnational non-governmental organizations and social networks seek to fill those gaps.

Since national states, however, continue to be the enforcer of last resort of social order as well as the most immediate potential protector of local interests against outside exploitation, they continue in many cases to be the target of protests and the site of contentious politics. Local activists make use of the extraterritorial organizations involved in transnational networks in order to pressure their states into making and adhering to agreements regarding the redress of particular conflicts within the context of the larger issues advocated by the transnational networks. Given that both opponents and allies of movement activists work within transnational frameworks, the political stance and cultural production of local movements necessarily also take on parts of those global discourses as well.

The involvement of movements with transnational networks, however, does not mean that they abandon the local nature of their demands nor of the construction of their discourses. Rather, it suggests that global mechanisms for organizing and for understanding the world are more explicitly fused into the discourses and practices produced by social movements. Globalization, in other words, weakens the epistemological connection between a unified nation and a singular state as the primary means of political identification, and allows for more diverse ways of seeing community and of developing and projecting identities. With the break in modernist hegemony, movement activists are able to articulate their position using "nation" as one of many cultural sites that correspond to their experiences of living in a local community while simultaneously being connected to much larger systems. They combine elements from these dual experiences to form identities and practices that are useful in meeting their demands. Because local beliefs and practices tend to remain more important to people in their everyday lives, however, this fusion, should not be interpreted as a privileging of the global over the local. That is, however, not to say that local culture is somehow pure and unchanging, rather it is that outside discourses tend to be assimilated according to the needs and conditions of local communities, while they simultaneously act to transform those communities.

Social movements are able to mediate the disjuncture between local, national and global identities by fusing them into a political praxis that, while clearly focused on the resolution of specific demands, nevertheless frames those demands around questions raised by larger issues. As people become involved in movements to resolve a particular conflict, they also become more aware of how that specific problem is informed by national and global issues as well. It may be impossible to improve municipal infrastructure, for instance, without involving national agencies, which in turn leads to a questioning of how financial and developmental priorities are established. In order to stop intimidation from being carried out by local police agents, it may be necessary to involve national and global human right organizations and also to make specific linkages between the need for repression and the demands of the global economy. Whatever the specifics of the case, social movements provide the mechanism through which people not only understand the relationships between local, national and global, but that they also provide a means to articulate a position on them, and a channel to work for or against particular projects.

This *involvement* in political *work* is an important step in the creation of identities, because collective identities need to be understood in terms of the process through which actors negotiate complex sets of relationships. In pointing out that collective identity is the means through which individuals within groups recognize each other and are recognized by others, Alberto Melucci (1995) argues that collective identity depends on the ability of a collective actor to "recognize the effects of actions and to attribute those effects to itself" (46). Movements create identity by providing a way through which people can actively make distinctions between themselves and their environment. Because oppositional activity heightens differences between the group of protesters and the society at large, it is key to building both the internal solidarity that leads to self-recognition as agents, and it creates antagonisms in their relationships with outside actors and groups leading to a distinct recognition from others. Melucci suggests that we should "see movements as action systems. They are not entities that move with the unity of goals attributed to them by their ideologues or opponents. They are systems of action, complex networks among the different levels and meanings of social action" (53). In other words, it is the ability to *act* in a manner that strengthens participants sense of agency which allows them to negotiate the "complex networks" of social relations and arrive at an awareness of themselves as unique: belonging to each other and different from others. In the context of globalization, local social movements offer a means through which local identity can be created and strengthened through collective action and self-awareness. This involvement in the specifics of that collective action allows participants to distinguish themselves in relation to their homogenized and globalized external environment. From this fortified, local collective identity, participants enter into external social relations from a new position.[4]

Because of the instabilities in identity formation caused by the vacuum created by the weakening of centralizing mechanisms, social movements provide a means to create new identities that are simultaneously local and global. That is, individuals and groups are able to reposition themselves and create new internal and external identifications within the various social networks that comprise their lives. On the one hand, due to an increased sense of agency, social movements help to create a sense of belonging to an expanded imaginary community, because local members are better able to see outside actors and organizations as potential allies. In other words, activists begin to see themselves as part of national or transnational communities marked by similar concerns and values. The work and rhetoric of global networks find a resonation in local conflicts, as activists forge alliances with groups from outside of their immediate face-to-face community. Not only do these outside allies bring important strategic support for the movement, but local activists can and do imagine themselves as belonging to, and participating in, those larger causes which cross through national boundaries.

At the same time, however, movements develop within the fragmented consciousness associated with globalization, which while facilitating involvement with transnational organizations and identities, also leads to a heightened importance of local elements in forging people's identities. Movements, therefore, also create a sense of belonging to a smaller community, one that is very much defined as much by its territoriality as it is by its difference from the *status quo* and from officially sanctioned projects. This local identity, therefore, bred of a confrontation with outside forces, challenges the homogenizing elements of national and global projects of modernity, because it values and perpetuates difference from the system.[5] Social movements, therefore, epitomize the kinds of dual consciousness that have been amply described as a product of globalization, because they not only correspond to the political and cultural realities that globalized systems have created, but because they actively encourage people to seek out and value local difference, while simultaneously creating transnational linkages to their struggles.

Transnational Advocacy Networks

These transnational linkages occur through what Margaret Keck and Kathryn Sikkink (1998) have labeled transnational advocacy networks. They argue that these networks make use of "principled and strategic actions" in order to pressure national states into accepting and adhering to international norms of behavior. These networks often develop when local and/or national authorities are unwilling to bend to local pressures, forcing activists to seek outside allies to pressure them in other ways. They have called this the boomerang effect: local activists, who are effectively blocked from proceeding at a national level, provide information to these transnational networks, which in turn by-pass national political channels to pressure them from other states, public opinion and international organizations, such as the Organization of American States or the United Nations. Rather than a centrally directed international movement, however, these networks are affiliations of local and national organizations, which they call nodes, working toward similar goals primarily by sharing information and coordinating political actions across national borders. The thicker the network, or the more local nodes in it, the more likely it is to succeed.

The importance of these networks in the current discussion is that "by blurring the boundaries between a state's relationship with its own nationals and the recourses both citizens and states have to the international system, advocacy networks are helping to transform the practice of national sovereignty" (1). Local activists challenge national sovereignty in three important ways: 1.) local activists look for and find help outside of national boundaries on issues that would seem to be the domain of national politics; 2.) the networks produce information that contradicts state information implying that states lie and giving international organizations other means to formulate policy; and finally, 3.) they force states to accept normative changes imposed by international organizations, brought about by pressure from domestic and transnational activist organizations (36). This re-negotiation of national sovereignty suggests that contentious politics creates identities outside of the state system, in that local activists are willing to seek out and accept outside help on certain issues, which, in turn, implies that local norms of conduct may supersede national ones and can be enforced by global mechanisms. They are acting, in other words, on a belief that despite their groundedness in smaller, face-to-face communities, they also belong to communities larger than the nation-state to which public officials can be held accountable.

Despite this challenge to traditional senses of sovereignty and local activists' willingness to (at least temporarily) inhabit this transnational space, we should not draw the conclusion that they are advocating the complete dismantling of the state. To begin with, the state continues to be an important and convenient target for contentious political action. It is more effective to draw causal connections between specific political actors and institutions rather than the more abstract processes that underlie complex social problems. Secondly, in the contemporary reality, it is still nation-states that must ultimately resolve the problems around which many movements are formed. Furthermore, in many cases, states are (theoretically) the only institutional force that can protect rights or safeguard populations against the predatory practices of global market economics that underlie activists' complaints. Finally, the nation continues to be an important category around which to mobilize as the idea of a global society is difficult to articulate, because there are few shared symbols around which dispersed people can imagine themselves as a community. Decades of state intervention, however, have created the necessary mythology for people to mobilize and relate to communities beyond their immediate regions. Instead of dismantling the state as such, by participating in these transnational networks, activists seem to be looking for a way to create and enforce a different kind of relationship with states around certain key issues.[6]

While many studies consider the importance of social movements on national and increasingly global political processes (Morris and Mueller 1992; Keck and Sikkink 1998), they are not so clear on the effects which participation in these movements have on the articulation of local demands or local identity formation. In other words, although the importance of the density of activist nodes in the formation and efficacy transnational networks cannot be underestimated, how do the networks affect the ways in which the people in the nodes understand their struggle, define themselves and articulate future political and cultural development? Two of the important transnational networks, environmentalism and human rights, played a clearly important role in the Tepoztlán conflict and demonstrate how local movements not only participate in transnational networks, but how they incorporate that experience into the specificities of cultural construction of their local societies as well.

Environmentalism

Ecology was one of the central framing issues in the conflict in Tepoztlán. Activists repeatedly claimed their rights to conserve nature and make sustainable use of natural resources as reasons to oppose the building of the golf course. They claimed that environmental impact statements suggested that the golf course would use over half of the town's water supply, and building on research done around other golf courses, demonstrated that the chemicals used as fertilizers and pesticides would leach into their food and water supply. By making use of such rhetorical frames, activists invited and made use of transnational environmental networks to provide political, informational and resource support for their struggle. This explicit linkage with the broader environmental movement, in turn, changed the terms of discourse within the town itself not only regarding the conflict with the golf course, but also more generally with questions regarding wise and acceptable future development within the municipality and the region as a whole. The incorporation of the global discourse of environmental protection into local practices, however, was marked by the subordination of the former to the latter as evidenced by continuing struggle over the meaning of local environmental policies and practices.

As with most transnational movements, the discourse that informs environmentalism reflects the heterogeneity of participants' backgrounds and relative positions within the global system. While it would seem almost self-evident that environmental or ecological refers to the protection and wise use of natural resources, the specificities of people's relationship to the environment and the physical and spiritual use that they make of it, creates a great deal of possible meaning for the term. Keck and Sikkink (1998), for instance, argue that "environmentalism is less a set of universally agreed upon principles than it is a frame within which the relations among a variety of claims about resource use, property rights and power may be reconfigured" (121). David Harvey (1993) furthermore, splits the movement into "environmentalists" and "ecologists." Environmentalists, he argues, tend to be interested in managing natural resources in an efficient way and fall almost anywhere along the political spectrum. Ecologists, on the other hand, adopt the more radical position that human activity needs to be considered from the perspective of belonging to nature rather than being outside of and managing it (2–3). These are obviously two very different projects concerning human relationships to nature, yet both find common ground under the broad project of protecting natural systems and making wise use of natural resources. This vagary serves both to strengthen and weaken the movement. On the one hand, a wide variety of beliefs and practices can be incorporated into environmental politics. Struggles of various indigenous groups around issues of land claims, for instance, are often times conflated by transnational environmental networks with projects aimed at preserving tropical forests. At the same time, however, a whole host of ideas and projects from the "natural" roles of men and women to dubious green development projects can lay claim to their soundness within the logic of environmental or ecological practices. This would be the case in Tepoztlán, where both CUT activists and KS supporters invoked the environment as a justification for their position. In the case of the activists, the golf course would do irreparable harm to the area, and in the case of KS, the golf course was a non-polluting industry that would rehabilitate abandoned and degraded lands. In most cases, of course, the development of environmental advocacy adheres to local concerns and thus represents a very heterogeneous set of claims and social positions.

Integrating, if even loosely, this wide range of local environmental movements has been no easy or automatic task. What began as conservation efforts, particularly among middle class activists from industrialized countries in the 1960s and 1970s, was often met with skepticism if not outright rejection by both government and non-governmental organizations (even those that would seem to be natural allies) from countries which had placed a great deal of importance on a developmental agenda that included industrialization. It seemed patently unfair, for instance, to propose zero growth agendas on world development, when most of the world did not enjoy the same level of physical comfort that inhabitants of industrialized nations did. How could Latin America, for instance, be expected to develop and compete in an industrial economy with the kinds of environmental restrictions that were not imposed on the United States or Europe when they were developing their industrial bases? Environmental politics were and continue to be viewed as a means to perpetuate inequalities between center and periphery.[7] More to the point, it was viewed as a new tool of imperialism. Harvey (1993) observes that

> control over the resources of others, in the name of planetary health, sustainability or preventing environmental degradation, is never too

far from the surface of many western proposals for global environmental management. Awareness of precisely that potentiality stimulates a good deal of resistance in developing countries to any form of environmentalism emanating from the West [25].

In the beginning, despite their best intentions, many northern members of the non-governmental environmental movement also fell into the trap of attempting to impose their vision of acceptable environmental practices over the lived realities and concerns of their southern counterparts, by dictating how other people were to use their natural resources. Environmental activism, in other words, was informed by contingencies of local (northern, industrialized, middle class) experiences and more generally circulating representations of international hierarchies that tend to obscure the imperialist power relations between center and periphery.

As the environmental network evolved, however, it found that it needed to forge more equal or horizontal relationships between north and south. As northern-based organizations began to collaborate with people based in the southern hemisphere, particularly around the issue of tropical rain forests, they also began to deepen their understanding of the complexities of the relationships between development and the environment. This engagement with southerly-based people changed the trajectory of the movement from one concerned with "conservation" to one concerned with "sustainable development," because it became more clear that the problems associated with environmental issues (overpopulation, depletion of resources, *et cetera*) had an important social aspect to them. As people in the south became important framing tools for the movement, their role also changed from one of informant or victim to one of partner.[8] Environmental movements, therefore, became important means through which local conflicts about land tenure, for instance, were framed. As people lost control over traditionally held lands, they also lost control over the more environmentally sustainable manner in which they were worked. Agribusiness and cattle ranching with their large-scale disruption of sensitive ecological systems replaced subsistence agriculture or forest resource gathering. Similarly, the need for environmental organizations to put a human face to their cause led to the linking of environmental concerns with indigenous rights movements (which encompassed both land tenure and cultural integrity issues). This linkage, in turn, gave international exposure to leaders of relatively small groups of people and allowed them to leverage that exposure for greater concessions from national governments on issues such as local autonomy, the creation of nature reserves and recognition of territorial claims.

Besides forging organizational connections, these transnational linkages also created important and problematic ideological conflations. For instance, the connection of "indigenous" with "environment" makes an implicit assumption that because indigenous people live "closer" to the land that they are automatically better stewards of nature. While indigenous groups have used this effectively to further their agendas for autonomy, it is obviously not necessarily true, and brings with it the dangers inherent in all essentialisms. It is not a big step, for example, to place indigenous people on the "nature" side of the nature/culture binary, which can just as easily then be used against them. This kind of essentialism, even if it is being used strategically, vacates the political work of indigenous people, by not accounting for the complex coalition building strategy upon which they have embarked. The blurring of these boundaries and issues, nevertheless, constitutes an important part of the political work of the various nodes of the environmental movement, as they attempt to frame localized conflicts within a more universalizing language. Furthermore, it shows how that framing returns to change the ways in which the local movements themselves reconstitute their own memberships. Environmentalism, in other words, becomes the language through which unwanted development projects can be opposed.

Tepoztlán is a clear example of how local nodes fit into the network, as well as how framing the conflict in terms of environmentalism has lasting effects on local populations. Well before the anti-golf course movement began, there were relatively strong pockets of environmental awareness and practices from different segments of the population in Tepoztlán, who in turn were connected to regional organizations in Cuernavaca and national ones in Mexico City. These environmentally concerned citizens focused on the two major poles of ecological activism: conservation of existing natural areas and sustainable use of resources. They tied a widely felt connection to local natural formations, such as the region's unique mountains, to the politicized discourse of environmental protection in attempts to influence policy over the use of local resources and the maintenance of the region's reputation for purity.

One of the most striking physical features of the town is the omnipresent mountains. Writers and residents alike have commented on the importance of the mountains to the identity of the inhabitants in terms of physical protection, mythology, spirituality and supplying of resources. It has even been noted in several places, that Tepoztecos have names not only for all of the mountains, but most of the hills and trees as well, and use these names and places in the telling of local history (Lomnitz 1982; Gallo Sarlat 1988; Rosas 1997; Soler Frost 1997; Sánchez Ascencio 1998).

Tepoztlán resident Victor Flores (1998), for instance explains this connection with the mountains:

> Tepoztlán is a paradise of the gods, surrounded by hills and mountains that rigorously and jealously guard the treasure of their history and their tradition. The hills have their own legends and symbolism, and form an extraordinary natural environment in this beautiful valley. They say that several forms of culture have flourished and perished in these hills, in their rocks and in their exuberant vegetation. This is one of the sacred places of the world, where people have been able to find refuge from the chaos. The hills give a vital energy, as if they had a magnetic force that can renovate or destroy. There are certain times and dates in which one can feel the vibrations throughout the body, that unite and contribute to the salvation of the soul and the equilibrium of everyday life [65].

Indeed, despite the influences of the pulls of modernity and cosmopolitanism, these localized and named natural formations continue to play a very important role in how Tepoztecos distinguish themselves from others, as nature becomes fused with notions of spirituality and place-based uniqueness (Demesa Padilla 1998; Tostada Gutiérrez 1998). The area is considered to be sacred by many different people for different reasons, but they all seem to be related to the area's natural surroundings. It is sometimes referred to as the "sacred valley" because of the numerous spirits said to live in its caves and mountains, as well as being the birthplace of the human/deity Quetzalcoatl. In addition, practitioners of various new age beliefs have found their way to the area, and claim that there are important energetic and magnetic properties to the mountains which create a unique area for the practice of their religions. Protecting these natural formations, therefore, is an important part of people's personal agendas.

Besides these spiritual connections, two very modern institutions reinforce the importance of natural conservation: the state and the tourist industry. In 1935, President Lázaro Cardenas created the Tepozteco National Park, which includes a good part of the municipality. As such, large tracts of land were declared off-limits to logging and other forms of exploitation. In 1985, President Miguel de la Madrid decreed parts of the land running from the Ajusco Mountains in the southern part of the Federal District to the low-lying areas of the valleys of southern Morelos to be the Ajusco-Chichinautzin Biological Corridor. A part of this reserve, dedicated to conservation of forests, the protection of the local aquifer and opportunities for scientific, educational and recreational opportunities, runs through the mountains of Tepoztlán (Aguilar Benítez 1994, 34). In addition, a prime factor in the booming tourist industry has to do precisely with the area's reputation for natural beauty. Since people are attracted to Tepoztlán primarily because of its reputation as being a tranquil, clean and pure place to relax, particularly in comparison to nearby Mexico City, protecting the environment is a key element of public life as it is seen as an important part of continued economic success. In order to protect that industry, therefore, it is important to preserve the sense and appearance of a relatively untouched environment. The conservationist edge of environmentalism, therefore, has very clear and important roots in the everyday life and economics of the town's inhabitants. Before and after the crisis, environmentalism in Tepoztlán has played an important part in the political landscape, as it has been necessary for the Tepoztecos to protect not only the actual environment but also their image as a natural place.

Similarly, the resource management side of environmentalism finds an important echo in much of the social conflict that has occurred in the town, particularly during this century. In the 1920s and 1930s, for instance, one of the underlying causes for political strife in the community had to do with how to make best use of the forests (Lomnitz 1982). One faction, made up primarily of ex–Zapatista combatants under the banner of the Union of Tepozteco Campesinos (UCT), advocated a (re)turn to communal and regional self-sufficiency and believed that the forests should be preserved for the internal needs of townspeople. The other faction, led by the "*centrales*" advocated integration into the national economy that had a great need, at the moment, for charcoal. After a series of political blunders and abuses by the UCT, the *centrales* gained control of the municipal government and formed a charcoal cooperative. Exploiting the postwar poverty in the region, the *centrales* made use of the fact that "many poor Tepoztecos would benefit in the short run by turning their forests into charcoal" (Lomnitz 1982, 172). By 1929, the cooperative had 500 members (out of a total population of 4,600), and was clearly the town's most important economic and political institution. For the next six years, the municipality's forests were cut and burned at an alarming rate. With the ascendancy to the presidency of the leftist Lázaro Cardenas and the fall in demand for charcoal, the backers of the UCT managed to bring an end to the clear cutting by having most of the remaining forest declared a National Park, and therefore, off limits to (legal) harvesting.

While not as stark as the charcoal issue, the question of natural resource use and management continued to be an important factor in local political conflict throughout the rest of the century. As tourism became an increasingly important part of economic life, the focus of the debate changed toward the question of sustainable development. Trying to avoid the pitfalls of many "eco-tourism" projects, a handful of Tepoztecos have been vigilant and vocal against the encroachment of development projects that threaten the region's natural appearance, which makes it amenable to tourism in the first place.[9] Serious conflicts erupted over issues of land tenure in the 1960s, for instance, with claims that the state's largest industrial complex, CIVAC, was being built on land illegally ceded from the municipality in the 1950s. Similarly, the Montecastillo real estate company's attempts to build a golf course on the same site as the one proposed in the 1990s was challenged (some times at gun point) by town residents who claimed that the company had illegally acquired communal lands and had tricked some residents out of their privately held lands. After escalating tensions resulted in the murder of one activist, the project was indefinitely suspended. Also in the 1960s, under the pressure of a growing population and a burgeoning tourist industry, the town's water supply system was revamped and taken over by the federal Hydraulic Resources agency, leading to a direct confrontation between angry townspeople and federal officials over the management of this natural resource.

The 1970s and 1980s saw developers attempt two major projects. The first was to build a gondola that would take people up the mountain to the pyramid of Ometochtli-Tepoztecatl, which overlooks the town and is one of the main tourist attractions in the state. Arguing that having cables running up the mountain would ruin the view and change the practice of climbing the mountain as an important part of the experience, people organized through neighborhood committees to successfully oppose it. In the late 1980s, developers wanted to build a scenic train route that would take people from Mexico City to and around the mountains of Tepoztlán. Using explicitly environmental arguments, local activists once again organized against the project, claiming that the digging of numerous tunnels would cause irreparable damage to the delicate ecosystem of the mountains. By 1990, the movement had made strong alliances with the rapidly developing national environmental movement, and cast itself as being one more of a series of ecological defenses against the neoliberal state. The project was finally defeated in 1991, only after local activists engaged in direct action against the builders by literally putting themselves in the way of heavy machinery and of pulling up tracks at night that had been laid down the previous day.

Given the central importance, then, of the environment, both in terms of conservation and resource management, in the collective consciousness of townspeople through this long series of political conflicts, it would seem a logical step on the part of movement leaders to frame the dispute with KS and the state government fundamentally as an environmental conflict. While there were many contentious local issues involved in this conflict such as unsettled land tenancy, electoral politics, a rapidly changing class structure and ambivalent attitudes toward tourism and outsiders, it was the environmental frame that became the most important. Most people, for instance, cited the threat to the town's water supply as their primary reason for opposing the golf course project. By successfully framing the issue in terms of the environment, activists were able to garner wide spread support locally as well as reach out to a much broader constituency. Building on their experience and contacts from past struggles as well as less controversial environmental projects, such as reforestation and the prevention of fires, the Tepozteco activists were able to draw political and ideological support from the environmental network. A number of national and transnational organizations, including Greenpeace, the Group of 100, the Global Anti-Golf Movement, Multinational Monitor, Green Warriors, Habitat, Pact of Ecological Groups, Environmental Studies Group, Save the Forests and the Sierra Club offered to support them by providing information about the ecological effects of golf courses and by publicizing their campaign in Mexico City and beyond. The environment, in other words, became an important label with which the movement could attract attention and garner outside support. Tepoztlán became, for a while, a center of regional ecological activism and a national and even transnational symbol of resisting unsustainable development projects.

Just as framing the conflict in terms of environmental protection helped to secure more wide spread support for the activists by making it an appealing one to people with very little physical connection to the place of Tepoztlán, it also effected the ways in which people approached the problem from a local level. Local people, in other words, take global discourses and transform them in order to use them according to the logic of their histories. At the same time, the introduction of those discourses change the ways in which people understand and explain their world. Just as the global environmental movement, for instance, tends to conflate indigenous rights issues with environmental ones, activists in Tepoztlán made significant use of an idealized vision of the town's indigenous past as a means to strengthen *local* solidarity and legitimacy for the movement as well as fit into global environmental images. Building on an increased respect for indigenous identity and political activism precipitated by the Five Hundred Years of Indigenous, Black and Popular Resistance Campaign and the Zapatista movement in Chiapas, activists began claiming the town's indigenous identity as well. Activists claimed to be acting on their indigenous roots as they attempted to find an ecologically sound manner for the town to develop. One movement participant, for example, explained her motivation for involvement, "Our ancestors gave us this land and through the generations, we have learned to care for it. It is our responsibility to defend it from exploitation so that it will be here for our children" (Interview, Tepoztlán, April 1999). Finally, the CUT placed its claims on the rights to convoke elections on Mexican law allowing indigenous communities to follow their "uses and customs" to select local leadership. Since most people in the municipality, however, would generally not identify themselves as indigenous, this newly found importance on an indigenous heritage can be understood in part through the legitimacy that being indigenous carries with it in terms of the framing work of the environmental movement. Under the logic of the global environmental movement, if Tepoztlán were an indigenous town, it would most certainly know how best to use its land, and therefore, make better decisions than the development company or the state.

This is a problematic stance as it clouds the issue of what an indigenous community actually is. After all, the majority of Tepoztecos do not speak Nahuatl, dress traditionally, work communally or in agriculture, as do most indigenous communities. The CUT, nevertheless, opted to build on an essentialist notion of indigenous identity promoted equally by official nationalist discourse, opposition intellectuals and the environmental movement. By adopting this strategy, however, they also limited discussion about other important and related issues, because all positioning related back to arguments about predetermined indigenous sensibilities. This essentialist strategy, for instance, makes continual environmental critiques difficult, as it posits a certain pre-existing "natural" knowledge about caring for the environment, which may or may not be part of a community's actual traditions or which may or may not be carried out in practice. Furthermore, some movement supporters were hesitant about using indigenous frames of reference, citing, for instance the dubious assertions that the present neighborhood system in the town is actually a direct descendent of the Tlalhuica/Mexica *calpulli* system. Likewise, one movement supporter questioned the uncritical adoption of an "indigenous identity," claiming that indigenous communities of past and present had and have strict hierarchies and gender inequities, hardly making them a "natural" model for democracy. She accused movement leaders of concocting the indigenous question as a means to stifle internal dissent and exclude certain community members from leadership positions, rather than using it as a mechanism to discuss democratic processes more broadly (Interview, Tepoztlán, March 1999).

Even the category of "indigenous" being naturally a positive environmental attribute seemed to be contradicted within the municipality itself. The village of San Juan Tlalcoteco, which forms part of the periphery within the municipality, for instance, is in many ways much closer to the traditional definition of an indigenous community. Many residents continue to speak Nahuatl, employ non–Western dress (particularly the women) and are dedicated to agricultural work. The majority of the residents of San Juan, unlike the majority of people in the rest of the municipality, however, favored building the golf course. For them, the environmental concerns were of less importance than those of day-to-day survival, and they believed that the project would bring employment opportunities. They refused, therefore, to cooperate with the CUT in the electoral process or other aspects of the protest (Rosas 1997, 41–45). That is not to say that community life and shared traditions and rituals are not and have not been a key component of Tepozteco make up for generations. It does imply, however, that the connections made by the transnational environmental movement between sound stewardship of the land and being an indigenous community, has clearly played an important role in developing this particular aspect of community identity in relation to the conflict. This identity, while effective for winning this particular conflict, could prove to be problematic when it comes into contradiction with other important issues, as suggested by some of the complaints expressed above.

Besides highlighting indigenous aspects of the town's culture, the anti-golf struggle also brought a greater awareness on the part of some citizens and officials as to the need to maintain ecologically sound policies as an overall development plan for the community. After winning a seat in the Morelos State Congress in 1997, former CUT leader, Adela Bocanegra, for instance, opted to head the state legislature's committee on Environmental Protection, because of her involvement in the anti-golf course struggle. While she had been an environmentalist at a personal level before the movement, as a result of her participation in the movement, she saw the need to work at a systemic level to make the kinds of permanent changes in policy and consciousness that are needed to improve the environment (Bocanegra Quiroz 1999). The Office for the Environment in the municipality has focused its efforts on better regulation and control of construction in environmentally sensitive areas, and has employed ecological arguments to persuade people not to build in restricted areas. This is an ongoing and much older conflict over land tenancy, in which communal lands have been invaded by individuals either from Tepoztlán or migrant workers from Guerrero or Oaxaca or lands disputed between Tepoztlán and the neighboring municipalities of Jiutepec, Tejalpa and Cuernavaca. One of the differences now, however, is that the land tenancy dispute is framed in terms of building on and inhabiting protected lands, which was one of the key framing issues in the golf course struggle. Finally, a number of citizen, non-governmental groups in the town have carried out various projects including a "Clean Tepoztlán" program to pick up litter, recycling in conjunction with an organization in a nearby municipality and education about composting, organic foods, preventing forest fires and educational programs about the Chichinautzin Biological Corridor. There seems to be some clear indications, then, that the discourses of environmentalism circulate among at least some of the town's inhabitants and that there has been some effort to transform those ideas into political practices and governmental policy.

The label of environmentalist, however, is a slippery one, and in the end conforms to local contingencies.[10] Despite the insistence on the importance of the environment, the meaning of ecologist is very different for many residents of Tepoztlán than it is for the large transnational organizations. One long time activist complained that less than two years after the crisis had passed that there was "virtually no environmental awareness in the town" (Interview, Tepoztlán, 1999). Although local people used that label, it was linked more to the realities of local social relations and local histories than to the more commonly held sense of conserving nature. Environmentalism here, he argued, "means something completely different than it does in the university and the international organizations. It is tied up with social conflict — people build where they should not and pollute the land and water. They think that it is their right because they are Tepoztecos, but they don't think people from the outside have that same right and they will fight them" (Interview, Tepoztlán, 1999). Indeed, the municipal government points to environmental and land tenure conflicts as important and related issues with which to be dealt. People commonly build on land that they own but which is in protected, environmentally sensitive zones. Part of that building can be attributed to this "lack of environmental awareness," and part of it is due to the lack of affordable land and housing as a result of the invasions from rich outsiders over the past 30 years.[11] The environmental label is brought out, in a sense, when outsiders, whether they be well-financed development corporations or squatters from Oaxaca or Guerrero, threaten a part of the land tenure system. It is a means through which certain people can be excluded from doing certain things. It is more difficult to apply that same standard, however, to long-standing members of the community.[12]

This contradiction between a declared environmental movement and continuing non-ecological practices is a useful illustration of how transnational discourses are appropriated by local activists for their own benefit. While it would certainly seem that movement leaders were sincere in their self-characterizations as environmentalists, and that other movement participants also considered their struggle to be about the ecological soundness of the municipality (wise use of water, for instance), it is also clear that the meaning of environmental became fused with other local discourses. The fact that it is acceptable for Tepoztecos to continue building in sensitive areas, use water unwisely, or keep polluting (the steadily increasing amounts of solid waste is of great concern and cost to the municipal authorities), while it is unacceptable for outsiders, reveals that although the environment is an important theme, it is connected to other local discourses and practices which look suspiciously on outsiders and privilege individuals and families with long histories in the town. That is not to say that people were untruthful about their position, rather that the concept of environmentalism as it is generally understood in academic or transnational activist circles took on different meaning within the context of the particularities of the town's history and this moment of struggle.

Human Rights

Another clearly important global discourse involved in this conflict is that of human rights. Like environmentalism, human rights discourse creates a narrative through which local activists can challenge not only specific governmental actions, but through which they challenge the idea of state sovereignty. This challenge is evoked both through a practical alliance of a broad transnational network of activists, and through an ideological mechanism in which human rights discourse creates an antagonism between the state and individuals, setting limits on permissible state actions in favor of the individual. Activists then fuse that limit on state sovereignty to their particular demands articulating their arguments in terms of rights that they hold against the state or the corporation.

As with environmentalism, the involvement of human rights organizations and practices had two fundamental impacts on the movement in Tepoztlán. On a practical level, the unfolding of the conflict necessitated the intervention of national and international organizations to secure protection for movement activists. Abuses by state forces such as unfounded arrest warrants, threats to physical well being, imprisonment, torture and eventually murder were countered by activating governmental and nongovernmental networks dedicated to the protection of human rights. Given the atmosphere of impunity and hostility emanating from the highest levels of the state government, it was impossible for activists to pursue local legal mechanisms for pressing their cases. One observer noted that at under the leadership of Governor Carillo, the Tepoztlán activists "were not confronting a government so much as a criminal organization backed by the repressive apparatus of the state" (García de Leon 1999).

In response, therefore, to egregious violations of human rights and the rule of law, organizations such as the Independent Human Rights Commission of Morelos, the Mexican Commission for the Defense and Promotion of Human Rights, the Center for Human Rights Miguel Agustín Pro Juarez, the State and National Commissions for Human Rights, Amnesty International, the Washington Office on Latin America and Human Rights Watch were contacted and involved in one way or another with the conflict in Tepoztlán. Because of the intervention of these groups, articles and opinion pieces were placed in national and international media and government officials were pressured from outside of the state in order to resolve pending human rights cases. Gerardo Demesa, for instance, was declared a "prisoner of conscience" by Amnesty International and received letters of support from people all over the world. Additionally, letters were sent on his behalf from the United States House of Representatives asking the state government to release him. Finally, even the federally appointed National Human Rights Commission eventually found in his favor, ordering his release and recommending that appropriate federal and state officials press criminal charges against the police and civilian authorities responsible for his imprisonment.[13] Furthermore, after the lethal police attack on activists in April 1996, the public outcry generated by human rights organizations through their relationships with the national and international press, was enough to force KS to cancel construction of the project. While the struggle to stop the construction of a golf course might not garner much attention from the global human rights community, particularly the parts of that community which are geographically removed from the area, by framing the dispute in terms of rights and drawing attention to violations perpetrated by state agents, the Tepozteco activists were able to make successful connections to, and include themselves in, the transnational human rights networks.

The action of building these kinds of border-blurring coalitions, however, serves not just to find allies in the fight against a powerful adversary. It also changes the scope of consciousness of the activists involved. Just as invoking organizations from the environmental movement moves the conflict from a strictly local problem to one that is involved in a larger, global process, so does the involvement of human rights organizations and rhetoric. In Tepoztlán, as repression became more and more acute in the conflict, activists began seeing themselves as part of the larger process of democratization in Mexico, as well as victims, or potential victims, of systematic human rights abuses. In order to successfully advocate for the specific demands of the movement, namely the cancellation of the golf course and democratic control over local politics, it became increasingly important to also advocate for the general acceptance of internationally accepted norms of human rights protection. By launching themselves into this struggle as well, activists were able to see themselves as part of a larger community working to restrict the actions of national states in regards to the means of coercion that they are allowed to employ.

Involvement with the human rights community serves to further the epistemological shift associated with the processes of globalization, because human rights discourse seeks to limit state sovereignty both by positioning individuals above unquestionable state discretion and by directly authorizing and encouraging the involvement of "foreigners" in the protection of individuals against state abuses. By following United Nations guidelines for the respect of human rights, for instance, activists increasingly undermine national laws and actions by appealing to international standards and instruments as a means of (self) defense. The creation of universally accepted and theoretically enforceable codes of behavior works toward the creation of a global consciousness in which people from vastly different cultural and geographical backgrounds are able to establish a common understanding for communicating with each other. Tepozteco involvement, therefore, with human rights organizations illustrated their ability to imagine themselves not just as Tepoztecos nor just as Mexicans, but also as members of a global community, with rights and responsibilities to and from other members of that community. Because of their actions on behalf of the defense of human rights (particularly their own), movement participants demonstrated their ability to think and act outside of the paradigm established by the system of nation-states. Indeed, by appealing to the universality of those rights, activists were very clearly negating the state's sovereign rights to regulate internal political affairs and to establish the order that it deemed most desirable. While they turned to the larger community to provide support for them in their struggle against state repression, they also contributed to that community by actively expanding the practice of human rights into the everyday lives of local community members and into the relationships between the state and civil society.

Like environmentalism, however, the ways in which that human rights discourse is acted upon corresponds very much to the local system into which it is being incorporated. Rather than simply rearranging the terms of rhetoric and perception into a totalizing narrative about human rights, activists use the terms of human rights to organize parts of their argument, but always within the parameters of local social dynamics, and always geared to a favorable resolution of the conflict at hand. Activists, in other words, invoke global notions of the universality of human rights protection, in order to strengthen their local movement, whether that be protecting the physical integrity of leaders or framing the problem in ways so as to gain wider public support. Human rights are also referenced in terms of other important local systems of meaning, such as those expressed by religious thought (particularly the active liberation theology groups in this case), the remembrance of abuses in past conflicts, heroic tales of those who have rebelled against authority and paid the price for their rebellion, or more broadly based political liberalization.

Within this local system, the universality of those rights, however, becomes somewhat muddied; and just as the abstract and utopian views of ecological harmony fall short of their implementation in everyday life, so do those of human rights. If Tepozteco activists claimed, for instance, that they had the right to be treated in certain ways by those in power, no matter how they expressed themselves, they did not always apply those rights to their own opponents. For instance, members of the deposed municipal government and communal land authority were forced from their homes and essentially banned from returning out of fear for their own safety. Likewise, those expressing support for the golf course were branded as traitors, their businesses boycotted and their homes vandalized. Shortly after expelling the municipal council, townspeople captured government officials holding a fraudulent meeting to attempt to ratify the permits issued to KS. Those individuals were held against their will for two days until state officials met certain demands. Federal and state security officials detected within municipal limits were sometimes subjected to physical mistreatment during their capture and detention. While in the larger scope of things, these may be minor issues and were carried out under the duress of often illegal governmental pressure, they nevertheless do represent violations of certain basic human rights.

The point here is not to try to show the shortcomings of the movement, but rather to explain how "global" discourses such as human rights become signified by the practices of local communities particularly during these moments of intense conflict where the reordering of hegemonic formations is underway. Despite this imperfection in implementing human rights ideals and the relative ease with which human rights as a category can be made to mean different things in different contexts, it does serve important discursive functions here that ultimately affect how social movements construct themselves and communicate meaningful ways for participants and observers to interpret events.

First and foremost, human rights discourse affects the construction of the narrative of events and hence the placement of agents within that narrative. Human rights movements exist because there exist serious and systematic patterns of aggression and intimidation on the part of states and other powerful actors. Part of that violence involves obscuring the truth, erasing certain events from official memory and rewriting the past. Human rights discourse, therefore, contextualizes itself primarily in the search for truth and remembrance. It seeks, in other words, to uncover the truth that states and other powerful actors attempt to hide. Secondly, and corresponding to the universality inherent in human rights, it attempts a legalistic decontextualization of issues and rationalizations of certain behaviors, because the circumstances almost do not matter. Simply put, under no circumstances can certain things be done to individuals. In the case of Tepoztlán, for instance, the economic stakes are irrelevant as is the context of a long-standing antagonism between state officials and certain members of the Tepozteco community. Even the overall context of political destabilization and transformation within Mexico are of little material importance in the application of human rights demands. The problem is clearly framed as one of the state committing bodily and/or psychological harm against individuals. Within this frame, the human rights community is able to garner more widespread support for not only this particular case, but for the larger goals of the movement as well.

The role of the local social movement within this discursive action is to place particular actors within the narratives that the human rights rhetoric has created. Since the first great challenge of the human rights movement is to accurately establish and document the truth, the search for the truth is the motor that propels its narratives. This truth is constructed through detailed and often legalistic testimonies of state violations of individuals' or groups' rights. By invoking this human rights discourse, therefore, movement activists in Tepoztlán not only attempted to protect themselves, but they sought to establish themselves as the tellers and recorders of the truth.[14] This is an important position to be able to stake out, not only because of the state's ability to hide and distort the truth through its manipulation of the mass media, but in a conflict in which right and wrong may not be immediately obvious, narratives that can convincingly claim the moral high ground and the objectiveness of the type conferred by the human rights movement are able to convey the correctness of their position in the conflict.

To better understand how this narrative works, I want to consider Gerardo Demesa's (1998) account of his arrest and imprisonment in his book, *No al club de golf*. He insists, for instance that "I tried to stick to the strictest reality" and "hope that my unique and true testimony may serve as an antecedent for future generations of my small country of Tepoztlán" (114). Furthermore, he hopes that the book "serves as a type of memory — that is why I put all the documents in it. I have to prove that what I say is the truth and not just my opinion. It should help to be a memory for the next time" (Demesa Padilla 1999). His book is filled with reproductions of numerous documents including letters from the non-governmental human rights community, newspaper clippings and the findings of the National Human Rights Commission, in order to verify his testimony in an objective fashion. He produced this book and its corroborating documentation as a means not only to explain what happened to him, but also to affirm his position as a holder of the truth. Borrowing not only from his own experience, but also from the discourse produced by the human rights movement, he positions himself as a recorder of the truth. He is fully aware that the state will lie to protect itself (as he shows repeatedly in his own case), and he is afraid that the true story will be consigned to oblivion as the state rewrites history for its own ends. By writing this book, Demesa hoped that his testimony, backed up by the photocopied documents to prove it, will make it that much harder for the state to impose a collective amnesia on the events in Tepoztlán and the serious violations of human rights that it has committed.

Certainly, claims to truth and altruistic motivations are not the sole property of the human rights movement. Even within Demesa's book he makes many references to his liberationist religious convictions as well as his communitarian philosophy. Nevertheless, the bulk of the book is clearly evidence that global human rights discourse is the driving force behind his writing. Of the 115 pages of text, a full 35 are reproductions of human rights interventions in his case, such as cards sent to him from members of Amnesty International from several countries, a letter on his behalf from the United States Congress, prison documents, human rights awards, photographs of protesters in front of Mexican consulates and the findings of the National Human Rights Commission. Additionally, he takes several opportunities to directly thank those who have worked on his behalf and hopes that they continue to struggle for the high ideals represented by the efforts on his behalf. Demesa, therefore, is very explicitly connecting himself to the global community through the question of human rights and using that position, along with its claims to truth and methodologies of documentation, to imply that not only is he telling the truth, but that the anti-golf movement itself, is acting in a profoundly "truthful" manner.

In his narrative, he goes beyond simply reporting what has happened to him, and presents himself as a symbol for the movement in general.

Following the trajectory common to this type of testimonial literature, he constructs his truth claims by presenting himself as a "loyal and disinterested" social fighter. He gives a brief biography of himself, which while unique, also comes to stand for the collective community experiences that he embodies. He explains that his desire to improve the social conditions of his fellow Mexicans comes from his "totally humble origins," and his experience doing his social service as a teacher among the poorest of his "Mexican brothers and sisters" (11). Upon his return to Tepoztlán, he used his teaching position to help other Tepoztecos organize and defend their ancestral land. As a teacher, he became very involved in the democratizing union activities of the 1980s and affirms that, "social struggle is not individualist nor partisan. Rather it is collective and of general interest, thinking always of the benefit of others. The most important and directing line of all social movements is to command by obeying" (16). He is, in other words, only a small part of a larger community. Throughout the book, he returns to the themes of being impartial, interested only in others and speaking only the truth. Because of his position as a human rights documenter and because of his organic connections to the community that he is representing (both in the book and in his political work), he is able to present an unfiltered voice of those people and of their struggles against exploitation. His only motivation, he claims, is to preserve the truth as accurately as possible as a means of furthering a collective project of liberation.

In this way, he is fusing the ideals of his communitarian ideology ("*patria chica*," "my Tepoztlán," "defending our mountains," *et cetera*) with the global discourse of human rights. He is telling the truth, which both because of the "pureness" of its origins and because of the strict documentation of the case, is beyond reproach. He manages in his narrative, therefore, to use the truth-telling power of human rights discourse to empower himself and his movement. If he is telling the truth about his own experiences, in other words, then his position in the political struggle must also be true. His side of this political dispute is imbued with the truth, meaning that the other side must some how be false. If they are lying about his treatment, then surely they are lying about the potential benefits of the golf course project. This question of truthfulness was no small matter as evidenced by the charges of lying and inauthenticity exchanged in the press by both sides throughout the conflict. Demesa uses his book and his position as a former prisoner of conscience to witness the truthfulness of his side by linking his political position to the accounting of that truth.

In addition to providing rhetorical truth statements, Demesa demonstrates the fragmentation of consciousness created through his use of the human rights rubric to short circuit the state's right to establish and control national identity. He clearly establishes himself as a local, national and global citizen, while attempting to disassociate the state from national identity. He is proud of his Mexicanness while remaining extremely critical of the state. Because human rights discourse (among of course the other elements of globalization) challenges the sovereignty of the state, Demesa is able to create an identity that allows him to seek new ways of understanding himself triply as a Tepozteco, a Mexican and a world citizen. He uses the tools of global discourse as a means to break with the totalizing project of the state. He shows how the state delegitimizes itself by failing to adhere to its minimal responsibilities. In this process of delegitimization, the state subsequently loses its right to speak for all Mexican citizens. Into that vacuum, therefore, he asserts the importance of local identity and social relations by recording this memorial for contemporary and future generations of Tepoztecos to remember their uniqueness and to protect their sovereignty versus the state and other powerful outside entities.

Local Agency in a Global Context

Although I have only analyzed two global discourses as a means to discuss this dialectic of homogenization and fragmentation, there are innumerable global, local and national discourses being fused to create identities that serve to create new ways for individuals to understand their places in the world. The importance of these two particular global movements is that they very explicitly erode state sovereignty in ways that are useful for local actors to exploit in their attempts to further their political and social agendas. They create frames, in other words, through which concrete actions can be developed and made meaningful.

I have also highlighted the importance that *local* actors have in reproducing transnational discourses. Much consideration of globalization concentrates on the obliteration of space by focusing on the ease with which people, ideas and practices travel and communicate. Such analysis minimizes the work that place-based people make of the transnational world to which they constantly and differentially relate. Rather than seeing local people as simply victims of global, neoliberal policies, this analysis demonstrates how they incorporate aspects of global realities into the local and regional social relationships that govern their lives. In the case of globalization, activists are able to challenge the rule of certain elite sectors by using the very rules of transnational logic that those elites have imposed for their own benefit. Social activists in general blame such global issues as free trade and economic restructuring, enforced by the extra-national institutions of NAFTA, WTO, the IMF and the World Bank, for much of the worsening poverty and social inequities that they encounter as a matter of course in their lives. Nevertheless, they take advantage of issues such as the eroding of national sovereignty in order to challenge the state and to make international allies. This process not only strengthens movements in relation to more powerful opponents, but because it poses serious questions about the totalizing project of the state, it permits activists to strengthen local identities and social networks.

While it is undoubtedly true that the commingling of different modes of production, semiotic codes and sensibilities of time produces the kinds of hybrid cultures very noticeable even superficially in places like Tepoztlán, it is not always clear how that hybridity can be effectively translated into meaningful and effective political action. In the Tepoztlán case, it seems, that, among other things, activists did successfully construct a position which articulated transnational discourses and movement resources with local ones in such a way that the local conflict was successfully settled in their favor, suggesting that cultural hybridity is not necessarily a politically neutral phenomenon, but rather one open to active political work. In the course of constructing the movement, leaders not only changed the meanings of globalized discourses of resistance to fit the needs of the community, but they also changed the ways in which local propositions about development and social relations themselves were articulated, further demonstrating that the political culture that develops along the hybrid lines outlined here is very much dependent on the historic specificities of the community involved.

4

Toward a Democratic Political Culture

Public Spheres and Activist Networks

We have an awareness of how power works and are willing to face it, because we want a life with dignity and freedom.
— Municipal Council member Malaquías Flores Pérez, 1999

While social movements are realignments of what Snow and Benford (1992) call master frames, and the hybrid articulations of distinct cultural discourses, they also challenge and attempt to force changes in concrete social relations. The construction of the political culture of movements takes place within and contributes to the structuring of very specific structures of power. Because they are on-the-ground embodiments of contentious ideas and practices, and not just imaginative creations, movements operate within the constraints and opportunities of existing power relationships. Likewise, the ideals and hopes raised by the movement need to be channeled through some sort of institutional process in order to be consolidated and last beyond the redress of the immediate grievance. It would have been one thing, for instance, for the movement in Tepoztlán simply to have stopped the construction of the golf course. It was another matter altogether for activists to give shape and materiality to their demands for democracy, and to be able to hold enough power to protect natural resources in the future.

The Tepozteco activists in the late 1990s were operating within an institutional context in flux. The centralized populist PRI-State was clearly weakened and in decline as it faced both elite and popular challenges to its legitimacy. As the state retreated from it dominance of social organizations, civil society came to play an increasingly important and contested role as the originator of political activity. That is not to say that the state simply stopped being important, as quite the opposite was true. The state remained a formidable opponent to many social movements, both through its repressive and cooptative abilities, but there were increasing opportunities to undermine the state's strength through openings created by its loss of almost absolute control. The state also played an important role in the Tepozteco and other movements, because as the prime organizer of public social relations, the state created myths of national identity and established the networks of local and regional relationships governing economic activity and political bargaining (Lomnitz 1992; Lomnitz 2001).

As the PRI-State was losing control over those processes, other actors were seeking to fill those gaps. While some of those actors came from other political institutions, much emphasis for opening and change emanated from organizations within civil society. Beginning particularly in the early 1980s, civil society played an increasingly important role in defining public relationships. Civil society became a field in which different ideas and practices were proposed and debated, and from which organizations arose that demonstrated a marked autonomy from the state.

As the PRI lost control over the state apparatus through the 1980s and 1990s, these organizations of civil society, which included but were not limited to the kinds of radical social movements like the one in Tepoztlán, began to demonstrate more competition and interaction with state institutions and actors, leading at times to a blurring of those boundaries. Social activists, for instance, became explicitly involved in electoral politics in large numbers in and after Cuauhtémoc Cardenas' 1988 presidential campaign, and as activists began winning midlevel elections the distinction between civil society and the state became slightly more difficult to discern. Also, the increased role of civil society, because it is not a centrally organized entity like the state, led to the blossoming not just of a single national public sphere, dominated by the mass media but multiple public spheres, which corresponded to the specificity of various communities' internal relations and relations with outside forces as well.

The growth and diversity of these public spheres, which straddled state-civil society distinctions contributed immensely to the evolution of a new political culture as part of the transition period. This new culture was not completely different than the old, as ingrained patterns of political behavior did not simply disappear, but attitudes and practices about politics and public life in general were debated in a new manner. An important development throughout the transition has been the "municipalization" of politics. As the state decentralized through the 1990s, funds and control were somewhat transferred from central institutions to municipal governments. In that sense, the locally and regionally oriented public spheres took on increasing importance, as citizens, both through their involvement in the state and in civil society organizations and movements, could more directly influence decision-makers who held direct relevance to their lives. Here, Tepoztlán offers an important example of how organized citizens were negotiating the uncertainties of political change, as they institutionalized some of the aspirations of the anti-golf movement by accepting compromises with the state in exchange for their participation. The experience of Tepozteco politics, once the movement had demobilized, also indicates many of the difficulties involved in putting into practice those ideals, as old habits and bureaucratic demands often took up much of the time and effort of activists-turned-politicians.

Social Movements and the State

Recent work and events in Mexico suggest that political transformation and democratization, in which social movements play such an important role, do not come all at once, but rather are the result of an uneven process (Foweraker and Craigs 1990; LaBotz 1995; Castillo and Patiño 1997; Zermeño 1997; Durand 2002; Alonso 2003; Olvera 2003). As the movement in Tepoztlán was unfolding in the late 1990s, the PRI was in its final stages as the hegemonic force in Mexican politics. An important element in that process was the rapidly changing role and level of influence of the national state, which found itself increasingly unable to maintain uniform control over its vast political apparatus. As neoliberal reforms weakened the PRI-State's ability to employ the kinds of clientalistic practices that it had utilized for the better part of the twentieth century, and as the state made some important (although limited) attempts at constructing competitive democratic institutions, the "rules of the game" were not entirely clear to most political practitioners, leading to greater political entrepreneurship on the part of both established politicians as well as citizen-based organizations.[1] This destabilization of traditional channels of political authority and control gave greater importance to regional and local actors in creating and taking advantage of political opportunities. Local social movements, therefore, were able to exploit this type of political opening to further their agendas and to democratize those spaces.

Contrary to many assumptions, however, regional political openings were not automatically filled with democratic forces. Cornelius (1999), for instance, points to "the survival and even strengthening of subnational authoritarian enclaves," as evidence that it was possible for federal level efforts at democratization to be ahead of local ones (3). The weakening of presidential authority as an important part of national political transformation, in fact, contributed in some instances to the strengthening of authoritarian politicians and practices, because, ironically, central political figures with a moderately democratic agenda were less able to challenge and control dissident politicians who were resisting even the mildest of democratic reforms. Morelos, under the leadership of governor Carillo (1994–1998), would seem to fit into this category. Even as his administration became increasingly intransigent on Tepoztlán and other issues, to the point of general ineffectiveness and embarrassment, federal officials were unwilling or unable to remove him from office, something which less than ten years earlier would have been unheard of. This suggests that there was an important level of political activity taking place below and outside of the control of national political actors and institutions. These subnational politics, particularly in an era of a weakened central state, did not necessarily conform to the prescriptions of national politics, suggesting that politics, even under authoritarian states such as Mexico's, is never quite the top-down process that it is often assumed to be. The relative autonomy of regional and local politics, therefore, provided an opportunity for locally based movements, such as the one in Tepoztlán, to successfully challenge policies and projects by organizing among local constituencies on issues over which they could realistically hope to have influence.

While the PRI-State had been portrayed routinely as an almost omnipresent force in political and social life, recent studies have suggested that the state was never as strong as many analysts (or politicians) believed it to be (Levy and Bruhn 2001). In his study of Juchitán in the state of Oaxaca, for instance, Jeffrey Rubin advocates a "decentered" understanding of Mexican politics. He demonstrates the importance of local and regional cultures to the deployment (or blocking) of national policies. He contends that while the central state did play an important part in determining power relations, politics always takes place within a particular, local context. He argues that, "politics is embedded in cultural meaning and practice and that what we traditionally label 'national' occurs in and through what we call 'regional'" (239). He places primary importance on the webs of social networks that constitute everyday life in the formulation of public policy and political relationships, and demonstrates the repeated failures of the federal government to impose several projects, because local political leaders (of various authoritarian to democratic stripes) were able to employ local culture to further the ends of *their* particular projects, which were often in conflict with federal plans. He points to the relatively autonomous political development of the region to argue that local and regional factors need to be seriously considered when examining the implementation of national policies. This autonomy can be seen not only in recent successes of the Coalition of Workers, Peasants and Students of the Isthmus (COCEI) to establish a democratic municipal process, but also to historic cases of post-revolutionary *caciques* sometimes collaborating with and sometimes resisting central authorities. His study suggests that despite the often times self-promoted image of the all-powerful state, there has always been another political process at play. This local process is in many ways more important than the federal one, because it is at a local and regional level that policies are experienced and carried out by people in their everyday lives.

Social movements such as the one in Tepoztlán or COCEI in Juchitán found themselves squarely in the middle of this tension between local meaning and practice and national attempts at homogenization and political control. As Rubin explains it, COCEI was successful because "...leaders not only spoke Zapotec with humor and skill, but they spoke the language of the regime as well" (272). Building on a long history of successful politicians, the leaders of COCEI, in other words, conversed easily in the language of people's everyday lives, understanding the cultural issues in which political problems are embedded. At the same time, because of their formal education and immersion in the culture of the Mexican state, leaders could translate those needs and demands into a language that the regime spoke, thereby building coalitions with other opposition groups and pressuring the state for concessions.

This ability, and indeed need, to speak a "double language" also played a crucial role in the Tepoztecos' ability to win the concessions that they were seeking. The CUT leadership, for instance, successfully used the terms of local discourse, while at the same time took advantage of their class positions and their contacts with national and transnational organizations to build broader support outside of Tepoztlán. They spoke the "double language" of local discourse as well as the language of the national regime. The importance of this bilingual and bicultural local leadership suggests that the state did not and could not function simply as a monolithic apparatus capable of imposing its will through a combination of co-optation and coercion. Rather its hegemony was created through on-going negotiations with local and regional discourses and players. In moments when the state was particularly weak, local and regional players had a better chance at asserting themselves and advancing their projects.

In a broader sense, the very existence of social movements outside of the state's ability to control requires a rethinking of the limits of conventional political culture. In her study of the *Movimiento de Damnificados* following the 1985 Mexico City Earthquake, Ligia Tavera-Fenollosa (1999) argues that movements with local and/or regional demands change the national political equation by promoting a democratic culture. While she notes that a democratic civil society does not lead automatically to a democratic state, it does "sensitize" states and political leaders to the needs and desires of citizens and creates self-confidence in citizens to demand services and accountability from the state. While much of this struggle occurs at the local level around very specific issues, the inclusion of new actors and new perspectives often has larger ramifications by forcing the state to deal with civil society in new and meaningful ways. The very existence of social movements, therefore, regardless of their success or failure, pushes the bounds of institutional rule by forcing the state to deal in one way or another with the demands of autonomous organizations and by creating a sense of citizenship and possibilities within movement activists themselves (Melucci 1995; Alvarez, Dagnino et al. 1998). Citizens begin to conceive of politics as something that can and does occur outside of institutional channels, and their efforts at bringing about local changes inevitably spill over into the formation and practice of politics even at a national level by adding to and changing the categories of political discourse.

The existence and success of the movement against the golf course along with the varying successes of other types of social movements, suggests an important shift in the ways in which the state was dealing with civil society. On the one hand, it highlighted a crisis in the Mexican state in regards to the state's ability to regulate public life. According to populist theories, the state should be able to channel this type of conflict by mediating between the parties involved (Vilas 1994). In this case, it was apparent that the PRI did not have the political resources to effectively reach out to disaffected citizens through its various mass organizations or official party apparatus. At the same time, the sort of heavy-handed politics used by Governor Carrillo was in conflict with more moderate PRI doctrine officially aimed at fostering a democratic transition, exemplified, for instance, by shifts in resources away from centralized bureaucracies toward municipal control, and negotiation with other political parties over new rules for electoral competition (Cornelius, Eisenstadt, et al. 1999; Poot Capetillo 2000). The inability for the national political apparatus to have much effect on either side of the political conflict in Tepoztlán underscored a very deep crisis within the mechanics of social control orchestrated since the Mexican Revolution. Although this crisis had certainly been exasperated by recent neoliberal reforms, it also suggested an underlying weakness in the construction of the national state from the beginning.

Although there were many indications of the PRI's inability to project and maintain centralized control over social conflicts, the state's relationship with land ownership is particularly enlightening and important especially within the context of the anti-golf movement. One of the pillars of the post–Revolutionary Mexican State had been its ability to control the use of natural resources (particularly land and oil), by claiming, in the name of the "people," to be the ultimate proprietor of them (Gilly 1994). Although this relationship with the land has antecedents reaching back to Spanish colonial administration, which wrested the right to control the ownership and use of the land from the *encomenderos* in the mid-sixteenth century, it is with the consolidation of the modern state in the 1920s that land became a key element in the state's claim to legitimacy and to controlling different sectors of society. It had been, until the early 1990s, one of the main mechanisms through which the state has successfully governed.

Land ownership was one of the key issues in the revolution, particularly in the state of Morelos. Emiliano Zapata and those communities that rose up with him were more interested in recovering and working the land that was stolen from them by the haciendas than they were with larger ideologies of democracy. "They did not want to vote in the first place, but to have access to their land," explains Warman (1988). From the beginning of the Mexican Revolution, the guerrilla armies of the south pressured repeatedly for land reform over and above political reform. Zapatista forces, for instance, abandoned Mexico City after their capture of it, since their interest lay in working their land and not reforming or running the national state. This disinterest in controlling the state is not surprising since most *campesinos* saw the state itself, whether it be that of Díaz, Madero, Huerta or Carranza, as the enemy. It had always been interference from the state that cost them their land, and they were fighting basically to be left alone.[2] Without the interference of a state that had always protected their opponents, they reasoned that they would be able to develop their communities and protect their ancestral lands.

While the revolution was extremely chaotic and destructive (Morelos lost half of its population between 1910 and 1920), there was a brief respite in 1915 in which the Zapatistas carried out a land reform project, based on communities' rights to collectively use the land in their territories (Hernández Chávez 2002). They attempted to put into practice their ideal of "autonomous municipalities" in which communities of peasant farmers could sustain themselves without political or economic interference from the metropolis. Disputes over territorial limits were worked out through community consensus, consultation with village elders, and long hidden colonial documents. Zapatista military leaders then enforced these agreements, and Zapatista militias obligated central authorities to accept community decisions regarding territory and land distribution, thus reversing the flow of knowledge and power that usually defined *campesino-*state relations. The fighting, however, returned by the end of 1915 and the land reform was abandoned as federal troops under Carranza's control entered the state and began attacking the Zapatista communes. The Zapatistas left their fields and returned to guerrilla warfare only to be gradually worn down and defeated over the next three years. By the end of 1919, Zapata was assassinated, and the "Liberating Army of the South," demoralized from hunger and the long years of fighting, was effectively disarticulated.

Although the Zapatistas had proven to be ineffective political leaders at a national level, they managed to force land reform and the restitution of the *ejidos* into the 1917 Constitution. While Carranza did little to enact this reform, his successor, Alvaro Obregón, who owed his political and military survival to the reorganization of the Zapatista militias in 1920, did begin the process of land reform throughout the country, with particular speed and thoroughness in the state of Morelos. This urgency in Morelos reflected the political reality that Obregón faced. Although his goal, despite revolutionary rhetoric, was not a radical transformation of social relations, but rather stabilization in order to consolidate the capitalist aims of the post-revolutionary state, he found that he needed to incorporate the remaining radical elements organized around Zapata's soldiers and ideals. On the one hand, he owed the Zapatista militias a favor as they had strengthened his military position allowing him to oust Carranza in 1920. On the other hand, he needed to pacify the countryside and incorporate the *campesinos* into his political organization in order to promote national stability. The land reform that he enacted, however, was fundamentally different than the Zapatista reform of 1915, because now the state, and not the communities, "owned" the land (Gilly 1971, 358). As Warman notes:

> ...behind the practical justification the political reason of the state was being advanced. The agrarian reform was not going to legitimize the historic right of the *pueblos* to the land nor strengthen their autonomy. It was not going to carry out acts of justice despite the legislation that authorized the government to do so. Just the opposite was happening. It was going to redistribute lands as a unilateral concession of the state, as a gift from the powerful who reserved the right to watch out for the fulfillment of its supreme order and to clearly

intervene in its administration so as to create a political client [152].

Rather than being a "right" which the *campesinos* had won through a military victory, land reform became a tool through which the new state would forge dependent client relationships with them.

The successful appropriation and redistribution of land through the next several administrations continued this client building process. The state more clearly defined itself, particularly in the Cardenas administration (1934–1940), as the legal arbiter of disputes involving land, by placing itself as the ultimate "owner" of the land through its representation of "the people" (Gilly 1994). At the same time, the state increased the dependency of its *campesino* clients through their incorporation into the state and party structure in the *Congreso Nacional de Campesinos* (CNC). The CNC, although itself a labyrinthine bureaucracy, became the only organization through which *campesinos* could mediate land ownership and credit problems with the state. The CNC and the various state agencies of the agrarian reform oversaw the distribution of credits and the redistribution of land and water resources. This corporative structure proved to be a valuable tool in maintaining control over this large and important sector of the population, and its success was due primarily to the state's legitimacy as the owner of the land and natural resources. Ideologically, this relationship was used to demonstrate the "revolutionary" credentials of the state as well as to foster political and economic dependence on the part of *campesino* sectors toward the state. The state, in other words, embodied the revolutionary aspirations of the *campesino* sector in regards to agrarian reform. Conversely, of course, loyalty to the party and the state were compulsory in order to receive any of the concrete benefits (credit, irrigation and land titles) of this revolutionary posture.

The effectiveness of this system, however, began to wane as early as the 1970s when more forceful methods of control were periodically employed against dissenting and dissatisfied *campesino* organizations. With the drastic economic restructuring following the 1982 economic crisis, however, the system began to fall apart. As the state was less able to intervene directly on behalf of *campesinos*, different organizations and orientations began to appear. The state itself recognized this change in relationship with the *campesino* sector and with its right to be ultimate owner of the land, by declaring the Agrarian Reform complete in 1992 and by changing points in Article 27 of the Constitution. The most important change was in the ownership of *ejidos*. Whereas before, *ejido* land was inalienable and could only be legally transferred through inheritance, the

Constitutional reforms, necessitated by Mexico's entrance into the North American Free Trade Agreement (NAFTA), allowed *ejido* land to be broken up and sold to outside interests. This change in the Constitution, while directly effecting *ejiditarios*, also implicitly recognized the change in economic regime in the country. The state was no longer an interventionist state, and property ownership rightfully resided in the private sector, not the public and communitarian ones. The state, in effect, ceded one of its pillars of legitimacy and control to the forces and logic of global economic restructuring.

This transformation represents a significant crisis for the state in that it could no longer claim undisputed legitimacy to control over land and natural resources. It is precisely this crisis that led to the ways in which the dispute in Tepoztlán evolved. Initial efforts by the Tepoztecos to solve the problem resided in appeals to the state, through both executive and judicial branches. The state, however, was unwilling or unable to resolve the problem along the communitarian lines advocated by activists. It was also unable to absorb the discontented factions within the town because of its lack of legitimacy in the eyes of many Tepoztecos. The state's inability to confront big capital in the name of local rights represented its turn away from its traditional role as arbiter of land disputes. The activists, in turn, therefore, took matters into their own hands, ultimately (and temporarily) displacing the state in the day-to-day functions of local governance. Social actors in this case demonstrated that in the absence of an interventionist state, they would assert their own claims to control natural resources.

Elements of this conflict illustrate that the neoliberal order adopted by the technocratic elite within the PRI put its ability to negotiate between various classes into jeopardy. As the state had been systematically reduced and had opened up the economy to transnational investment, it could no longer effectively intervene in the economy nor provide subsidies as a means of political control.[3] It abandoned nationally oriented development policies and defunded virtually all types of financial support to "non-competitive" economic and social sectors, which in turn severely eroded the PRI-State's ability to successfully negotiate resolutions to land and other types of conflict.

This inability to successfully incorporate marginalized groups into the dominant economic strategy highlighted a second important crisis, this time an ideological one. The post-revolutionary state relied heavily on a communitarian discourse, in which it portrayed itself as the protector and patron of the people. The people, of course were always left rather ambiguous, as was the way in which the state was protecting them. Nevertheless, marginalized groups successfully petitioned the state using their position as the people, in order to gain certain advantages. Although the Mexican state has always pursued a strategy of economic modernization of a markedly capitalist stripe, it also successfully created and manipulated myths about the revolution and the protective relationship between the state and the people, in order to create the types of political subjectivities and organizations that it required to govern. With the adoption of neoliberal ideology and programs, it was increasingly impossible for the state to maintain the legitimacy of those myths. In fact, the political subjects that the PRI-State was trying to create turned many of those state-created myths against it. The use of the myth of Zapata by indigenous people in Chiapas is a clear example of the "people" (poor, *campesino*, indigenous) turning state sponsored myths back against the state. This schism then, between the state and the people that it had created, represented a very serious crisis in, and renegotiation of, the hegemonic order led by the PRI for the previous seventy years. It suggested a disruption between the heterogeneous and contradictory nation and monolithic pretensions of national mythology and partisan political practices. This breakdown in stable political institutions also made the rules for gaining and exercising power increasingly less clear as the state was forced to abandon the corporatist categories as useful channels of power, facing instead, an increasingly diverse civil society with multiple demands of representation.

The appearance of many different types of movements in Mexico, particularly beginning in the 1980s contributed greatly to the destabilization of the PRI. Because of the highly diverse nature of these proliferating organizations, the state was capable neither of systematically meeting all of those demands nor systematically co-opting their leadership (Foweraker and Craigs 1990; LaBotz 1995; Castillo and Patiño 1997; Zermeño 1997; Díaz-Barriga 1998; Lomnitz 1999). The move away from the totalizing impulses and abilities of the Mexican state and the disintegration of rigidly guarded social sectors gave rise to a burgeoning civil society from which the state was continually challenged to respond to citizen needs. This process partially pushed political discourse out of the realm of the strictly institutional and into the realm of civil society.

Social movements provided one means through which these multiple identities and demands sought to represent themselves to the state and the public in general. Unlike the traditional corporatist social sectors organized by the PRI, however, by the 1990s, movements usually emphasized the need for solutions to specifically local problems within a broader context. The specificity and contingency of these movements made them difficult to incorporate, as they suggested a way of doing politics that was organized locally, horizontally and dependent on the face-to-face knowledge of participants. This tended to encourage (although it certainly did not guarantee) more democratic and open forms of organizing. As local movements branched out and formed alliances with other movements concerned with similar issues, they increasingly began to practice a coalition politics that allowed for experimentation with negotiation and agenda setting (Greene 1997). It also was a means through which local activists began to put into practice political ideas that were only tangentially connected with the state at all. While that is not to say that all social movements were inherently democratic or progressive, it does mean that members of civil society practiced politics outside of a closed institutional system. This extra-institutional politics was furthered by the generally provisional nature of social movements, making them less susceptible to wide-scale cooptation. This relative autonomy of locally based social movements, therefore, would not only contribute greatly to the unraveling of PRI dominance, but would make the reconstruction of a post–PRI political system difficult to enact at the national level.

Civil Society as Discourse and as Social Field

Although state structures laid the groundwork for organizing, and the weakening state provided the political opportunities for activists to put forth new proposals, civil society played a multifaceted role in the conflict in Tepoztlán, which highlighted important political and scholarly debates at the national level. Civil society's importance sprang both from the associative organizations existing within the community as well as discourses about civil society that were circulating among activists during the 1990s. From an organizational perspective, the many autonomous associations present in Tepozteco social life provided a vital means of communication and consensus building for the movement. The movement was able to draw upon the diverse strengths of different organizations and to communicate its messages efficiently through neighborhood networks established during previous conflicts and/or run through church organizations. At a discursive level, movement supporters cast themselves as representing civil society and as embodying the democratic impulses of the population against an arbitrary and authoritarian state. Under this logic, the movement was acting to defend society from the colonizing tendencies of the central state and transnational capital. By positioning itself as civil society, the movement claimed to represent the entire community, as if that population were acting of a single mind.

The ways in which the term civil society were deployed in the conflict in Tepoztlán reflected national debates about the nature of civil society and the changing relationship between citizens and government. As often happens in oppositional rhetoric, civil society was often conflated with a singular popular movement. Supporters repeatedly equated the term civil society with the people in a homogenous project of self-determination. It linked the idea of citizenship and democratic participation with a politicized and mobilized citizenry. Many movement participants talked about how "we" or "the people" beat a "very powerful business" and a "corrupt government." In most descriptions of the struggle, there is this sense that "almost everyone" was with the movement, suggesting that civil society in fact had an opinion and a specific project that it was able to carry out,[4] and insinuating that those who did not oppose the golf course were agents or dupes of the state and not really part of civil society. Furthermore, within the contemporary national political landscape, the movement was able to project itself clearly as a movement *of* civil society against the state, linking it to broader efforts of political reform. One long-time human rights activists characterized the conflict in Tepoztlán as "a great victory for civil society over the state, as democracy advances in even the most repressive of situations" (Interview, Cuernavaca December 1998).

This has been a common, and problematic, posture of many opposition movements throughout the transition period. Since the PRI-State had so thoroughly controlled public associations throughout most of the twentieth century, many critics of the regime began to personify civil society, portraying it as an actor in resistance to the state. The problem with this position, however, is that it tends to flatten out the complex heterogeneity of civil society, which must more accurately be understood as a social field in which individuals and organizations attempt to push particular agendas and build support for specific projects.[5] In a democratic society, except in rare occasions, civil society does not so much as *act*, but, rather, is the field where individuals and groups organize to promote their interests, and, in the case of political projects, attempt to win support for their proposals. In other words, groups act within civil society, but civil society as a whole does not really act. The appropriation, therefore, of the mantle of civil society by movement activists and supporters was an attempt to magnify the breadth and depth of their support and to widen the frame of their issue from the particular conflict to a broader vision of how society should be organized.

The exact meaning of civil society represents a never-ending debate among both theoreticians as well as political activists in the context of contemporary Mexican politics. Enrique Brito (1997) notes "the difficulty in arriving at a definition of civil society that is acceptable to everyone, not only because the phenomenon is analyzed from a variety of perspectives, but also because it deals with a dynamic reality which is constantly changing" (186). Building on a series of definitions from Gramsci through Habermas (1987) and Cohen and Arato (1992), Brito comes up with an operative definition of civil society as "the groupings of citizens organized as citizens to act in the public field in search of the common good, without interest in personal enrichment, without looking for political power nor institutional connection to a political party" (186). This working definition attempts to make a clear distinction between the state, political parties, private economic initiative and "other" organized groupings in society. There are four key elements to this definition. First, civil society is *organized*. In other words, it is not just individuals or undifferentiated masses, but rather it consists of organized citizens. Secondly, civil society works in the public field as opposed to the private. Organized citizens attempt to voice opinions and make changes in public social relations. Thirdly, civil society works for the common good, rather than for personal gain. This differentiates it from private enterprise. Finally, the fact that civil society does not work for political power or affiliate itself institutionally with a particular political party, differentiates it from the state and other political institutions, which in the end seek to promote their own interests rather than necessarily that of the public in general.

This working definition is helpful in many ways and somewhat restrictive in others. On the one hand, it sheds light on the ways in which the concept of civil society is defined and used in contemporary Mexican politics, in which civil society takes on the characteristic of an oppositional political movement. The insistence on civil society being that which is not the state describes to a great extent the ways in which civil organizations frame themselves in the contemporary political context. In an era marked by widespread distrust of political actors and institutions, claiming to be the opposite of them, obviously, has a certain amount of ideological capital (Lechner 1997). Furthermore, given the state's historic ability to colonize and control virtually all public political spaces, the simple assertion of autonomy from the state is clearly an important political stance.

Using the term this way, however, tends to misrepresent the complexity of civil society, by failing to recognize civil society as a very heterogeneous entity. Furthermore, suggesting that it always works as a foil or safeguard against the state, political parties and business organizations does not pay heed to the ambiguity inherent in that heterogeneity. The collapsing of diversity causes analytical problems, as very different political and social positions are made into a monolithic whole. This points to another problematic aspect of Brito's definition in that he stresses that organizations of civil society work for the common good rather than personal or partisan gain. While this distinction differentiates the actions of groups of citizens interested in promoting the general welfare, with those associated with the state and private business, the altruistic nature of organizations of civil society is rather problematic. People organizing in urban neighborhoods for improved infrastructure and for more honest and efficient police protection, for instance, certainly do constitute civil society, as do business people organized through a Lion's Club or Chamber of Commerce. Although, their claims to be non-state actors working collectively toward a common goal make them both constitutive of civil society, they most probably do not share a similar position as to the role that the state should play, for instance, in allocating public resources. It becomes rather unhelpful, therefore, to consider civil society as just popular organizations working on a progressive agenda. Since civil society is extremely heterogeneous, different organizations are going to have very different visions of the common good, and therefore, are going to struggle amongst themselves for social, political, economic and cultural advantage to promote their vision.

Furthermore, the separation of civil society from the institutions of political power proves to be elusive in practice. As Olvera notes, there is not always a clear distinction between the state and civil society, as actors and organizations cross back and forth, both in terms of position and orientation of programs and policies (2003, 43). The PRI historically created various organizations through which citizens could express their opinions and attempt to influence policy. Although these organizations were generally used to maintain control over the constituencies involved, they were also forums through which individuals could give voice to their concerns and develop an agenda that would benefit their social sector. The National Action Party (PAN), which has traditionally championed conservative values and pro-business agendas, claims to represent civil society through its promotion of liberal economic measures that seek to privilege the private sector over the state in economic policy. Finally, the PRD seeks to represent civil society through its connection with a wide variety of progressive social movements. There is a great deal of cross-over between organizations of civil society and the PRD, as many social movement activists use the PRD as a platform to push their agendas for social change into political institutionality.

This last case proves to be very complicated, because as a matter of practice these social organizations, while very active politically, have ambiguous relationships to political parties. At times, some organizations

are openly antagonistic to all political parties, due to histories of co-optation and manipulation. They equate collaboration with parties, even those
in the opposition, with a recognition of the state's legitimacy, and fear that
such a move forces them to play by the state's rules, which ultimately sup-
ports the *status quo*, and will lead to their absorption into the system. At
other times, however, some organizations seem willing to create at least
temporary alliances with political parties in attempts to further their agendas, realizing that political parties are necessary channels of mediation
with the state which they require to consolidate their victories. Most organizations, however, jealously guard their autonomy and are quick to criticize their allies (particularly the PRD) for violating democratic norms or
for attempting to incorporate them. Given the history of political co-optation in post-revolutionary Mexico, this insistence on distance between
"civil society" and "political party" is a key element in the identities of civil
organizations. Perhaps rather than making a clear distinction between civil
society and the state, organizations of civil society, must also be understood as forming points of articulation and mediation between citizens and
state institutions (Olvera 2003). It is through the autonomous organizations of civil society that pressure can be brought to bear on officials and
agencies to implement policies desirable to citizens, and it is likewise
through these associations that consensus can be established and ideas
promoted.

The civil society debate, despite the ambiguity that it has generated,
is an important one because the term holds much capital in the contemporary political process. Those on the left have attempted to frame the issue
in terms of the state versus the people, and equate the people with civil
society. In this case, a conglomeration of progressive movements and non-
governmental organizations represents civil society. One of the dangers of
construing civil society as that which is not the state is that it imbues civil
society with subjectivity and as a protagonist in political conflicts. Civil
society is often described as "awakening" and "confronting" the state in
an ongoing struggle for power, and thus, a political actor, capable of opposing the state and developing its own program of nationhood.[6] It creates
two sides: the state and civil society. Civil society is imbued with all of the
values that the state does not have, including democracy, respect for human
rights and an impulse toward a more equitable distribution of wealth.

The very diversity of positions within civil society, however, makes
such a position rare. Olvera argues:

> Only in a highly symbolic field and in extraordinary circumstances
> can "civil society" claim a collective moral representation: in campaigns

against dictatorships, against crime, against the violation of human rights, against the impunity of the political class, against hunger, for free and fair elections, for indigenous rights, for peace, for a dignified life. Outside of those circumstances, that a group or network or sector of civil organizations claims a supposed representation of civil society is a political error that can have serious consequences [2003, 32].

Instead he insists that civil society is not a collective or homogenous actor and that in and of itself it does not carry any particular political or reformist program. Furthermore, the relationship of civil society to state and economic institutions is not uniform and depends entirely on the specificities of the societies involved, but is related to the development of modern societies and depends on the existence of a market, the state, the rule of law and freedoms of expression and association (Olvera 2003, 28–30). As such there is clearly a relationship between autonomous civil societies, the rule of law and functioning democratic states, but the specificities of those relationships depend on the history of the society involved, meaning that civil society as an abstract notion in and of itself does not create democratic relationships, but connotes the ability of individuals and groups to negotiate their relationships to each other and to powerful political and economic institutions. It is more accurate to consider it a "field" in which actors, both individual and collective, operate to create public opinion, to demand redress from the state for certain grievances, and to propose a project of community or nation. It has critical *potential*, and it is dependent on the actions of the various organizations within it as to the democratic influences that it does or does not have on the state.

If we understand, therefore, civil society to be the public and semi-private spheres of life in which people organize, make decisions and carry out projects outside of the immediate control of the state, then the possibility of a viable civil society is relatively recent in Mexico. Historically the state has so efficiently controlled organized public actions that it severely impaired the ability of citizens to act independently. Under the state that was consolidated after the revolution, the government effectively monopolized all public association of society by organizing interest groups into sectors represented both in the party and in the state resulting in populist-corporatist state and society. Carlos Monsiváis contends that "for a long time, (civil society) referred only to the fiction that the state tolerated the non-existent or always insufficient autonomy of the governed" (1987, 78). In other words, although there existed some sort of field of social relations outside of state control, actors in that field had little hope of effecting serious public change without intervention from the state, because the state itself was actively organizing and controlling civil organizations.

The broadening of the autonomy of organizations in civil society and the weakening of state control over those associations, would seem to be promoting the possibility of democratic opening, because they become increasingly stable and reliable ways for citizens to express themselves and to pressure the state to implement policies that benefit their constituencies. The foundation for these organizations as Olvera notes is the various social movements that provide citizens with the consciousness of advocacy and the space to learn and improve on the tools of communication and political involvement (2003, 38). In the case of Tepoztlán, activists affiliated with the CUT successfully portrayed themselves as representing civil society against the state, and contributed to the autonomy of civil society by breaking the PRI-State's control over municipal politics and energizing other types of public associations.

The Tepozteco Public Sphere

If civil society is the semi-autonomous field in which non-state actors operate, then the public sphere is the means through which they communicate and articulate proposals and analysis. By public sphere I mean an arena in which citizens can freely express their opinions and discuss possible actions without fear from state intervention. The public sphere, however, is not simply a neutral space for discussion, but rather a highly contested one in which various actors, representing what Habermas calls the "system" and "life world" compete for the formation of public opinion and the legitimization of public policies (broadly understood). Communication through the public sphere is one of the key elements "in the reproduction and transformation of cultural traditions, collective identities and social integration. Communicative action also permits a collective critique of systemic social problems by rational-moral actors drawing on the normative structures of their life world" (Miller 1993, 27). This "collective critique" drawn from the complex interaction within civil society contends with systemic needs and precepts in the public sphere as different groups negotiate a collective identity and project. Social movements insert themselves into the public sphere as the point of articulation between specific demands and broader political/cultural projects. They provide the means, in other words, for groups of citizens to communicate and act with other like-minded groups and individuals in attempts to influence public policies, particularly when their positions receive little institutional representation.

Analysts generally refer to a single, national public sphere through which matters of public importance are discussed and refined. The nation is the prime referent in discussions of public spheres, because it is believed that policy and cultural debates only make sense within the parameters of national political discourse. In his analysis of the public sphere in Mexico, however, Claudio Lomnitz (1999; 2001) argues that there are really several public spheres that need to be understood in terms of region and access to means of communication. He is skeptical that a national public sphere even makes much sense given the dynamics of contemporary society. Lomnitz insists on Mexico being a nation built up of different communities organized through several regions and class sectors. Although the state has built a myth of a homogenous national identity, local and regional interests continue to dominate people's lives and influence the ways in which they form and articulate opinions about political matters. What is more, in an era of mass communication, the creation of a national public sphere requires access to the mass media. Clearly, many elements of civil society do not have access to those media, and certainly not as active participants. This type of fragmentation as well as a general lack of access to mass media precludes an effective national public sphere. He sees the creation and strengthening of regional public spheres, therefore, as an important process of Mexico's modernity, because the diversity of regional systems reflects the deep democratic potential of a reconstructed Mexican state. Instead of a single party forging a monolithic nation, the growing importance of regional public spheres allows for the wide variety of Mexican communities to define themselves and articulate their attitudes toward "national" policy. He points to "new" social movements as playing an important role in the development of regional public spheres, because their very instability and intimate connection to people's everyday lives make them almost impossible for the state to incorporate into a particular sector, allowing them to maintain a certain amount of autonomy from state control (1999, 203–204).

One of the contributions of social movements to promoting democracy is not so much their ability to make quick and decisive structural change, but rather their communicative power based in people's everyday experiences. Instead of addressing people as political objects to be won over, they reach out to and construct individuals as important communitarian subjects. Social movements generally appeal to "neighbors," "colleagues," "friends," *et cetera*. In other words, they appeal to and affirm deep, personal identities, rather than abstract or overtly political ones. It is from these semi-private positions that an urgent matter of public interest is engaged. This is a powerful combination as people align a question of public policy with their own lives. Operating through one or more public spheres, therefore, protagonists of social movements articulate political positions by using the languages of local, regional, national and transnational discourses in a grammar which makes sense to people in their everyday lives. They appeal to the concreteness of their lives rather than the abstraction to which formal politics often appeal. This engagement with people at a personal level makes public issues more important and real to them and, in that process, politicizes a series of other social and communicative networks. This creates a markedly different type of public sphere than is often considered in political analysis, because the modes of communication, as well as the potential impact on national policy, are vastly different in these networks. They correspond more directly to the specificity of local and regional cultural systems rather than to the parameters of national political discourse.

Building on various communicative networks, the conflict in Tepoztlán produced a very active public sphere. As Lomnitz suggests, the public sphere developed along already established lines of communication unique to the history and relationships of the municipality. In many ways, especially during the first few months of the conflict, the movement did evoke a kind of idealized public sphere. Nightly meetings were held in which news was discussed and in which strategies and tactics were debated. As state institutions had been removed from the town, there was obviously little interference or fear on the part of participants about reprisals, as long as they remained in town. While discussions focused primarily on immediate concerns, there was also an implicit and often-times explicit critique of the larger structural issues that directly affected people's lives, suggesting that people had concrete opinions about questions of social organization beyond the limits of the municipality.

The growth and consolidation of this public sphere was limited both by external and internal pressures. There was reasonable fear that state authorities, using both physical coercion and its control of most of the mass media, would retaliate and attempt to squelch the growth of dissent being expressed at these public meetings. The ability of the movement to physically isolate itself from attack and to develop communication networks outside of the media would seem to confirm Lomnitz's contention that local public spheres are of utmost importance, because they are able to evade the kinds of restrictions which a powerful state can impose on the mass media, and because they conform to the cultural expectations of local populations.[7] Even within the confines of the town, however, this ideal public sphere had its limits. While many opinions were discussed, the parameters of that discussion were very clear. Open support for the golf course, for instance, was not permissible public speech. Golf course supporters' homes and business were often spray painted with "traitor" and boycotted. This would clearly not be conducive to an absolutely free exchange of ideas nor the growth of unhindered communicative networks. Nevertheless, it did create a space (with limitations) in which "civil society," with all of its contradictions and imperfections, could discuss issues of public importance and laid the groundwork for making future office holders accountable to the public for their actions.

These kinds of public discussions obviously did not occur in a vacuum, but were built on the already existing communicative networks of groups and individuals. These webs are contingently constructed both through explicitly political relationships as well as those relationships created through the routines of everyday life. Activists utilize these webs to build support for their movement by recruiting members and attempting to sway public opinion in their favor. These types of networks or webs constitute the often fragile means through which politicized and organized civil society works. Alvarez, Dagnino and Escobar (1998) argue that

> the term "social movement webs" (in contrast to the more common "networks") conveys the intricacy and precariousness of the manifold imbrications of and ties established among movement organizations, individual participants, and other actors in civil and political society and the state. The "web" metaphor also enables us to more vividly imagine the multilayered entanglements of movement actors with the natural-environmental, political-institutional, and cultural-discursive terrains in which they are embedded [15–16].

In other words, understanding the use and creation of networks of support within civil society as a multilayered and at times tenuous process helps us to better analyze *how* activists successfully carry out their struggles, by pointing to the articulation of multiple and contingent social positions present within movements.

In Tepoztlán, activist webs reached deeply both within the community as well as to outside allies. Throughout the conflict, it was clear that activists had very little hope of success without utilizing and thereby strengthening and broadening these webs. They needed the informative and solidarity support of like-minded individuals and organizations throughout the region and throughout the world, as well as the solid support of respected local individuals and organizations. Anti-golf club activists successfully accessed local webs of power and public opinion by taking advantage of family, neighborhood, church, professional and other networks of prestige. They were also able to access networks that had been established in previous conflicts. The *Comité de Barrios*, for instance, was formed during the struggle against the construction of a gondola in the 1980s, and led the fight against the scenic train in the early 1990s. CUT leaders were drawn from this committee and its already existing networks were used to mobilize support throughout the struggle. Similarly, CUT activists won the support of the neighborhood *mayordomos*, who assisted the movement by providing logistical and communication support, as well as lending it legitimacy as it confronted state officials.

At the same time, they were able to access those networks that exist outside of the town. Many of the CUT leadership, for instance, were linked to outside communicative webs either through their professions or through their activism in other types of organizations such as the reform wing of the teacher's union. Activists in Tepoztlán, in other words, had important and varied connections with activists from other organizations. At the beginning of the struggle, local environmental activists used their connections with national and international NGOs, such as Greenpeace, to help them orient their analysis of the ecological and political affects of golf courses around the world. Likewise, throughout the struggle, activists relied on contacts with national and international organizations to "get the word out" and to organize pressure from outside of the town.[8] Intellectuals residing in Tepoztlán wrote articles or produced political cartoons that circulated through various national media outlets, making this very local issue present in the formation of national public opinion. It is through extensive networks of civil society that movement activists were able to articulate a broad response, and attempted to influence national public opinion about their concerns. It further demonstrates that the public sphere is not *just* what happens at a national level nor is it reducible to simply public opinion. Rather it is the interconnected communicative webs through which people construct and express opinions about public matters. These webs must necessarily hold an important local component, and given the realities of national public life in Mexico, regional and local cultural practices are key components in the construction and functioning not of one, but of several, diverse and interrelated public spheres.

Weaving a Local Web

A prime example of how webs of activism are woven through multiple public spheres can be illustrated through one of the members of the CUT directorate, Carlos.[9] Although not a native born Tepozteco, he married into a well-established and politically active family, and as a long time

Depiction of a growing activist web, showing a Chinelo embracing a Zapatista and urging civil society to participate in an upcoming referendum, Tepoztlán, 1999.

resident, had been a highly visible member in past struggles such as the fight against the scenic train in 1991. When it became apparent that KS intended to build the golf club, he, along with seven other residents formed the initial organization that would become the CUT in order to educate themselves and townspeople about the risks of the project and to begin mobilizing opposition. The CUT leadership divided their work into various commissions, and he headed the press and public relations commission. His paid work at the time was as an advisor to the PRD bench in the state congress, where he analyzed economic issues and legislative proposals.

His previous job, however, had been as an information analyst for the Center for Meetings and Dialogue (CED) in Cuernavaca, which serves as an umbrella organization for many popular organizations in Morelos. Sergio Mendez Arceo, Cuernavaca's famed "red" bishop, upon his retirement, founded CED so that the pastoral/political work of liberation theology would continue to have an institutional foundation after he was forced (by age) to relinquish the diocese.[10] CED provides a regional level mechanism for progressive popular organizations to support one another, and it is usually the physical site for regional and statewide meetings on issues including popular education, human rights, women's empowerment and environmental protection.

The connection between liberation theology and the anti-golf movement was also no coincidence. Participants repeatedly pointed to the "historic" Base Ecclesial Communities (CEBs) as one of the organizational foundations of the movement. Carlos is an active participant in a base community in his neighborhood. During the conflict, the parish priest gave his support to the movement and encouraged parishioners to support one another and to defend the town.[11] Members of the CEBs whom I interviewed stressed that the communities helped and strengthened the movement within the *barrios* and villages by convincing people to come out to demonstrations and by keeping people in touch with each other. One leader of the CEBs noted that "they were the motivation for many. Most people who were involved are poor, but they supported with what they could. They're the only group that has managed to stay articulated" (Interview, Tepoztlán, 1999). The struggle, in turn, made the communities stronger by creating a greater sense of internal cohesion and by facilitating links and connections with other outside groups.

Besides providing communicative networks, the practice of liberation theology in the town also contributed to the willingness of people to take risky positions and to stand up for what they considered to be issues of social justice. During a Good Friday commemoration that I observed, for instance, a woman leading the service asked people to reflect on the death of Jesus in terms of contemporary issues:

> Jesus was crucified by those who have power, for being a rebel. Even though it happened two thousand years ago, it continues every time someone is hurt, killed, slandered, or shunned for standing up for what is right, for being a voice for those with out a voice. We need to look upon the human rights violations in our own country, state, municipality and village and see Christ in that [Tepoztlán, 1999].

By reflecting on their religious beliefs in this way, members of these Base Ecclesial Communities contribute a sense of *obligation* to the protection of human rights and to work toward making substantive social change. This dramatically alters the public sphere, in that the discussion of these types of political issues moves beyond the realm of "politics" to become framed in religious discussions and debates in everyday life. These politicized religious reflections in which the communities are involved contribute to a greater radicalization of political positions. Much of the political analysis done by CEB members posits local disputes within a larger socio-economic context. One CEB member, for instance, argued that

> part of the problem originates in the U.S. [...] I don't know if you are with them or not, but I have to say that they are mixed up in everything;

like the massacres in Kosovo. Since Mexico is the gate to the U.S. and Latin America, well, it is very important. The people in the CEBs understand how that works and what the dangers are. It even says it in the Old Testament where people were killed by empires. They had to fight wars [Interview, Tepoztlán, 1999].

The CEBs, in other words, contribute to discussion and action within the public sphere both by maintaining communicative networks and by framing radical political issues in religious terms.

The other important block of support for the movement came from women. Virtually all observers and participants in the movement noted the importance of women at demonstrations, guarding barricades, pushing the limits of the debate, and seeing to the countless logistical details involved in moving and feeding hundreds and even thousands of people. Although Carlos, obviously, is not a woman, his wife is very involved in a number of women's organizations in town. Using, in part, the confidence that his wife has developed with other women, Carlos was able to collect and publish an article of interviews with women in a publication sponsored by CED on the golf course conflict. In these interviews, women expressed their opposition to the golf course and their need to participate "as women" in the movement, because it was necessary to protect the future of their children. This is significant, because although women were unquestionably important in making the movement successful, their views and voices were often excluded from public debate. By publishing these interviews, Carlos was hoping to help facilitate the dissemination of these women's positions on the golf course issue.

The role of women in this movement also highlights some of the ambiguities in discussing public spheres. In Tepoztlán, only one woman, Adela Bocanegra, emerged as a very public, and ultimately elected, leader in the movement. When I asked her why she thought this was so, besides the obvious continuing problems of sexism, she mostly attributed it to the fact that most women simply had more important things to do than run for public office. She noted that women are the primary care givers at home, and that their families come first. During moments of crisis, women were able to organize themselves and get their work done at home early, so that they could be out at demonstrations all day. She believes, nevertheless, that their voices are heard through the influence that they wield on the men in their lives. Although they themselves may not run for public office, they debate the issues among themselves and see to it that the men who do hold office understand their positions (Bocanegra Quiroz 1999). The public sphere that women in this case occupy is decidedly different from that which men occupy. There are women's political groups, such as *Mujer Tepozteca*, which, although it has historic ties to the PRI, has been a contentious organization working for "women's" issues over and above partisan ones. Nevertheless, the public sphere in which women seem to have the most influence is a mostly informal one. Women, for any number of reasons, generally do not run for public office and do not make the speeches at public events. Nevertheless, none of the women that I spoke to expressed a deep dissatisfaction with their abilities to influence public debate.[12] This suggests that public spheres extend through and beyond various social networks, including those that are not often associated with arenas of public influence.[13]

These informal networks can also be seen at play through the ways in which Carlos interacted with his neighbors. Despite not being a native born Tepozteco, he was continually greeted with "*compadre*" by his neighbors when we would walk down the street together. This is a sign of respect and shows a certain level of trust. This trust is not just the result of his leadership on political issues in the town, but reflects his involvement in other kinds of communicative webs as well. While I was conducting fieldwork, for instance, Carlos's neighborhood was involved in a project to improve road conditions and water storage. Discussions of these issues occurred frequently on street corners, stores and in more formally convoked meetings at the neighborhood church. Carlos's willingness to participate in these projects increased levels of *confianza* (trust) between him and his neighbors. Furthermore, these neighborhood and kin ties (Carlos's in-laws are long time residents of the neighborhood) are strengthened by their active participation in the neighborhood festival, which brings everyone together for several days of celebrations, mass, and shared meals, as well as his participation in collective work, such as tending to the chapel's corn field. The closeness of these networks was indispensable in creating and sustaining the anti-golf movement as it provided for both a means of disseminating information as well as establishing the needed levels of trust to discuss and act on risky political opinions.

Activist webs were also important at a larger regional and national level. Outside of town, as a result of his work with CED, Carlos had established a sizable number of contacts with various other opposition organizations and movements as well as the local media, which he utilized to gain favorable publicity and protection for the movement in Tepoztlán. Of particular importance to the movement was the active involvement of various non-governmental human rights organizations. Statewide, the Independent Commission for Human Rights of Morelos (CIDHM) coordinates human rights efforts and provides front-line documentation work on human rights abuses. They offer legal advice, seek to educate the public in general as to their human and civil rights, and maintain strong contacts with national and transnational human rights organizations. Many active members of CIDHM are also long time members of opposition parties, such as the Revolutionary Workers Party (PRT) and are involved in a number of other efforts aimed at creating social change. CIDHM often times collaborates with CED, and Carlos was able to use his personal contacts with the leadership of CIDHM in order to facilitate communication of human rights issues within Tepoztlán to the larger community.

The press contacts that he had developed during his work as information analyst at CED proved to be very useful to the movement, as well. He was able to get the CUT's version of events to sympathetic people in the press as a means to counter the propaganda produced by the governor's office. Most of the Morelos press was indebted politically and financially to the PRI and to the State, and often ran articles of dubious credibility that favored the stance of the government on controversial issues. Carlos was able to use the trust that he had developed with certain journalists to quickly counter those types of negative stories. In this way, he helped to create the shield that the press provided against more draconian repression from the state government.

Furthermore, his job as advisor to the PRD bench gave him immediate access to statewide political leaders, who were sympathetic to the struggle in Tepoztlán, and who allowed him the time he needed to work on movement issues. He helped to influence the PRD's position on Tepoztlán and on developing a statewide strategy for opposing the governor. This level of political support from the legislature was very important as it put pressure on the governor, from yet another angle, to keep him from carrying out more drastic policies. It also led to the governor's eventual ouster, by keeping the issues of human rights and criminal behavior high on the priority list of PRD politicians. Through this one person, therefore, we can see how these "activist webs" are created through different movements of civil society, reaching through community level networks, regional social movements, the press and even into the political parties and the state itself.

Movements not only uses these far reaching activist webs to help them in organizing their campaigns, but their very use of them reinforces certain social relations and creates new connections, thus amplifying the reach and importance of the webs themselves. The protests in Tepoztlán originally received some support from Greenpeace, for instance, but as the movement grew, so did its outreach to other environmental groups. These new connections continue to bring support and interest to the community around environmental issues, exemplified by a series of environmental initiatives in the town, including a small recycling and composting project, greater interest in the national park, an active reforestation program and projects to avoid forest fires. Finally, the human rights crisis brought closer ties particularly with the non-governmental human rights commission, as it worked to free prisoners and to provide legal assistance to Tepoztlán activists who had been legally and/or physically attacked. These new ties, while responding to immediate crises, nevertheless continue to exist and serve as a conduit for further civic actions. Such further actions could be seen, for instance, in the March 1999 Zapatista Consulta in which the *Comité de Barrios* (an organization that was greatly strengthened by the anti-golf struggle) set up 20 polling places in town and collected over 4,500 ballots, in which people overwhelmingly expressed their support for the protection of indigenous rights and for a peaceful solution to the conflict in Chiapas. In 2001, these same organizations pushed the PRD controlled Municipal Council to join a lawsuit seeking to nullify laws regarding indigenous rights, which the EZLN denounced as counterproductive.

Activists involved in these webs often cross the boundaries between civil society and the state, suggesting that the distinction between state and civil society is not always a clear one. During the conflict, members of the state legislature attempted several times to mediate. While there was certainly some self-interest in those overtures, the ties which that attempted mediation created would prove important over the next several months as citizens attempted to negotiate a new position for the town with the state government. The 1997 elections also saw to a greater convergence between movement and state as several movement leaders were elected to local, state and federal office. Once in office, the webs in which they were enmeshed played an important role in how they created themselves as politicians. State representative, Adela Bocanegra, for instance, became head of the Environment and Natural Resources committee, making use of the network of environmental activists who helped in the anti-golf movement. Her involvement in the Tepoztlán struggle has led her to be a strong advocate for environmental issues at the state and national level, thus creating another layer of "web" in which she, as a local social activist, now has an integral role in formulating and carrying out state environmental policies. In an interview with her, she explained that her interest in environmental issues is directly related to the movement in Tepoztlán, in that she began to see ecological problems as social and political ones demanding collective action rather than just individual efforts. Furthermore, she recruited environmental activists from non-governmental organizations that she had come to know during the course of the struggle to serve on her staff, thus further blurring the boundary between the state and civil society (Bocanegra Quiroz 1999).

Finally, the seemingly a-political networks in the town, which constitute the foundation of local public spheres, were reinforced and changed as a result of the movement. Historically, the division of the town into eight neighborhoods organized through church related *mayordomías* has been critical in the construction of people's sense of community. It has served as the primary channel through which neighbors most frequently have public interaction, and neighborhoods developed their own unique identity in relation to other neighborhoods. This organizing was also a means through which intracommunity rivalries were expressed, enforced and ritualized through festival competitions such as Carnival. Many anthropologists had noted a decline in the importance of this system as a source of rivalry, and a general decline as a means to form community cohesion (Lomnitz 1982; 1999). Salazar Peralta, for instance, notes that although the *mayordomías* originally served as institutions in which "distinct levels of economic, political and spiritual lives of indigenous towns converged," by the 1980s, those institutions were losing their importance and their prestige (227). The series of environmental/developmental struggles, however, which took place in the town from the early 1960s through the golf course struggle, have contributed to regenerating the importance and prestige of those neighborhood institutions. They have served both as a mechanism for political organizing, and as a means of differentiating Tepoztecos from outside interests. In discussions with me, many residents pointed out their neighborhood institutions with pride and considered them to be an important means of social reproduction. Annual neighborhood festivals, for instance, bring back Tepoztecos who have moved to other areas of Mexico or even to the United States. So while the main function of the *mayordomo* continues to be the reproduction of neighborhood traditions and rituals, that reproduction takes on new meaning as a kind of resistance to national and global homogenizing cultural influences.[14] Furthermore, the *mayordomías* have become important institutions for meditating political and civic issues as well, be they the militant opposition to development projects or the more mundane projects of water collection and forest fire prevention.

Consolidating Change and Institutionalizing Politics

The decision on the part of many movement leaders in Tepoztlán to pursue political office illustrates one of the strategies that activists deploy as a means of consolidating social and political victories. It also raises questions about the interface of state and civil society in the pursuit of democratic change, as individuals moved from the realm of civil society and autonomous social organizations to the state. Furthermore the divisions that the decision to reintegrate with the state caused within the politicized community in Tepoztlán indicates that the question of participation is not clear cut and that there continues to be much debate about the wisdom of compromise with the state. Within the larger context of an overall opening of the national political system, social activists around the country have increasingly faced the dilemma of how to consolidate their victories and to promote their proposals for change. The debate among activists, as was reflected in Tepoztlán, has been whether compromising on some principles to participate in the state system or whether remaining outside of the system to pressure it from without is the most effective means of enacting the more broad-reaching ideals of movements concerning democracy, human rights protection and the reorganization of economic benefits (Rodríguez Araujo 1996; Alonso and Ramírez Sáiz 1997; Labastida Martín del Campo and Camou 2001; Meyenberg Leycegui 2001).

Perhaps the obvious answer to institutionalizing change would be militancy in a (radical) political party that would contest for state power. Political parties, regardless of their ideology, however, are often seen as part of the state-system, and therefore are not trusted by many activists. Politicians are seen as being out for themselves, and although they may have long resumes as social activists, as soon as they become politicians their loyalties and perspectives change. This perception is certainly not unfounded as the Mexican government has a long and well documented history of co-opting movement leaders, further eroding the confidence of many activists in cooperating with any attempts to institutionalize their struggles (Vélez-Ibañez 1983).

In Tepoztlán, as in many places throughout Mexico, politicians are generally looked down upon. Politics is seen as an inherently corrupt and "dirty" profession. While there are a few exceptions to the rule, it is generally understood that in order to be a successful politician, one must be in one way or another "on the take" or beholden to a higher and more corrupt political official. The only clean politicians are the ones who refuse to play political games and are, therefore, forced out of office before the end of their terms and are, hence, ineffective (Lomnitz 1982). This distrust of the state and politicians not only applies to government officials, but to opposition parties as well, because it is assumed that people involved in institutional politics are attempting to better themselves, while using a rhetoric of representing the interests of the majority (Schedler 1999). Social movements have had an ambiguous relationship with political parties, generally eschewing outright, long-term alliances as a means of maintaining their autonomy and their moral position.

In their analysis of the intersection of social movements, NGO's and local government, Jonathan Fox and Luis Hernández (1992) argue that the most important change within Mexican civil society since the mid 1980s has been the "transition from an exclusive emphasis on protest toward efforts to build concrete social and political alternatives" (167). This change from contestation to proposition has not been an easy one, as movements have wrestled with questions about their autonomy while pursuing an often times frustrating process of gradually opening small holes in local and national politics (168). Despite failures at national level organizing, activists have had moderate success at the municipal level, since that is the level of politics which is most real to people in their everyday lives and the level at which activists most effectively operate. They note that "the municipality has become a key arena of conflict between civil society, which tries to occupy the space, and the central state, which treats is as merely the bottom layer in the regime's vertical hierarchy" (169).[15] This municipal level struggle, therefore, takes on more meaning than simply winning a political office, as it becomes symbolic of civil society's ability to appoint political leadership in opposition to the central state's attempts to maintain vertical control of the entire political apparatus. In their struggles, therefore, to consolidate victories and to implement proposals, rather than simply protesting, social movements have often turned to seeking political power by contesting for municipal level offices.[16] The step between movement and public office is no simple one as it involves a reconceptualization of the movement. No longer is it simply a matter of advocating against certain policies, but it requires a larger picture of what it means to form effective democratic governance by negotiating differences among local populations and political groups.

In addition to this sea-change in thinking, there are legal requirements that activists tend to see as restrictive. According to federal electoral law, all candidates, even those for local office, must run on the slate of a registered party. This direct involvement with a political party often runs counter to movements' beliefs about autonomy and the functioning of the state. Movement activists fear that their alliance with a national political party will force them to subordinate their local agenda to national priorities. Although many studies of opposition municipal governments, particularly those of the PRD, have found that there is often a great disjuncture between national political ideologies and programs and local formulations of them, local communities generally have enough experience with co-opted leadership to be wary of direct involvement in partisan politics (Rubin 1997; Zermeño 1997; Bruhn 1999). Throughout this transition, then, between "movement" and "partisan" politics, activists attempt to keep the two domains separate. As demands become more complex and systemic, however, this separation becomes increasingly difficult to maintain.

In the case of Tepoztlán, it was difficult to completely separate involvement with partisan politics and civil society even from the very beginning of the conflict. Much of the CUT leadership, for instance, had ties to or sympathies with the PRD. The movement's martyr, Marcos Olmeda, was one of the local party founders in the early 1990s. Adela Bocanegra, who initially organized the CUT and was at various times its spokesperson and chief negotiator, ran for municipal president on the PRD ticket in 1994 and won a seat in the State Congress in 1997. Members of the *Ayuntamiento Libre* whom I interviewed in 1996, while denying any official party militancy, expressed clear sympathies with the PRD project and saw it as a viable and desirable option to the PRI system. This flirtation with the PRD opened the movement up to attack from the state government and KS who charged that it was simply a front for the PRD, particularly given Adela Bocanegra's visible involvement. This is one reason why she, and the rest of the CUT leadership, opted not to run in the 1995 elections and why none of them chose to run for municipal office in the 1997 elections. They wanted to make a clear distinction between themselves as citizens working for the "betterment of the people," and them as political party activists. By not running for office, they were showing that they were not interested in partisan or personal gain.[17]

The attempt to separate partisan politics and social movement activism, however, does not mean that political parties were not interested or involved in the conflict. The parties, particularly the PRD, the PRI and the Morelos Civilista Party (PCM) all attempted to take advantage of the process in one way or another. The PRD, as a political party, for example, attempted to intervene in the conflict for what would clearly seem to be its own gain. As the crisis was developing, the party attempted to position itself as an intermediary between the CUT and the state government. When the CUT refused to yield on the question of local elections, state-level party officials were critical of their radical stance and their unwillingness to compromise. It would have been in the PRD's interest for Tepoztlán to have held regular elections in 1995 or 1996, because, as the center-left opposition party and with important ties to the CUT leadership, they would surely have won handily in local elections.

The PRD was, of course, not the only party to attempt to take advantage of the situation in Tepoztlán. During 1995 and 1996, the PCM offered their "registry" if the town would hold officially sanctioned elections (Rosas 1997, 84). There was very little support for the offer and virtually no presence of the PCM in Tepoztlán. Finally, the PRI, which obviously suffered a serious setback through the conflict, managed to maintain a presence within the town, as almost all of the political organizations in the municipality had some sort of affiliation with the PRI prior to the crisis. Even as the movement managed to consolidate its strength in opposition to the golf course by incorporating visible PRI members, the party itself continued to exist. In the 1997 elections, it won the second highest number of votes, and regained the municipal presidency in 2003. Throughout the negotiations, the governor kept insisting on a formula in which the PRI would gain at least a portion of the seats on the *Ayuntamiento*. At one point the *Ayuntamiento Libre* and the CUT leadership agreed to cede three of the seven seats to the PRI, in exchange for the government meeting their other demands. In other words, throughout this process, the PRI and even the CUT, in the end, looked toward solutions that were based on political party representation rather than direct democratic decision making.

All of these attempts by the political parties were effectively defeated by townspeople through various Popular Assemblies, which came to embody the voice of civil society during the conflict (Quero 2003). In the end, the *Ayuntamiento Libre* was forced to serve out its term and the CUT leadership was severely criticized for attempting to barter off the people's right to democratically choose their own officials. This strong anti-party sentiment was problematic when, in 1997, all municipal and legislative offices came up for elections. The town was forced to decide whether to follow national norms and hold new elections, and thus regularize their legal status or to continue their protest. Since most of their demands had been met, after much deliberation and debate, the Popular Assembly decided to participate in the elections. Many people were skeptical that participating in officially sponsored elections, however, would be at all helpful or desirable, since they would be forced, under IFE regulations, to affiliate with one of the national parties. There was fear that the PRI would steal the elections or commit the types of fraud that had historically prevented opposition candidates from being elected. After much discussion, the CUT leadership was able to convince a majority of the Assembly that they needed to regularize their situation by participating in the elections and that their high level of organization would prevent the PRI from using its electoral tricks to sway voters. Three days before the required deadline for the registering of candidates, the PRD agreed to lend its registry to the

CUT, and a slate of candidates was selected through the system of *barrios* and public assemblies which had been used in the 1995 elections.

This temporary alliance with a political party has been a relatively new but increasingly common strategy used by social movements involved in electoral politics. Fox and Hernández note that few popular organizations advocated electoral participation until the late 1980s. Realizing, however, that legal options were limited, organizations began to seek out ways in which they could work with national political parties and continue to maintain their autonomy. They credit COCEI in Juchitán for pioneering the kinds of "flexible tactics and alliances" (1992, 176) that would be used in Tepoztlán and other municipalities in the 1990s, as they sought to consolidate political and social gains. COCEI carried on a militant campaign in Juchitán from the 1970s based on class and ethnic demands. Building an alliance with the recently legalized Mexican Communist Party, they won municipal elections in 1981, and managed to maintain a critical voice not only toward the state and federal government, but also toward their partisan allies. Although that experiment ended with the military occupation of Juchitán and COCEI's violent ejection from public office, the movement learned to build other alliances both within and outside of the municipality and returned to office in a power-sharing arrangement in 1986 and electoral victories in 1989 and throughout the 1990s. Throughout their experience, COCEI has had to form an alliance with a national party (most recently the PRD) in order to be allowed to field candidates. While those alliances have proved fruitful for both sides, COCEI has not been reticent to criticize national party policies, and has balked at entering fully into the party. Similarly, Bruhn (1999) notes in her study of PRD governments in Michoacán that some municipal officials, elected on the PRD slate "often exaggerated their distance from the PRD" in their attempts to continue pushing local concerns over national policies and to maintain loyal bases of support among their constituents (43). She found this trend repeated in Oaxaca, Veracruz and Guerrero, where a "PRD municipal president openly declared that she was not a member of that political organization" (43). In all of these cases, the elected officials stressed their ties to, and origins in, civil society rather than their careers as professional politicians. The strategy was to find acceptable ways of working with parties when they needed to, while not being swallowed up by them.

In Tepoztlán, movement activists negotiated an alliance with the PRD in which the town chose its own candidates according to their uses and customs, and the PRD named them as their slate. The PRD promised that it would not interfere with the local dynamics and would not impose candidates or agendas on the municipality. Then-national party president, Andres Manuel Lopez Obrador, himself a social activist from Tabasco, told leaders of the CUT that this model was as an example for how elections should occur, and that the PRD was "privileged" to be able to participate in this way (Interview, CUT leader 1999). The party tensions between local and national concerns in this case would seem to be leaning toward the local. The national president even suggested that the party should be a coalition of local movements united to help each other out, rather than a centrally directed political party. That however, is not the way in which the party has developed, as it has been marked by serious internal struggles and behavior reminiscent of machine-style, clientalistic politics.

Because of this type of behavior on the part of political parties, even those with sympathetic agendas, many activists continue to view parties with suspicion, if not outright hostility. This distrust of parties led to a split within the municipal government and the progressive political groups in Tepoztlán by late 1998. Even before the conflict had been resolved in 1996, the movement was divided among four tendencies. The CUT/PRD faction, while seeking the cancellation of the golf course and the right to self-determination, continuously pursued a "pragmatic" strategy of compromise with the state in order to move the town forward. A more radical faction headed by the teacher Ariel Bárcenas took a less compromising position, insisting on autonomy and continued confrontation with the state. The PRI faction, although discredited, had not altogether disappeared and attempted to work as an intermediary between townspeople and the state and, in particular, worked to secure the release of political prisoners as it positioned itself for an eventual return to municipal politics. Finally, the largest faction were people who were not as interested in political positioning, but who wanted to end the conflicts — both the internal one and the one with the state — as quickly and efficiently as possible (Quero 2003, 160).

After municipal politics returned to normal functioning, these splits were reproduced as the majority of Tepoztecos demobilized themselves from active political participation and the various political groups began positioning themselves to win the Municipal Presidency, which is up for election every three years. The split within partisan politics was most obvious beginning almost as soon as the constitutional government took office in 1997. Several municipal officials, elected on the PRD ticket that year, for instance, did not consider themselves to be members of the party. They were openly critical of the party organization, and insisted that they were elected on the "People's Slate," with their participation with the party being merely a legal technicality to fulfill IFE regulations (Martínez Zúñiga 1999).

Many radical activists complained that the PRD, simply because it was a political party, constituted part of the state-system and therefore could not be trusted. They argued that it is by nature an undemocratic institution interested in furthering itself and its leaders. Since the "People's Slate," however was run under the PRD registry, Tepoztlán officially became a PRD municipality. The state and federal officials who were elected sat on the PRD benches in their respective legislatures, and the municipal government was affiliated with the other PRD municipalities in Morelos. While the People's Slate/PRD held power, the relationship between the PRD and the municipal government became ever closer. At a very fundamental, structural level, the PRD and the municipal government shared certain resources and support personnel. The municipal PRD office, for example, did not have a phone, but party workers could usually use one in the municipal offices. Likewise, support personnel worked both for the PRD and some government agencies, some times being paid by one entity to do work for the other. Many people began to turn to the PRD for help resolving legal issues, rather than going through official channels. Such practices were clearly established by the PRI, in which one would need to go through party channels in order to expedite the resolution of problems with the state or federal bureaucracy, but carried through into the new government.

It is precisely these types of clientelistic practices and attitudes that the more radical activists in the movement feared. They believed that the *Ayuntamiento Libre* represented a type of autonomous municipality advocated since the time of the Mexican Revolution, and believed that by letting their guard down, the people had allowed the state, through the PRD, to regain control of local politics. They pointed out that with the waning of the crisis, townspeople were more willing to let the politicians handle the political problems and withdrew from the day-to-day political struggles, leading to a marked decrease in public participation and democracy. According to the analysis of a long time environmental activist, part of the government was attempting to live up to its democratic and communitarian mandate, whereas the other part was reverting to the old way of doing things and attempting to build the patron-client relations that existed under the PRI, only now under the banner of the PRD. When asked about differences between the PRI and the PRD governments, one elderly campesino activist stated bluntly, "there is no difference; they're all assholes" (Interview, Tepoztlán, July 2001). In part, these political practices and attitudes would seem to be due to an entrenched political culture not only on the part of officials but also of the citizenry, which, according to several municipal officials, was confused by the new rules of political conduct and frustrated by the slower pace of democratic processes.

Not everyone, however, shared the perception that working with political parties, particularly the PRD, was inherently a bad idea. Many community members believed that allying themselves with the PRD and becoming active members in the party was the only viable option for securing the gains of the movement. They seemed skeptical of the idea of a truly autonomous municipality not only because of the severe financial and political problems of the *Ayuntamiento Libre*, but also because of the reality that Tepoztlán is enmeshed in a series of regional, national and increasingly transnational relationships, which preclude the possibility or even the desirability of being autonomous in the original Zapatista sense.[18] One movement activist explained that there really was no choice but to join a political party if the ultimate goal of the movement was to effect permanent change in local politics: "There exists a rule of law in Mexico, and under that rule one has to work through the political parties. If you ignore the parties, you can't participate in the system and you leave the state in the hands of the PRI and the corporations" (Interview, CUT activist, 1999). As Fox and Hernández have noted, this attitude is widely reflected as social movements move from their protest phase of single issue advocacy to a broader phase which proposes more permanent reform to electoral and political practices and institutions (1992, 190). Many of the local PRD members, for instance, believed that they were participating in a national democratization movement, and that participation in a political party was necessary to consolidate democratic change at a national and institutional level. Grassroots party members talked about "joining the movement" rather than "the party." They pointed to a long history of political fraud and marginalization at the hands of the PRI-State as their reason for joining the party and hoped that their participation would help bring about change not only for themselves but also for the nation as a whole.

In Tepoztlán, the experiment with social movement and partisan alliance does appear to have allowed for a relative amount of openness on the part of municipal authorities to listen to the needs of citizens. When asked in 2001, what the biggest political change people could attribute to the anti-golf movement, most people responded by saying that they were less afraid to voice their opinions. This assertiveness is compared to the old system in which people reported that they were less likely to oppose projects, or in which projects would simply be started without consulting them first. There seemed to be a greater sense that since the municipal government was elected by the people and not imposed through fraud and manipulation, that the people had a greater right to be heard and that officials needed to be more responsible to the citizens. Interviewees claimed to be more willing to confront elected officials when they were unhappy with their performance. One neighborhood, for instance, held an assembly to consider removing their representative from the council, because they did not believe that he represented their interests well. Another neighborhood was angered over the construction of a communications tower in their neighborhood. Many seemed to believe that it would act as a giant lightning rod during rainy season and thought that the emissions would cause long-term health problems. They threatened to take it down if the municipal government did not rescind its permits. Although it was not clear exactly who had the authority to remove the cell phone tower, it does show people's unwillingness to accept unwanted projects and to demand that their elected officials "do something" about it.

While this type of assertiveness on the part of citizens would certainly seem to be a welcome step in the development of local democracy, because it demonstrated a certain level of citizen autonomy from government agencies, officials and other observers complained that many citizen demands were unreasonable or impossible to fulfill. State legislator Adela Bocanegra attributes this, ironically, to people's involvement in the anti-golf club movement: "They believe that since they were with the movement that they have the right to demand immediate resolutions of their issues. The problem is that they want to do it in an individual way, rather than seeing the problem as one for the community" (1999). This sense of raised expectations was a serious problem for both the *Ayuntamiento Libre* as well as the following constitutional governments, as they were unable to meet all of the demands of the citizens, and unable to balance different political factions within the town, which led to increasing dissatisfaction with PRD officials and repositioning of political parties as they attempted to sway people toward their candidates.

Nevertheless, the popularly elected government was generally credited for making good efforts toward consulting people about public matters. In April and May 1999, for instance, the municipal government began planning a new central market, as the current system of setting up stalls in the main plaza had become unwieldy. Before committing to any plan, however, a series of meetings was held with market vendors, communal land holders and the public in general to solicit opinions and to explain the need for a new market and the various proposals that the municipal government was entertaining. Clearly, the members of the *Ayuntamiento*, who were all visible activists against the golf course, had learned some lessons about the importance of incorporating public opinion into policy decisions, and seemed to be committed to the idea of participatory democracy as an outcome of their social movement experience. As the complaints by more radical community members would suggest, however, the tensions between democratic processes and autocratic structures and practices have not been easily resolved despite good intentions and efforts in that direction.

This uneasy alliance between movement and party raises important questions about the possibilities of democratic government in Tepoztlán as well as the direction and speed of democratization in Mexico in general. Kathleen Bruhn contends that although opposition parties have been winning municipal elections throughout Mexico, especially since 1988, it is not clear that those victories necessarily contribute to an overall deepening of democracy at the national level. She points to the serious problems that PRD governments in Michoacán have faced in trying to establish themselves as viable and effective democratic alternatives to the PRI. She notes that central authorities maintain tight control over all budgetary matters and can effectively subvert municipal authorities' abilities to carry out promises or even take care of day-to-day business by restricting funds. The PRI, even after its loss of the federal state apparatus, continues to be a formidable opponent because of its strong connections to a wide variety of social organizations and municipal employee unions that can cause further problems for opposition municipal authorities as they attempt to implement their agendas. She further argues that PRD governments, because they often are composed of uneasy internal alliances generally lack the kind of party discipline necessary to amplify local victories into regional or national successes. These internal divisions have caused numerous problems at the local level between elected officials who find themselves caught between trying to be fair and effective administrators and party members who expect to receive some of the spoils of electoral victories (Bruhn 1999). Finally, the lack of political and administrative experience can be daunting, as movement activists are generally unprepared for the kinds of bureaucratic responsibilities associated with running a municipal government.

Tepoztlán clearly has experienced many of these tensions. The *Ayuntamiento Libre*, in particular, was hard hit by both the state's ability to cut off its funds and the lack of experience of its leadership. While they were generally credited with doing a good job and for trying hard given the circumstances, people were quick to point out many of the problems that the *Ayuntamiento Libre* experienced. They were unable, for example, to carry out any public works projects with out soliciting volunteer help and donations of materials. Municipal employees often went unpaid, and there seemed to be a general chaos regarding matters of day-to-day governmental duties. After the golf course was canceled, the *Ayuntamiento* tried to resign and lost much of the political cohesion that it enjoyed in 1995 and the first half of 1996. This would seem to fit Bruhn's model of opposition municipal governments as being rather ineffective when facing a hostile central state. With the legal elections in 1997 and the resignation of Governor Carillo, much of the hostility between the municipality and the state government receded. In fact, Tepoztlán enjoyed a closer relationship with the state government than did the other opposition municipalities in the state, receiving a fair amount of state funding, while the other municipalities suffered through partial financial boycotts (Martínez Zúñiga 1999). Council Member Asciano Cedillo attributed this fairness on the part of the state to the fact that the state government was now "afraid" of them, because they had been such effective and militant organizers. While the issue of the state's fear might be hard to judge, effective local and national organizing does seem to have played a role in the new governor's attitude in that his predecessor's handling of the crisis in Tepoztlán had become an embarrassment, one which he quickly wanted to put behind him.

If the constitutional *Ayuntamiento* after 1997 successfully managed to circumvent the financial hostility that other opposition governments faced, many officials found that it was one thing to be an activist and another to have the responsibility of governing. Supporters and critics alike of the 1997–2000 *Ayuntamiento*, for instance, pointed to a series of administrative errors and general lack of experience on the part of officials as a serious problem in the day-to-day functioning of the town. The Municipal President himself acknowledged such shortcomings in his annual state of the municipality report (Bello 59). A common assessment of the *Ayuntamiento* was "that they are honorable, hardworking people, but they really don't know what they are doing" (Interview, Tepoztlán 1999). Such administrative incompetence presents dangers to the ongoing process of democratization, because faith in new politicians becomes slowly eroded. Some residents complained that once elected, officials became bureaucrats and governed just like previous officials, because that is all they know how to do. Conversely, others complained about inefficiency because the new officials did not play by the old rules, making it unclear how to get certain things accomplished. Either extreme discourages people form being visibly involved in political activity, as the outcome of that involvement is not very clear. As one resident explained: "if people do not see any differences, then they will become apathetic, and stop trying to change things" (Interview, Tepoztlán 2001).

This dilemma raises questions for social movements that advocate fundamental changes in governance. How does one govern? Negotiate with the state bureaucracy? Build coalitions? Do business with opponents? Run and finance political campaigns? The Mexican state is highly centralized and bureaucratized and learning the basics of negotiating those bureaucracies and fulfilling the minimum legal (and paperwork) requirements of office can easily take one or two years on the job. Local offices are held for three years and reelection in proscribed. If movements are proposing to generate new politicians and encourage new people to run for political office — as a way of avoiding the "traps" of the political parties— they need to consider how to successfully train newly elected officials to succeed in their jobs (Fox 1994; Zaragosa n.d.). This has been a problem throughout the country, as well-meaning and capable officials spend much of their public service simply learning what it is they are supposed to do, and do not have much time to implement creative alternatives to the political process.

The dependence on larger structures of the state once again brings into question the possibilities of autonomy once a movement has passed beyond the satisfaction of immediate demands. Although the movement in Tepoztlán made much rhetorical use of the autonomous municipality, the ways in which the *Ayuntamiento Libre* did and did not function, as well as the constant negotiations between the CUT, the *Ayuntamiento Libre* and various state and federal agencies belie the possibility of a truly autonomous municipality. Even beyond the necessities of bureaucratic and administrative demands, Tepoztlán is very much enmeshed in a series of social and economic webs that increasingly connect it with and subordinate it to outside forces (Lomnitz 1999). The movement itself was dependent on outside allies in other movements and the press to provide a shield against repression and to pressure KS and the state government to change their positions. It seems unlikely that the Tepoztecos alone would have succeeded in defeating the project and defying the state government indefinitely, without the explicit assistance from outside sources. The final event which led to the cancellation of the golf course, after all, was the national outcry against the police attack on the caravan, and not, necessarily, any one specific thing that the movement did.

Furthermore, those webs of relationships are reproduced within the community itself. Although the movement was able to form a strong sense of identity and unity as a *pueblo* under attack from outside enemies, that unity was artificial. Within the town there are various political factions and local elites that are constantly competing for power, that hold very different opinions and worldviews and that have and favor competing relationships with outside interests. The whole question of autonomy, therefore, is quite debatable not only in terms of practicality but also in terms of definition and desirability among the politicized groups of Tepoztecos themselves.

The ambiguities between "movement," "party," and "government" in the conflict in Tepoztlán are illustrative of tensions at a national level, and raise important questions about the parameters of democratic reform. Is it possible to find a balance between the necessary (and at times burdensome) commitments of participative democracy and the kinds of representations required by institutional politics? How can people's voices be effectively heard while not demanding all of their time and attention? Can local democracy function within a larger, semi-democratic system? Clearly, there are well-grounded fears that the "institutionalization" of a movement into a political party and into a state system of partisan politics tends to deflate the movement and to lead to a certain complacency among movement members. This allows for and encourages a return to "politics as usual," although, perhaps, with different faces. At the same time, however, it is clear that people cannot maintain the kind of energy that they need to sustain the movement over a long period of time, while carrying out the other routine demands of everyday life. People simply cannot make the time to be informed about and carry out every decision of day-to-day governance. As happened in Tepoztlán, movement members get burned out and have to return to the rhythms of everyday life. In the end, they would rather leave the business of everyday government to their elected officials. Many radical activists in Tepoztlán, however, saw this retreat from daily involvement as a step backward.

What this movement does contribute to democracy, however, is a greater respect on the part of elected officials for their constituents, and a greater sense of assertiveness on the part of regular citizens to organize and make their voices heard. Although the movement, in the end, opted to return to the established rules of political conduct, including a certain reabsorption into the state system, it did so on its own terms. It successfully broke the chain of political domination that the PRI had wielded in the town for 70 years, and established new norms of acceptable political behavior. Although there remains a certain sense that politics is dirty, it is now acceptable to be a politician, as long as you are not a professional politician. The officials who were elected in 1997 were elected because they had won respect in their struggles against the golf course, not because of their positions within a political party. They proved to a great majority of the municipality's electorate that they were primarily interested in improving Tepoztlán, rather than forwarding themselves. In other words, politicians can be acceptable if they align themselves with a project perceived to be one of civil society, one that is looking for the common good, rather than individual or partisan gain. That acceptance, however, is neither automatic nor universal, but dependent on their behavior in office and their abilities to construct and evolve political coalitions, and the mixed success of the PRD in the next two election cycles— a narrow victory in 2000 and a loss to the PRI in 2003 — suggests that it was not able to fully integrate the desires of civil society into its model of governance.

5

Atenco

The Struggle Continues

"This is not democracy. This is a farce."
— FPDT supporter, July 2003

The election of Vicente Fox and the advancement of the transition to democracy that his election represented, did not, however, put an end to the contentious politics and cultural struggles represented by the Tepoztlán movement. Those types of movements continued despite the institutional reforms, suggesting that the demands of those communities for recognition, participation and more equitable economic distribution continued to go unmet.[1]

In Atenco, on the outskirts of Mexico City, a relatively small group of *ejiditarios*[2] who opposed the construction of a new international airport, because they would be forced to give up their ancestral lands, stunned the nation by bringing the transition government's most ambitious infrastructure plan to a standstill. By using arguments about their rights as a unique community, the *ejiditarios* not only questioned the wisdom of building the airport, but also challenged the legitimacy of the neoliberal state to pretend to represent them. Like their counterparts in Tepoztlán, they occupied and created a hybrid cultural space between global, national and local influences, to give voice to a different vision of their local and national communities.

The case provides a compelling argument demonstrating that the political cultures growing up around the so-called transition to democracy, while related to that process, also corresponded to the specificities of local histories and relationships.

Yes to Land! No to Airplanes!

Like Tepoztlán, the conflict in Atenco was sparked by the proposal to undertake an enormous development project. In the case of Atenco, however, the political and economic stakes were even higher, as it involved the construction of a new international airport that the Fox administration had promised to be its major infrastructure project and upon which it had staked its legacy as a new and more efficient government. Arguing that thirty years of studies and debates had finally culminated in the decision to relocate Mexico City's international airport, the Fox Administration announced on 22 October 2001 that it had named Texcoco as the site for the new airport and that it would expropriate the *ejido* lands of nearby communities and begin construction as soon as possible. Although potential economic, technical and even environmental questions had been excruciatingly detailed and resolved, administration officials greatly underestimated potential political resistance to the project by not adequately consulting with the *ejiditarios* of the area, who were less than enthusiastic about turning their cornfields into runways.

From the government's perspective, the need for a new airport was obvious and the rationale for selecting the area around Atenco was sound. To begin with, the airport in Mexico City has outlived its utility. It has only two runways that do not permit simultaneous operations making it exceedingly difficult to keep up with ever increasing demand for more flights in and out of the capital. Because the airport is located in the middle of the already overcrowded city, there is no room for expansion at its current location, it represents significant safety risks, and it greatly contributes to Mexico City's notorious pollution problems. How to improve the airport has been a contentious issue over the past three decades, and Vicente Fox vowed to change the political culture of corruption and indecision that had marked the PRI's handling of the problem.

Armed with the results of numerous technical, economic and environmental feasibility studies, the Fox administration made the case for Atenco. Being a former lakebed, the Texcoco area has the most open and level area around the Federal District (DF) metropolitan region, which would allow engineers to build one of the largest airports in the hemisphere. The plan called for six runways, allowing for three simultaneous operations and was estimated to be able to accommodate over 100 million passengers a year. The operating capacity would not only be more than sufficient to handle traffic to Mexico City, but would have the added advantage of allowing officials to promote it as an intercontinental hub connecting South and North America.

Located some 35 kilometers from Mexico City and already well connected through existing highway infrastructure, it was also the closest of the finalists to the metropolitan area. The plan revealed by the government envisioned the airport anchoring a commercial and industrial corridor, further integrating the region into Mexico City's attractive economic orbit. The area, however, was also sufficiently large and far enough away from Mexico City that it would resolve the crowding and environmental problems of the current facility. Of the 16,000 hectares expropriated for the project, most would be set aside to provide a natural buffer to absorb pollution and protect residential areas from potential accidents. It was hoped that the project, therefore, would not only create a more viable airport, but that it would also improve the environmental health of the entire region. Financially, the government proposed that the private sector would contribute approximately seventy five percent of the estimated 18 billion peso (1.8 billion dollar) construction costs. The benefits from the project would be almost immediate, as its construction would create some 32,000 jobs and then 12,000 permanent jobs at the airport and an additional 40,000 indirect jobs as the airport became functional (Lajous 2003, 115).

In order to make this vision a reality, however, the government needed to expropriate 5,376 hectares of *ejido* land, the majority of it from the municipality of San Salvador Atenco. The project planners, despite their detailed studies of the proposal, did not expect and were incapable of dealing with the depth and determination of opposition from the Atenco *ejiditarios*. As discussions and speculation about the airport project gathered steam throughout 2000 and 2001, opponents of the project in Atenco, led by seasoned activists Ignacio (Nacho) del Valle and Jesús Adán Espinoza, began organizing against it. Building on their experience in previous campaigns and suspicious of the state and federal governments' intentions, activists began talking with *ejiditarios*, warning them that if the area was chosen for the airport, they would lose their lands and their way of life. They argued that over the past twenty years, small agricultural producers had been losing their markets and their lands, because the government refused to help them with credits, favoring instead big capital and export sectors. They saw the airport proposal as yet another example of the government supporting the already rich at the price of the poor and as part of a continued attempt to force modernization of the economy at the expense of peoples' traditions and livelihoods.

They began organizing against the proposal by forming various committees through communications networks established by the Ejidal Commissions, which are responsible for the governing of the collectively administered farms in the area. They used these committees to identify local leaders, to keep *ejiditarios* updated on developments, and to request information from government officials asking them to clarify the search process and how a decision might affect them. As press reports indicated that the government was growing closer to making a decision, activists working with *campesino* organizations in the *ejidos*, as well as allies in nearby Chapingo University, began drawing up contingency plans for their reaction to an unfavorable decision. The day that the expropriation order was issued and it became known that the price set by the government would be 7.20 pesos (US $0.72) per square meter of land, the nascent movement expelled Atenco's Municipal President, Margarito Yáñez, for supporting the project, and blocked the highway connecting Texcoco and Mexico City. The following day, the affected *ejiditarios* held an angry demonstration in Texcoco to denounce the inadequacies of the price and the process through which they would lose their land. Although they were offended at the price, one movement participant explained, "The protest was never about getting a higher price, even though that is what they said in the papers. It is not like they came with an offer to buy our land. They were trying to steal it. The land was not for sale, though. How could we sell the land when it is our life?" (Interview, Atenco, July 2003).[3]

In the absence of elected authorities after 22 July, activists, calling themselves the Peoples' Front in Defense of the Land (FPDT), convened public assemblies as the ultimate decision-making body for the community, like their Tepozteco counterparts had six years earlier. The public assembly, which met in front of the closed municipal offices, was the mechanism through which ideas were debated, strategies decided upon and difficult positions reaffirmed. They grew out of the *ejidal* system's tradition and structure of consultation, in which all members had the right to have their voice directly heard in matters of collective interest. Although the Ejidal Commission has elected officers, it is the assembly that makes and ratifies all important decisions. Turning now to public assemblies, rather than through representatives, to make decisions, therefore, was a logical step for movement organizers. Additionally, in the eyes of many FPDT supporters, assemblies represented the best example of democracy in action, because the decision-making was not left up to a handful of individuals who might have their own interests in mind rather than the common good. Furthermore, public assemblies gave all participants a stake in the process and strengthened their commitment to carry out the protest until the very end. Although the assemblies were theoretically open to everyone and its decisions binding, decisions were made by those that showed up, meaning that those who did not agree with the protesters and who were afraid to voice their opinion at these meetings, had little chance in influencing decisions. Nevertheless, protesters argued that in making collective decisions everyone had the right to be heard and the responsibility to attend and make their case.

After months of preparing and debating, organizers were ready from the beginning of the conflict to have the assembly approve a two-pronged strategy to defeat the airport. One course of action involved generating legal appeals, which had to be filed shortly after the expropriation order had been issued. The second was direct action involving symbolic protests, civil disobedience and public challenges to the President to come and debate the issue. Working with sympathetic attorneys, the *ejiditarios* immediately filed appeals to the expropriation order, claiming they were issued in an unlawful manner. In order to expropriate property, for instance, the state is required to prove that the benefits to the public good resulting from that expropriation outweigh the harm caused to property holders. In their appeal to of the President's 22 October decree, the *ejiditarios* argued that the state failed this test because it never specifically explained the details of the public good, it merely asserted it in its order. They also questioned the "public" nature of that good, arguing that the great participation of private interests indicated that a relatively small group of investors would reap the most benefits and not the public in general. (Frente de pueblos en defensa de la tierra 2002). Because, the *ejiditarios*, however, did not trust the court system to adequately protect them, they also immediately began organizing a series of increasingly disorderly marches and rallies in the area and in Mexico City to pressure the Fox Administration into rescinding the orders (Manrique Mendoza 2003). Always dressed with a red handkerchief around their necks and with their machetes in hand as a symbol of their profession and their strength, Atenco demonstrators became increasingly visible in the region as they confronted regional, state and federal officials. On several occasions, they attempted to march to the presidential residence, Los Pinos, to discuss the matter directly with the president. When police prevented them from reaching the President, they issued numerous invitations for him to come to neutral venues to publicly debate the merits and legitimacy of the proposal. When Fox repeatedly failed to appear at the designated time and place, the protesters increased the number and severity of their direct actions, periodically blocking the highway connecting Texcoco to Mexico City, organizing sit-ins at various state and federal agencies and even one day shutting down the current Mexico City airport for half an hour as they marched up to its front gates to press their case directly with airport users.

Because their attempts to engage public officials in a meaningful dialogue about the airport went unfulfilled, the protests continued throughout

2001 and 2002, making the region increasingly difficult to govern. The direct actions came to a final confrontation on 11 July 2002 when state police violently stopped a protest march of 100 *campesinos* on their way to deliver a message to Governor Arturo Montiel, who was on a working visit to the area. As one Atenco participant describes it: "We were going to tell Montiel to stop the project, when we were attacked by the Preventive Police. Many of them were dressed in civilian clothes. They hit us with batons, rubber bullets and tear gas. They just beat everybody." In the melee between police and protesters, the FPDT's leadership was captured and sixteen protesters were badly hurt. One man, Enrique Espinosa died two weeks later, officially of complications from diabetes, although many of the protesters believe that the head injuries he received that day from the police ultimately caused his death. In the confusion afterward, the *ejiditarios* withdrew to the main plaza in Atenco, which had served as their headquarters since the previous October, and in assembly decided on a radical plan to resolve the situation. Over 1500 protesters now broke into several groups and blocked the highway and hijacked two Coke trucks and two gas tanker trucks. "We weren't going to let them fuck with us," one participant explained later. "We were going to show them that we were serious. We hijacked the tanker trucks and threatened to blow them up. If they were going to come kill us, we would take a lot of them with us. We were fucking tough." Another group went to Texcoco to demand the release of their comrades. Failing to get any response, they captured three state officials, including the Assistant Attorney General and brought them back to Atenco. The state police, backed by federal law enforcement agencies and a task force of the Armed Forces surrounded the town and the stand-off began.

By the morning of 12 July, the Texcoco-Lechería highway that runs through Atenco had become a parking lot. In the middle of that parking lot, FPDT activists kept watch over a barricade of burning tires, the smoldering shell of a car and debris blocking the road. The bottles taken from the commandeered Coke trucks had been turned into dozens of cases of Molotov cocktails and fires burned close to the tanker trucks, ready to make good on the *ejiditarios'* threats to blow them up. Townspeople were attentive for the signals of rockets and church bells to take up their positions and fight the police. On either side of the 5-mile long back up, various police units, including the feared, militarized Federal Preventive Police were fortifying their positions and waiting for their orders to end the roadblock and rescue the hostages.

Negotiations for prisoner exchanges carried on for several days, and Atenco became a national focus of political concern. By the 12th, the largest national television network, Televisa, had arrived and began broadcasting live from Atenco, where protesters quickly made use of this national forum to explain their case and strengthen their resolve. Leader David Pájaro quickly took the initiative from the Televisa reporter to make his case, and the cameras depicted the protesters, indeed, as regular farmers and townspeople, not as the guerrillas or anarchists as they had been described in the press and by some government officials (Lajous 2003, 141). On the 13th, support from various social groups such as students from the UNAM's General Committee on the Strike (CGH), Mexico City's urban movement, the Francisco Villa Popular Front, and activists from Tepoztlán came to show their support for the Atenquenses and to provide an outside presence to help deter police aggression. By the 14th, the government had decided to avoid violence and released the FPDT prisoners, by changing the charges against them and making them eligible for bail, which the state government itself paid. Interior Minister, Santiago Creel, announced that once the stand-off was resolved, the government would reconsider the airport plan. By the following morning, all of the hostages were released and the Atenquenses celebrated their victory.

On 18 July, a commission of *campesinos* was finally received in Los Pinos in order to settle the airport dispute once and for all. The government made a final offer for the land, raising their price from seven pesos per square meter to fifty. At this point, however, after enduring such a long struggle and the violent repression of their protests, the *ejiditarios* were clearly not interested in selling at any price and declared that only the definitive cancellation of the airport would satisfy their demands. On 1 August, the Fox administration officially reversed the expropriation orders and announced that it would seek another solution to the airport problem. Declaring, "The Government of the Republic considers that no project should surpass any human life" (Lajous 2003, 157), Fox attempted to rescue some dignity from this critical defeat by highlighting the democratic credentials of his administration.

Like Tepoztlán, however, the cancellation of the project was not the end of the story. During the course of the conflict, the protesters had accumulated a series of new grievances and new perspectives on how to organize their community. As in Tepoztlán, there was a human rights issue. The FPDT insisted that the government not only indemnify the family of Enrique Espinoza, but that it also publicly assume responsibility for his death. Citing medical findings, the government insisted that his death was due to uncontrolled diabetes and refused to accept that the head injuries he received in the confrontation with police caused his death.[4] Secondly, the protesters demanded that the charges against them be dropped completely. Noting that their actions were motivated by their desires to protect their land and as "social fighters," they argued that they should not be held criminally responsible for their actions. As FPDT leader Adán Espinoza explained, "We're not criminals. How can the government claim to be democratic when they label us as criminals and threaten to put us in jail?" The outstanding charges weighed heavily on those accused, not only because of the ever-present threat of being imprisoned, but also because as a condition of their bail, they were forced to appear before a judge on average three times per week, making a return to everyday life nearly impossible. One of the charged FPDT members complained in July 2003, "I've been to over 150 hearings in less than a year. They need to make a decision, instead of making us run around. If we fail to appear, they will put us in jail. That, and we have to pay our lawyers, somehow. They have been very good, but we have not been able to pay them."

Finally, the question of democracy rose to the forefront once the airport had been cancelled. Atenco's elected officials had been run out of town at the beginning of the conflict, and after the events of 11 July, the assembly had declared Atenco to be a "municipality in rebellion." As the immediate jubilation of their victory wore off, community members turned to the equally difficult task of reconstituting their political society. At this point, divisions within the community began to appear more forcefully than they had during the protests. Many community members wanted to return to normal and negotiate a return of the elected officials. FPDT members, however, had become radicalized through the conflict and refused to let former officials back into office, arguing that they had been traitors to their community. Furthermore, they questioned the type of larger society into which they were to be integrated. What kind of society attempts to steal the land of some of its poorest members? What kind of legitimacy does a government have that sends armed men to beat unarmed protesters? The disillusionment with traditional politics manifested itself again in Atenco, when in October 2002 the public assembly, urged on by the FPDT, declared Atenco to be an autonomous municipality. Like the Zapatista autonomous municipalities in Chiapas, the assembly in Atenco declared that Atenquenses alone had the right to determine their form of government and refused to recognize the sovereignty of state and federal governments over any of their natural resources and internal decision-making processes.

The organization of this new autonomous municipality, however, was never very clear and the divisions within the community continued to grow, as the town existed in an institutional limbo. There were no police and no government funds to finance projects. Representatives of the town, selected by the assembly, met with state officials to resolve some matters of everyday importance such as traffic regulations and school funding, but with no official standing, they did not have much influence in those negotiations. The first test of the resolve of the municipal government came on 9 March 2002, when elections were to be held for local government. The FPDT repeatedly declared that they would not permit elections, because they already had an elected government and because their demands for restitution and clemency had gone unfulfilled. Election day was marred by violence as the FPDT successfully shut down enough polling places throughout the municipality to force the state government to annul the results. The violence around the election also pointed to the tensions within the community about how to proceed. While the FPDT certainly never had complete support for its protest, it did enjoy widespread backing while it was clearly defending land rights. After the airport was cancelled, however, its support began to wane, particularly as it continued to advocate radical political positions. When I asked one local merchant her opinion of the movement, she commented, "The people in the movement, you know, are generally good people. They have good intentions, and protected the land and stood up for the community. Some of them have just taken it too far. They mean well, but people are tired of this now." Others, however, were not as kind. One small businessman, who was in favor of the airport all along, vented his frustration at the ongoing conflict:

> You can't dialogue with the *ejiditarios*. They are very uncultured people, not educated. If you were to go to any zoo, whatever zoo and you went to the ape cage to have a dialogue. What would happen? Nothing. It is like this trying to dialogue with them. They are not people; they're apes. They don't understand what is happening. It has been like this since the Conquest. You cannot negotiate with those Indians. They're *pendejos*, we say.

These tensions continued and sharpened over the next several months, as the community's status remained unresolved. Activists were unsatisfied, because they continued to feel persecuted by state authorities and felt that the entire political system was rigged against their interests. Many Atenco residents were unsatisfied, because they saw the FPDT as being overly stubborn and wanted a return to institutional normalcy. As both sides hardened their positions, anger and distrust came to mark much of the public discourse around resolving the issue. Part of the problem was that in the absence of credible elections, both sides could claim to be speaking for the entire community. One mechanism, therefore, for returning to normal and potentially resolving some of these tensions, was elections to decide definitively which faction had the greatest support and to begin rebuilding institutional relationships with government institutions. By the time of the July 2003 general elections, however, the FPDT and its many supporters were still adamantly opposed to elections, and the bitter conflict in Atenco had become the center of electoral disputes around the country. At the national level, these midterm elections were being seen as a test of the new democratic culture supposedly ushered in by the ascension of Vicente Fox. The reality, however, was quite disappointing for supporters of the transition. Critics of the Fox government noted its failure to accomplish virtually any of its goals, and politics-as-usual was generally seen as a corrupt process in which parties competed for power through ever-sophisticated marketing techniques, but did not really represent the population. The record sixty percent abstention rate around the country that day seemed to indicate that something was indeed wrong with the transition process. One commentator noted in the Mexico City Daily, *La Jornada* that, Mexico was becoming "a democracy without people" (Hernández López 2003).

These anxieties about democratic reform, or lack thereof, also found their way into the discourse of FPDT activists and their supporters as they made their case for boycotting and shutting down the elections on 6 July (Stolle-McAllister 2005). Noting again that their demands concerning their legal status and compensation for the victims of police violence had not been met, the FPDT vowed not to allow elections to take place. Echoing critiques from radical sectors within Mexican politics, they charged that the elections were a fraud and a sham. Speaking in a press conference before the elections were to take place, Nacho del Valle insisted that,

> without full freedom and the right to self determination, there will be no elections. We cannot pretend that there is a rule of law when none exists. First, we want freedom and then as a people we can decide the form of government that we want and how we want to hold elections. It is ridiculous to talk about elections without freedom. How can we hold elections, if we are threatened with jail and violence? No, we will not allow elections until we are all completely free.

The critiques, however, went even further than just complaints about particular policies or grievances about unfair governmental action. A deeper criticism emerged from movement participants, who noted that the political process was being controlled not by "popular will" but by moneyed interests. Adán Espinoza pointed to all of the electoral advertising, heavily subsidized by the government, as a prime example of the real purposes behind elections, "Look at all this electoral trash: they're spending 15 billion pesos (1.5 billion dollars), that is about half the budget for poverty programs. How does that help us? How many schools could you build? Hell, we don't even have an ambulance in this county of 40,000 people." The purpose behind the elections, therefore, was not to select true representatives that would fight for the rights and needs of communities, but rather to shore up a corrupt, undemocratic system. The parties and the state had decided that promoting their candidates was more important than fulfilling basic human needs. This led some people to conclude that the democracy they were being offered was an illusion, because the parties, indebted to the system and to money, could not possibly represent the population. As one FPDT sympathizer explained on Election Day:

> It is very difficult to make changes in the government. Even an individual with good intentions, once he gets into office loses little by little to the logic of government, which is on the side of the rich. They control everything. It would be better if they left us alone to govern ourselves. We already know what we need and what we should do.

Another FPDT member argued:

> The politicians come around only before the elections. They promise you anything and everything. Then, they go away and you never hear from them again. We are not stupid. We know they cannot fulfill those promises. Why should we vote for people who we don't even know and who don't know us? How can they represent us in the government if they don't know who we are or what we need?

Clearly these two perspectives indicate grave doubts not only about the Fox government and the transition, but also about the entire process of representational government being promoted by the backers of the transition.

After several confrontations with PRI members and other residents wishing to exercise their right to vote, the FPDT did effectively shut down the elections again that day. Despite threats from government officials to "enforce the law," there was no official attempt to force the elections to take place, which would have provoked a potentially violent confrontation between police and angry residents. The conflict, however, continued unresolved for several weeks. State officials, seeing that they would not wear down the Atenco opposition, opted by the beginning of August to drop formal charges against FPDT activists. The federal government, however, brought charges against them for disrupting the elections in

March and July. In an assembly that Fall, the residents of Atenco decided to permit special elections in October for a Municipal President and Council. Although the FPDT was against the elections, now because of the federal charges they faced, they respected the will of the assembly and permitted the elections to take place. They did, however, boycott them and urged other community members to do the same. On 12 October elections finally took place, with no violence and no attempts to impede them. The PRI candidate, Pascual Pineda won with 51 percent of the vote to the PRD's Germán Nuñez's 35 percent. The FPDT's position was that these, like previous elections, were a sham because the parties controlled them, and they seemed relatively unconcerned that their archenemies in the PRI had won over their nominal allies in the PRD. For them, party politics was a capitulation to an unfair and undemocratic state.

Although they allowed the elections to take place, they also vowed not to permit the newly elected government to take possession of town hall until federal charges against them had been dropped, and the government promised to fund productive projects for the region.

> We won't let him come and be president. I don't think he is really afraid of us. We won't do anything to him. But, he is afraid of his own conscience. He knows he is not the legitimate winner. There were 36 voting stations. He lost in 33 of them, but won the elections. Well, how can that be? It was the old PRI tricks. They bought votes and pressured people in the small communities. So, we still don't have a president.

On 1 December, there was once again violence as FPDT members physically blocked Pineda and his PRI backers from taking office. After a day of fighting and dozens of injuries, both sides agreed to a pact of fifteen points, which included an official request that the federal government drop its charges, promises to fund various projects, the dissolution of the "Vivo V" paramilitary police unit operating in the municipality, the prohibition of any officials from the last government from serving in the new one, and the appointment of non–PRI members to the municipal council. The next day, the new municipal president entered his office, opening the municipal government for the first time in 25 months.

Defining the Community

Like in Tepoztlán, the movement developed along the lines dictated to it by the hybrid culture in which it operated and to which it contributed.

The town itself is physically located at the edge of the Federal District's metropolitan area, and according to Lajous,

> is classified as somewhat marginalized. Nevertheless, its nearness to the metropolis confers on it singular characteristics. Many of its inhabitants live a hybrid reality, between tradition and modernity. In the backyard of a much richer zone, they have access to education and employment in the Federal District, but have not lost their love for the land, their traditional forms of organization or their identity as Texcoco peoples [2003, 118].

Indeed, the contradiction in this model was quite evident among Atenco residents. One middle class businessman characterized Atenco as a "bedroom community. You should see the lines of people waiting for the bus here at 5 o'clock in the morning. Almost everyone works in Mexico City. Despite what the protesters say, this is not a farming community anymore." This version was, of course, disputed by residents who do in fact make their living working the land and providing services directly to the agricultural community. Even many of those people who either work the land and/or who were members of the FPDT admitted, however, that it was very difficult to subsist purely through agriculture. When I asked, for instance, what FPDT members' occupations were their answers were often mixed, such as "farmer and electric repair," or "my father works his plot and I help out," or "I am a dentist, but I grow some corn on the land that my family owns." This is not to deny the important connection between land and identity, but rather to highlight that Atenco, despite the image portrayed by the movement, is not strictly and only a farming community. It is a mixed community facing the pressures and opportunities of urbanization, while trying to maintain their unique identity and control over their historic natural resources.

As was the case in Tepoztlán the particularities of Atenco's hybridity derived from the specificities of its history, its position within regional, national and global webs of power and economics, and the internal dynamics of social relations within the community itself. The juxtaposition of these different worldviews, as well as the uneven use of them to create identities and consolidate political strategies, suggests that the world visions and political cultures developing in Atenco were very much dependent on the particularities of the moment and the abilities of residents and leaders to articulate their needs and desires. At the same time, the continuing divisions within the community also indicate that the process of forming hybrid cultures is not uniform, but is, in fact, highly contentious.

Protesters continually insisted that local rights and local concerns drove their movement. Their two major claims to their land had to do with ancestry and with their continued use of it. In a document issued in March 2002, after President Fox failed to appear to debate the merits of the airport, the FPDT claimed that the rights of *ejiditarios* to maintain control of the land superceded the federal government's, because "our origins are pre–Hispanic and therefore we have the natural right and the conviction to defend that which belongs to us" (Frente de pueblos en defensa de la tierra 2002, 1). The document then recounts the history of the movement of people into the valley in 968 CE, concluding, "The inhabitants of our communities have descended from the Chichimecas and the Toltecs, that is from warriors, artists and learned people. We can say proudly that we are authentic natives of our villages" (Frente de pueblos en defensa de la tierra 2002, 4). Residents similarly pointed to their parents' and grandparents' participation in the Mexican Revolution as the means through which they gained eternal access to their lands, "The Revolution of Emiliano Zapata gave us our *ejido*. The land is ours, not to brag about having, but to work" (*Lands Yes!* 2002). This strategy established the local as the key to granting legitimacy.[5] By asserting themselves as the original inhabitants, they were claiming rights guaranteed to indigenous peoples under Mexican and international law, which protect their right to self-determination and their natural resources from being usurped. Secondly the Zapatista discourse which residents deployed by pointing out that their lands are a product of the Revolution, posited them as the products of the noblest intentions of the nation and insinuated that removing their properties would be a betrayal of those high ideals.

The question of an actual indigenous legacy, however, might be questionable. Almost no residents of Atenco speak Nahuatl, nor do they practice many pre–Columbian rites. Unlike Tepoztlán, where the preservation (or re-creation) of indigenous culture plays a very visible and important role in community identity, those overt practices are not as visible in Atenco. In fact, many people seem unaware of the exact nature of their heritage. One FPDT participant, for example, pointed to the town's church, "Have you been in our church? It is very big and very beautiful. At one point, we must have been an important town, or why else would they have built such a big church?" Another FPDT activist noted frankly,

> Before the movement, we really did not know much about our indigenous ancestors. We learned a little in school, but most of us never really went to school for very long. You probably know more since you have been to university. Isn't that strange that foreigners would

know more than we do? But, since the movement, we have learned to take our land more seriously and have begun to realize that we inherited a lot from our ancestors. They knew how to protect and care for the land, and, although we didn't know it, we have saved some of that knowledge. We are trying to learn more now about our heritage; to learn from their wisdom.

It is quite probable that much of this pro-indigenous discourse has been picked up from the Zapatista movement in Chiapas, which is ironically imported here to make very local claims about rights and responsibilities. It also, however, reflects a desire to distinguish them as much as possible from the neoliberal invaders who want to steal their lands. The movement, then, serves, in part, as a catalyst to encourage people to think differently about themselves and their history.

An integral part of this discourse of local identity centered on residents' connections to the land that they collectively owned and worked. The land not only provided an economic grounding for many Atenco residents, but also constituted an important part of their identities and social networks. The *ejidos*, which were the results of their parents' and grandparents' participation in the Mexican Revolution, created a community of producers as well as political structures, such as the Ejidal Commission, through which people related to each other. Taking away their land, therefore, not only threatened to deprive people of an immediate economic resource, but also of the social and cultural structures that had grown up around it. As one FPDT document put it, "We rose up with machetes in hand because we are *campesinos* and *campesinos* without land are worth nothing" (Frente de pueblos en defensa de la tierra n.d.). Taking their land, therefore threatened to break a key element in their identities as well as the politicized discourse of being direct descendents of indigenous people. If they no longer held the land, then they would no longer be able to make those ancestral claims, and they would cease to be themselves as a community.

In addition to these ideological concerns, the *ejiditarios* insistence on maintaining control and ownership of their lands also represented pragmatic concerns about where and how they are to live. Many residents viewed the expropriation as unfair, not only because they were offered an insultingly low price for their parcels of land, but also because those lands are their homes and their livelihoods. One resident explained that he decided to join the movement after understanding the potentially devastating effects that the expropriation would have on his own family. "I was never involved with politics, and to tell you the truth, had not thought much about the airport. But, one night I came home from work and found my mother crying that this would be the last crop that my father harvested. He has worked the land all of his life. What was he supposed to do now? It just wasn't fair to take all of that away from him." Many of the Atenco activists pointed out that the land not only represented their current livelihoods, but also their futures and their children's future. "The money would only last for a little while. And then what would we do? We may always be poor farmers, but at least we, and our children, will always be able to feed ourselves if we have our land. That is something that many of us have taken for granted, and having it threatened has made us more aware of that." Theirs is not only a spiritual connection to the land, but also a highly pragmatic one. Arguing that their lands have been inherited from their grandparents and are being kept for their children, not only emphasizes their historic connection to their territory, but also represents what they see as their best hope for a livable future. As James Russell (2003) points out, in the current economic situation of the country, where the price of food has vastly outpaced the production of jobs and the rise in salaries (which have actually declined in relation to purchasing power), "it would be irrational for peasants willingly to give up or sell the land from which they derive a basic subsistence. Even apart from their cultural attachment to it and considering only economic interests, the often meager subsistence that they derive from the land is far better than what they could hope for in the paid labor market" (23).

Locality, however, also has to do with social relations and not just history and economics, and, as in most places, those social relations were contested and sometimes conflictive within the community itself. Political, class and geographic divisions and tensions in Atenco have long, complicated histories. These tensions came out during the conflict in name-calling, distrust of motives, charges of working with outside forces for nefarious ends, threats and sometimes physical violence. Nevertheless, those relations constituted the bedrock foundation for the movement and finding a way to "be a community" was always an important aspect of activists' and opponents' discourses. At the height of the election tensions in July 2003, I asked residents with very diverse opinions what they liked about Atenco. And almost without exception they answered "tranquility" (which had obviously been absent for the past two years) and "shared traditions." All sides believed, as did this more or less neutral merchant, "Our traditions are very important. For the Festival of San Salvador in August, people will put aside their differences and get along. Everyone will leave politics out of it, at least for a few days. None of this will matter."

The authenticity of that community was one of the primary points of contention throughout the conflict. Since both sides in the conflict claimed to be representing that almost mythical community, yet they had very different visions about how the community should either deal with the airport or proceed afterward, they needed to find an explanation for those differences. The answer, for both sides, was that the other represented only a tiny fraction of the population and was being manipulated by outside forces. Airport supporters, for instance, argued that the FPDT, besides being belligerent and seeking personal political gain, was really a front for outside groups. A report produced by the *Centro de investigación y seguridad nacional* (Center for Investigation and National Security or CISEN) charged that the FPDT was being supported by the *Frente Popular Revolucionario* (Popular Revolutionary Front), the political arm of the *Ejército Popular Revolucionario* (Popular Revolutionary Army—EPR) and was intent on establishing a "Marxist-Leninist-Maoist party, that would begin a popular war" from its "base camps in Atenco" (Lajous 2003, 105). As proof the report noted the large number of radical political groups that supported the movement as well as

> the alliances with foreign organizations, like the International Brigades of the Basque Country, the fraternal group of Sendero Luminoso called the "Support Committee for the Popular War in Perú[...]. At a meeting on the 29th of June there were present twelve foreigners from the United States, Spain and Germany. Finally, the text points out that: "The strategy utilized by (these groups) might use members of environmental organizations as a 'shield' to counteract in some way the actions of the state and federal forces of public order" [Lajous 2003, 105–106].

Although most Atenquenses did not believe this level of paranoia, FPDT opponents did insist that outside forces were manipulating the movement. They pointed to the very visible presence of their allies from around the country, particularly the student leadership of the UNAM's 1999 strike and the Villa Popular Front from Mexico City. Many FPDT opponents claimed that these two groups unnecessarily radicalized the somewhat naïve peasants and were provoking them into taking ever more extreme positions in order to serve their own ends. Another opponent bluntly blamed the PRD, especially Mexico City mayor Andres Manuel López Obrador:

> When it started, it was all paid for by the government of Mexico City. They put their trash out there, and they did not want to lose that land. What else are they going to do with the 20,000 tons of garbage they

dump there everyday. They paid the *ejiditarios* to agitate and cause trouble. López Obrador got his start in politics by disrupting the oilfields in Tabasco and his party the PRD is a very violent one. They turn to violence and intimidation to get their way. [...] These outside groups pay them. Now those from here travel all over the place to protest. They go to Hidalgo, the DF and Veracruz and Tabasco. They have to be getting paid. They say they are poor *campesinos,* but they don't work their land. They spend all their time doing politics. Someone has to pay their bus fare to the DF, for their propaganda, for their upkeep. Someone has to be paying them.

If their opponents tried to discredit their authenticity as Atenquenses by claiming they were merely agents of outside forces, the FPDT likewise claimed that they actually represented the majority of their community and that their opponents were in fact the puppets of outside forces. They were either traitors bought off by money, or they were pawns of the state PRI's powerful political machine. When I asked FPDT members who opposed them in the town, they replied, "groups organized by the PRI. They give them money and building materials to come out against us. On Election Day it was PRI shock troops and Vivo 5 [a paramilitary police unit] who were throwing rocks at us, and hitting us. Some of them are not even from here." Another respondent noted, "[Governor] Montiel hates us. He sends spies to the assemblies, and then they try to divide people by spreading lies, paying people and intimidating them." During the blockades of balloting in July, FPDT members taunted those wanting to vote by calling them "Traitors," and "These are the ones who screw the nation." Part of the conflict in Atenco, therefore, became identifying the community itself. Both sides claimed that the other was somehow inauthentic and acting, consciously or not, as agents for outside powers.

But, it was also telling that this fight over community was not just a matter of political positioning, but a truly heartfelt battle. After the conflicts on Election Day in July, while some FPDT members were proudly nursing split lips and black eyes, one protester commented, "I was nervous about confronting people from town. They are all organized by the PRI — manipulated by PRI operatives. But, it's not right that we fight among ourselves. I would rather just confront the police." The dispute seemed to be causing great strain and harm to the community that, even in these very conflicted times, many seemed to want to preserve and reconstitute. Outside pressures, however, were making that reconciliation extremely difficult by encouraging internal fighting. As one woman yelled at news reporters covering one of the many confrontations in July 2003, "Stop taking pictures and go away! You are just encouraging them, both sides. We don't want you here anymore. You only come when there is trouble and you make it worse. Let us settle this ourselves."

Building Wider Networks

Given the involvement of outside actors and pressures, however, solving problems "by themselves," would be extremely difficult. As was the case in Tepoztlán, the local proved to be the intersection of many different and sometimes far-reaching ideas, practices and relationships, which were, obviously, instrumental in touching off the conflict, but also important in the ways in which activists designed their strategies.

The proposal to build the airport in the first place corresponded not to local needs or desires, but rather the needs of the country, particularly the country's elites, as it becomes increasingly integrated into global economic relationships. Realistically, none of the Atenco *ejiditarios* would ever use any of the airplanes that, if the proposal had succeeded, would have been soon landing on their cornfields. This irony was not lost on protesters as they identified the cause of not only their immediate grievance with "capitalism" and "neoliberalism," but, indeed, blamed these global forces as the foundation of the many structural problems that keep them in poverty. "Fox came into office promising to help the small producers, argued on Atenco resident. "But what has he done? Nothing. It is a total disaster in the countryside. We have no support. All the help goes to the big companies." A middle class FPDT supporter commented:

> The biggest problem is capitalism. They pretend there are elections, but these do not change anything while the capitalists decide everything. The parties and the elections only serve capitalism. It is what makes us poor. We have a lot of wealth here, but where does it all go? We buy from abroad; we buy technology, that's ok. We have some money from oil, but now we can't feed ourselves. It is a problem when you can't support yourself as far as food goes. All of the technology is good [he says, pointing to the cell phone on his belt], but you can't eat it. If I could do it all over again, maybe I would work full time in the field. Feel the dampness of the earth and see the green, green corn leaves. See all of the fruit in the market. Well, it is something, isn't it?

The structural problems, in other words, come from the outside world and the solution, therefore, must lie within the community itself. Self-sufficiency and an almost idyllic view of agricultural production are important themes, for this man. The irony, of course, is that he is also a product of that outside world that he holds as responsible for the structural poverty of his hometown. He has a professional career, studied in Mexico City and is literally connected to a global communications network by a piece of technology on his hip.

Despite, therefore, their insistence on local autonomy and self-sufficiency and their blaming of problems on exploitation from outside systems, movement activists were also part of networks for social change that ran through their town, which connected them to other localities and other struggles. The movement's critics were not incorrect in pointing out the number of outside organizations that came time and again to support the protesters in Atenco. Their support was critical for maintaining morale for FPDT members during particularly hard times and for giving them logistical and strategic assistance when they needed it. FPDT members, however, insisted that these outside forces were only there to help, since they were all involved in fighting against the same enemies, and since meaningful social change would only occur by working together with like-minded groups and individuals. One movement leader noted, "Well yes the CGH [student strike committee] has been a great supporter. But they say that the CGH tells us what to do and manipulates us. That's just not true. With all due respect to those kids, I think that we have taught them some things about organizing and resistance."

FPDT leaders were also keenly aware that a positive media image was an important part of their struggle. Participants complained that they were often unfairly portrayed in the media, particularly on television. As the movement gained momentum, leaders sought out sympathetic reporters, such as those working for the Mexico City daily, *La Jornada*, and actively nurtured relationships with them. They were able to call press conferences that were well attended by print, radio and television outlets. They were even able to take advantage of sometimes hostile television reporters to get their message across, such as during the crisis in July 2002 when David Pájaro upstaged Televisa reporters to broadcast the movement's message live to the rest of the country. Being media savvy in the global age meant that appearance was as important as substance. At press conferences, FPDT spokespeople were careful to present their visual image — machete in hand and bandana around the neck. Although there were definitely identifiable and important leaders, they made efforts to have others speak as well in order to portray the more egalitarian aspirations of the movement. Women had important leadership positions in the movement, and in a break with many other movements, they were accorded speaking time at press conferences and from the podium at rallies. While this reflects the workings of the movement, it also reflects an understanding of wider progressive movements and an attempt to portray that image to those audiences as well.

This hybridity of local and non-local also manifested itself in diverse leadership and tactical issues of the movement. The two predominant leaders of the movement were men, for instance, but several women also played important roles, not just in logistics, but also in planning and speaking. Although the movement was portrayed as a peasant movement, the leadership of the movement itself was a mixture of classes. As mentioned earlier, in terms of class, the *ejiditarios* themselves were in a state of fluctuation from strictly subsistence agriculture to more diverse forms of employment. Because Atenco is on the edge of the urban/rural divide, people of mixed professions live there. The leaders of the movement, therefore, although drawn from peasant sectors, also included professionals such as lawyers and doctors who provided their services and expertise to the movement's development. The tactics employed by the movement were also derivative of their mixed and fluid position. They used the by now standard tactics of blocking highways and demanding meetings from government officials to resolve issues. They also raised the stakes by detaining government officials and private sector employees who were working directly on the airport and frequently confiscated their equipment, including surveying tools and pickup trucks. Communication, too, reflected this mixture of strategies. One FPDT leader explained, "When we want to get everybody together we use our traditional forms of communication. We shoot off rockets, and post signs around town to let people know about assemblies. Word goes out through neighbors. If it is an emergency we ring the church bells and everyone comes running. Well, that and of course, cell phones."

Like the movement in Tepoztlán, the one in Atenco resulted from the combination of different factors and influences circulating within the community. The movement focused clearly on the local aspects of the conflict and framed it as greedy outsiders trying to "loot" their lands. From a wider angle, the airport was just one in a long series of actions in which the rich of Mexico and the transnational capitalist world were attempting to use their power to take more resources and wealth from the poor. FPDT leaders attempted to build internal cohesion to the movement by portraying a clearly defined "us" (poor, Atenquenses, shared traditions etc.) against a very powerful, harmful "them" (capitalists, the state, political parties). Those labels, however, were not always as clear as movement supporters depicted, as some Atenquenses did support the airport, because they thought it would be beneficial to the community, and some outsiders helped their cause immensely. In fact, the outside world, organized by other social movements and informed by the press, played a pivotal role in securing their victory. By the time of the July 2002 violence nearly 70 percent of Mexicans in a national survey supported the *ejiditarios*, making it politically difficult for the government to forge ahead with it at the cost of the *ejiditarios'* community (Russell 2003). Furthermore, the ample press coverage, with its image of police violence made repression of the movement an equally unappealing decision for the new government, as it was trying to consolidate its democratic credentials nationally and globally. In order to avoid more violence and a politically fatal public relations disaster, therefore, the Fox Administration was forced to cancel the project and anger its supporters, who represented the very global project that FPDT activists claimed to be the root of their problems.

Specificities of Atenco's Hybrid Political Cultures

The contours of the political cultures developing in Atenco as a result of this conflict, therefore, were shaped by the contingencies of the context in which the movement took place, as well as the specificities of the protagonists involved in the conflict. The national political landscape changed dramatically in the time between the Tepoztlán and Atenco conflicts. Tepozteco activists and their supporters framed their political arguments around the authoritarian practices of the PRI. For them, their movement was part of a national one demanding democratic control over state apparatuses and the removal of the PRI from power. They were able to take advantage of the political opportunity created by instability within the PRI to isolate Morelos Governor Jorge Carrillo and hold him up as an example of the corruption and lack of respect for the rule of law, which characterized the PRI's long tenure in power. By 2001, of course, the PRI, while still an influential player in national politics, with the largest share of seats in Congress and still very much in control of its state machinery in the State of Mexico, was not the bogeyman of pre–2000 opposition politics. The FPDT *ejiditarios*, while clearly pointing fingers at the state and regional PRI, could not simply lay its complaints at the feet of authoritarian rule. Instead, the movement's frame shifted from the PRI to critique the transition process itself.

The shift in control of the national state from the PRI to Fox's faction of the PAN provided the first substantial opportunity for the movement. Although the Fox government was widely seen as being a legitimate democratic institution, having won free and fair elections, it clumsily handled the entire airport project. If the neoliberal–PRI had lost the capacity to effectively communicate with its base, the neoliberal Foxistas never had the capacity to begin with. In the case of the expropriation, for instance, although Texcoco was widely known to be one of the preferred sites for the airport, the Fox government never consulted the region's *ejiditarios* about the impending expropriation. They never offered to negotiate a fair and reasonable price for their lands or attempt to alleviate other anxieties about the proposal that the small landowners might have. Instead, and in the fashion of its PRI predecessors, the Fox administration simply handed down an edict, and, as Fox himself did in December 2002, congratulated the Atenco *ejiditarios* for "winning the lottery." This political blunder arose in part from the lack of experience of the officials involved, but it also resulted from their ideological blindness to differing cultural concerns. For them, land was simply a commodity, and in their analysis, the land in question was of minimal productive value, so the Atenco *ejiditarios* should indeed feel grateful that the government was going to help them dispose of those properties for more cash than they could reasonably expect to attain trying to sell them on the open market. It was an obvious win-win situation.

Such optimism, however, failed to account for attitudes expressed by many *ejiditarios* that "the land is our mother. You do not sell your mother." Nor was it capable of foreseeing the determination and political abilities of a relatively small number of people to organize, publicize and eventually defeat such an important project. Furthermore, officials in the Fox administration had apparently believed their own campaign rhetoric about "change" and failed to understand an entrenched political culture based around myths of resistance, and the practices of negotiating that took place through generations of personal and patron-client politics. Instead of trying to bring elements of the community on board, or attempting to persuade them in terms other than money that the project was worthwhile, the government stuck to its neoliberal discourse and strict interpretation of the rule of law and simply insisted that it was within its rights to expropriate the land at the price it determined.

Part of the ideological baggage surrounding the transition to democracy that accompanied Fox's ascension to the Presidency was that the PRI was, in a sense, an outlaw government. Since it had historically acted arbitrarily and ignored the rule of law, one of Fox's major promises as President was to respect it. This meant not only ending blatantly corrupt practices and beginning investigations into past human rights abuses, but it also meant strictly adhering to the letter of the law, rather than being open to politically expedient interpretations of those rules of conduct. In this case, for instance, the Fox administration came up with its 7 peso per square meter price, not necessarily out of spite for *campesino* sensibilities, but based on technical studies of the value of the land. They determined that the land was generally not improved upon by such things as buildings and irrigation and that the soil was too saline to be very profitable. In its view, the land was unproductive, hence its low price, and given the legal stipulation that the state had to pay the fair market value for land that it expropriated, federal officials saw no reason or way to offer more money or to negotiate under the threat of civil disobedience. The political reality, of course, is that the land was more valuable than that to the owners, and that as soon as construction began, the value of that land would skyrocket. The current owners of the land were well aware of that, yet the Fox administration insisted that it would stick to the legally determined price, rather than a politically negotiated one. To do otherwise, would have been a return to the old ways of PRI politics. Although the administration did eventually raise the price to fifty pesos per square meter in a desperate attempt to save the project in July 2002, the damage was already done and the *ejiditarios'* position was cemented. That is not to say that they would have necessarily sold out at an earlier time, no one will ever know, but it would have changed the parameters of the conflict.

This adherence to the rule of law and to at least nominally democratic practices also helped the *ejiditarios*, because it limited the coercive actions of the federal government. In the old days, it would be imaginable that local and regional PRI operatives backed by the implicit threat of force from the federal government could have more easily, and violently, disrupted the movement from the beginning. Throughout my interviews with FPDT members, although they were always wary of the federal government, it was the state government and state security forces, still controlled by the PRI, that they feared and hated most. In the culminating conflict in July 2002, it was the state police who initiated the violence against marchers, and although federal security forces were deployed to the area, the Interior Minister, Santiago Creel, ordered them not to intervene. The civilian authorities even refused to act on the military's assertion that the FPDT was a front for guerrilla groups. There was no daring rescue of hostages. There was no massive repression of the movement. The protesters were never physically dislodged from their two-year occupation of the town offices. The new state, in other words, would respect citizens' fundamental human rights.

This position cost the Fox government dearly in terms of both its economic development strategy and its own political capital. In not forcing the *ejiditarios* to obey the law, some critics contended that the government was allowing itself to be held hostage to a violent minority, and were in fact sacrificing the rule of law (Aguilar Rivera 2003; Lajous 2003). Within Atenco, FPDT opponents felt that it was ludicrous that the government drop criminal charges against activists in return for them allowing elections to occur.

> Those in the FPDT want them to drop the orders against them. But how can you? We live under a rule of law. One cannot commit crimes and not pay the sanction. Some of them even stole private cars. They destroyed public and private property. They robbed those Coke trucks. Where did all the Coke go? That was not just a protest. They are criminals. I want to know why the government doesn't just arrest them.

The Fox government, therefore, found itself in an impossible bind over its public support for the respect of the rule of law. On the one hand, it demanded that it respect the life and physical integrity of the protesters, and not make politically expedient deals negotiated outside of the stipulations of the law. On the other hand, it was forced to deal with how to handle the breaking of laws, such as the blocking traffic, kidnapping officials and disrupting federal elections. In the new political reality, through which officials in the Fox administration were unable to successfully maneuver, their win-win proposal for the airport turned into a costly defeat for them.

The political culture developed by the movement, therefore, was in part structured by the realities of the new political institutions being formed through the transition process. The ineptitude of federal officials in their political handling of the case, as well as the unwillingness of those same officials to be dragged into a potentially bloody and delegitimizing conflict, gave fuel to activists' rhetoric and provided them a certain degree of physical protection as they pushed the limits of their protests. They then used those structural opportunities to expand their arguments away from just the airport, to a wider critique of the political process in general.

Because Fox's administration issued the expropriation order, he was the primary target of FPDT rhetoric. Members and sympathizers pointed out continually that Fox had promised to help the small agricultural sector, but that they were generally ignored, while the true beneficiaries of the Fox's policies were big capitalists and foreign investors. In its Manifesto, for instance, the FPDT asserts:

> The Fox government, that promised so much, does not know how to fulfill those promises. In his campaign, Fox said that he would help the countryside, that he would see to the regularization of the land, and that he would give support to production. But he has done none of that. Fox is more interested in staying good with foreigners than

in supporting the country's *campesinos*, so that the country can move ahead [...] They have abandoned us; the government has not seen to our needs, they only come when they want us to vote for them. On top of everything else, now they want to take these lands to build an airport that does not benefit us; they look to help the rich by sacrificing us [Frente de pueblos en defensa de la tierra n.d.].

Although this is clearly a condemnation of the Fox administration about the airport and about its alliances with national and transnational business interests, over the course of the conflict, the frame moves beyond a critique of particular policies and personalities, a common practice in any political system, to a more profound critique of the entire transition process.

One supporter claimed, for instance, "Elections are not democracy because they do not represent the people. Atenco is a model because it is popular power. They consulted the villages and neighborhoods through assemblies and then they decided on an action." Another FPDT member commented, "Before, I thought well of the parties and of democracy, but it was all an illusion. The parties serve only to control people." Another Atenco resident, who was fairly critical of the movement, believed "all the parties are corrupt. No, the transition has not changed anything. The country is no more democratic now than before." This is an important step away from a critique of particular policies, because it is an assertion that the transition, which to date has been generally characterized as successful because of its opening of the electoral process, has not really been democratic. In fact, many critiques from academics, activists and regular citizens charge that despite the change in government, "nothing has really changed."[6] Or in the perspective of many FPDT activists, things have even gotten worse. Since the transition seemed to benefit them neither economically nor politically and since its directions seemed out of sync with the cultural desires of many Atenco residents, it is logical that, as Lajous asserts, "at the political level, there were few possibilities that the conflict would be resolved, because the protesters, those that belonged to the most affected *ejidos,* were not looking to improve their position but rather to change the political system" (153).

The fundamental problem with the transition in Mexico, according to FPDT members, was that the government was not capable of representing them. The parties were beholden to powerful economic interests, and professional politicians were either dependent on the parties or interested only in their own power and advancement. One member of the movement leadership explained, "for those in the party, it is just another job, but it should be something special; it should be wanting to help the people pull themselves forward." If movement members distrusted politicians and parties, because they were cynical and not representative, they turned instead to direct dialogue and participation as a means of making decisions. In an interview, FPDT leader Adán Espinoza argued that the assemblies, and, obviously, the people who attended them, made all of the important decisions: "We don't want to just have a small committee that goes in the back there and decides what to do. If someone has an idea or a problem, we bring it to the assembly and let everyone decide what should be done about it. Or decide if something is a good idea or not." Like similar movements throughout Mexico, especially since the 1994 Chiapas uprising, the Atenco activists employed a discourse of local autonomy as a model of democratic government. Since politicians, who do not know them and therefore cannot possibly represent them, do not offer a viable form of democracy, direct democracy, at least at the local level, is a logical solution for them.

This was a similar strategy as the one employed in Tepoztlán, where, at least one of the movement factions also consciously advocated breaking with the state and operating as an autonomous entity, subject to the will of the municipality's inhabitants. In Atenco, the actual shape of that autonomous government was never clear, but the idea was attractive to many members of the movement, if not to the population as a whole. One FPDT member explained it this way:

> Autonomy is not independence. No, we don't want to be here isolated and by ourselves. We are Mexicans and Mexiquenses [residents of the State of Mexico]. We don't want a Republic of Atenco. We want to keep all of the rights and obligations of being part of the nation. Nobody, not even the United States can be completely independent. We participate in the nation. We pay our taxes and demand what is fair. But, autonomy is the right to decide internal matters according to our own way. Nobody can come into your house and tell you, you need to do this or that thing. No. It is the same here. If we don't want the parties, why do we have to suffer through them? If we don't want elections, why should we be forced to hold them?

This notion of local autonomy clashes with official political culture, which while respecting some local rights, ultimately holds that the federal state has sovereignty over political institutions and over natural resources. The argument, then, of the activists in Atenco, was not just about the airport, but was also a challenge to the legitimacy of a form of government. The transition considered and has attempted to correct some of the problems inherited from seventy years of one-party rule, but it has not considered these other, perhaps deeper, questions about fundamental representation and control over resources.

To counter the state's claims to legitimacy, FPDT members invoked their rights as "original inhabitants" and noted the state's inability to meet their needs. Their claims to be direct descendents of the area's original inhabitants were neither spurious nor merely an ideological move to distance themselves from their neoliberal opponents, but rather they represented a fundamental challenge to state sovereignty. By invoking their indigenous status, they were also claiming specific rights in national and international law that give special protection to indigenous communities. In particular, a movement communiqué notes that the expropriation

> transgresses Article 169 of the International Labor Organization (ILO) that was recognized by Mexico as a constitutional norm, where it was established: Peoples have the right to be consulted when legislative or executive measures are intended to be adopted that could affect them (article 6); that they can not be subjected to economic and political development processes that affect their lives, beliefs, institutions and welfare, nor the lands they occupy or use in any manner (article 7) [Frente de pueblos en defensa de la tierra 2002].

Their assertion that the government is violating at least part of that pact by ignoring the needs and desires of their community would seem to place sovereignty with local inhabitants rather than the national state and demonstrate the incapacity of the current, nominally democratic state to deal with the contradictions of a heterogeneous society. The protesters' demands, therefore, are limited not only to the debate about the merits of the airport project, but also contest the legitimacy of the state to carry out the project or to claim to represent them in any meaningful way. The frame, in other words, shifted from debating policy to debating political processes more generally, and subsequently criticizing the nature and direction of the transition to democracy as a whole.

Another important aspect contributing to the specificity of the movement came from the experiences of its leadership. Like in Tepoztlán, the movement leadership did not spring spontaneously from an undifferentiated mass of impoverished farmers, but was cultivated over years of other struggles and with connections to other movements and institutions. In the words of one FPDT supporter, "To tell you the truth, some of the *compañeros* have some experience with this sort of thing." Indeed, Atenco has a long history of social struggle, and leader Nacho del Valle has been a member of a group called United Inhabitants of San Salvador Atenco, formed in 1969, shortly after the repression of the student movement the previous year. In 1995 del Valle and his organization shut down the highway and held a government official in protests demanding greater access to public transportation and to the "*tortibono*" program, designed to help low income families buy tortillas (Lajous 2003, 128). In addition, its location both physically and culturally between the countryside and the city, has given activists in Atenco knowledge of, and access to, a number of other movements, including the one in Tepoztlán six years earlier, that they have supported in numerous ways over the years. Similarly, their position at the cultural and economic edge of urban/rural populations gave the Atenco activists cultural access to these different life experiences. Like their Tepoztlán counterparts, they were able to move between these spheres to communicate with very different constituencies, while creating a distinct culture of their own that appropriated elements of those different cultural processes. These hybrid positions and participation helped movement leaders develop strategies and tactics and also led to the construction of a wide network of solidarity.[7] These connections and experiences with other social groups helped encourage the movement leadership to take radical stances and to articulate their political demands in terms of autonomy.

Unlike Tepoztlán, however, it was the more radical faction of the movement that held sway in the assemblies. In Tepoztlán, the CUT leadership, in the end, opted to compromise with political parties and to participate in the state system. In Atenco, although the movement leadership did have some connections with PRD activists, it opted for the more radical stance of autonomy and rejected potential PRD allies. When elections were finally held in October 2003, this anti-party stance ended up helping the PRI, because movement members did not participate in the elections and enough of them abstained to cost the PRD, who would be more logical allies, the election. Their analysis that collaborating with the state, even through alliances with opposition parties, would lend legitimacy to the transition process nationally, led the Atenco activists, in other words, to continue developing a political culture at the margins of institutional politics. They negotiated with elected officials, on issues of law and order, economic development, and municipal logistics, such as school repairs and traffic problems, while continuing to develop some of their own educational, political and cultural programs. There are numerous reasons why the conflict ended differently here than in Tepoztlán, but clearly the national political context, the deep seated animosity between movement leaders and regional officials and the radical ideological orientation of movement leaders all contributed to the formation of the particular, hybrid political culture of the municipality and the concrete social relations that have resulted from the conflict and from the development of that culture.

Negotiating for Respect and Recognition

The movement of the *ejiditarios* demonstrated that part of the puzzle facing citizens and politicians as they contemplate the direction of the transition has clearly to do with resolving the question of representation in the pluricultural reality of Mexican society. The Zapatistas in Chiapas since the middle of the 1990s have most eloquently put that question forward. Indigenous communities throughout the country have joined them in their demands for respect for cultural difference and recognition of their rights to determine the best way for them to live. Interestingly, as both Tepoztlán and Atenco have shown, that question of cultural identity is not limited to those communities specifically recognized as indigenous. Both of these communities are predominantly *mestizo*, yet they used the discourse of indigenous rights to identify themselves, to make claims against the state and transnational capital and to build wider networks of solidarity and support. Culturally, these communities have successfully negotiated the fluidity of identities and practices created by mobile societies, promoted by modernization programs and made possible by wide communication networks, to name themselves as culturally distinct peoples. They are not generic "indigenous" peoples or generic "peasants" but rather Tepoztecos and Atenquenses. And, although these identities tie them strongly to particular territories and bind them to specific groups of people, they are also very much a part of the larger world, which they often criticize for infringing on their sensibilities, their organizations and their well-being. They do not seek to be islands isolated in a fluid sea of globalizations, nor do they want to be independent from the nation, from their compatriots or from the more widely shared values and myths that also make them who they are. They want to be respected for being part of those larger communities, but also distinct from homogenous identities and extractive economic relationships.

The challenge, then, for the transition, is how to incorporate these particular, hybrid, distinct and sometimes contradictory cultures and groups into a viable and governable nation. The Tepoztlán case demonstrated that authoritarianism no longer works. The Atenco case suggests that neoliberal democracy may not work either. In trying to respect the rule of law, the Fox Administration found itself in an impossible situation, as it could neither convince nor coerce this very small group to make sacrifices for what it saw as the greater good. Atenco, however, was not the only challenge to governability. By 2004 there were dozens of hot spots demanding autonomy and different relationships between communities, the state and transnational businesses. Increasingly, communities have tired of waiting for the "Government of Change" to implement those changes and have taken matters into their own hands. The logic of the current transition is tied to neoliberal economics, export markets and the harmonization of social and economic relations with standards set by transnational corporations and supranational organizations like the IMF and the World Bank. The clash, however, comes when communities realize that those economic relations have very little benefit for them, and that the global is only *part* of their specific cultural make-up. In order to be successful, it would seem that the new institutions must be able to negotiate between the multiplicity of demands, visions and practices that constitute Mexican society.

Appendix

Social Movements and the Construction of Contingent Hybridities

In this book, I have been arguing that contemporary social movements in Mexico are fundamentally hybrid political/cultural formations that respond to the centrifugal and centripetal forces of contemporary social relations. They simultaneously deploy multiple kinds of tactics in order to achieve both material and ideological ends. Importantly, the cultural spaces that movements occupy are clearly marked by the influence of several and at times contradictory discourses, which people assimilate in their everyday lives. Movement activists, therefore, are adept at moving between and synthesizing these multiple communicative and symbolic systems in order to define themselves, define the goals of their movements and communicate with various types of audiences in order to most effectively press for the redress of their demands. This process, which comes from a mixed cultural background, itself contributes to the further creation of particular hybrid cultures through the experiences gained by participants in the movement.

Throughout the book, I have been concerned with two interrelated questions in the study of these two communities successfully challenging the imposition of development projects. How is conflict expressed and articulated in a pluricultural nation, such as Mexico, when that nation is ruled my a monocultural state? This question supercedes the demise of the PRI as the ruling party, because although the PRI party structure no longer controls the state apparatus, the discourses used throughout the negotiation of the transition tie the reconstruction of the state almost exclusively to liberal and modern structures, leaving out other important voices and modes of thought and organization. The second, and obviously related question is how have these microsocial movements contributed to the current transition to democracy and what critique to they offer to that process? The answer to both questions lies in understandings social movements not just as attempts to sway public policy or to express economic grievances, but also as cultural phenomena. They are processes through which identities, values, symbols and the circulation of power are interrogated and recast. They create new subjects, who, as they articulate a different vision for their societies, also express a new vision of themselves. In Mexico of the late twentieth and early twenty-first century, although the tension between acknowledging difference and seeking assimilation is one of the issues that defines social and political struggles, it is one of the issues least addressed by the transition to democracy.

The question of pluriculturalism is a hotly debated one, as one can easily observe not only conflicting cultures but also processes of accommodation, resistance and domination. These questions have been recently taken up in the literature concerning subalternity and hybridity. While I find both of these concepts useful, in this book I have argued that what movements of citizens, such as those in which the myriad of organized political and social activity in Mexico over the past several decades are involved, create hegemony based not entirely on the domination of subaltern groups nor the negation of dominant society by those same groups. Instead, it is a creative articulation of discourses emanating from the concrete experiences of individuals and communities that have inevitable links to both, or more accurately several different, cultural systems. This process is often described as cultural hybridity. The critique of hybridity that I have endeavored to put forward here is that the process of hybridization is neither one of equal mixing of differing cultures nor is it necessarily one in which the stronger cultural group ultimately dominates. Rather the process of cultural creation is a fundamentally contingent one (Stolle-McAllister 2004). That is, it is dependent on the specific needs, desires and capabilities of the community in question. This contingent hybridity, in other words, conforms, to certain extents, to be what communities need it to be in a particular moment. Rather than simply dissolving differences, and thus conforming to hegemonic formations, hybrid thinking and practices allow for a challenge to that domination by providing points of articulation from which marginalized groups participate in larger social structures and communicate with other marginalized groups, while maintaining their differences from the system and from each other.

Hybridity

In the context of Latin American cultural studies, the notion put forth by García Canclini (1995) concerning hybridity has become the point of departure for discussing the complex heteroglossia of contemporary Latin American society. He argues that contemporary Latin American modernity must be understood in terms of not only the juxtaposition of different symbolic orders and temporalities, but an awareness that because that heterogeneity forms an integral part of people's quotidian experiences, it has to be studied as a single, highly diverse, cultural system. It is a process, in other words, which incorporates peasant artisanal production, transnational movies, telenovelas, "art," indigenous social relations and global cosmopolitanism into a (some times chaotic) system of multiple meanings. While the concept of a cultural mixing is certainly not new to Latin American cultural analysis,[1] García Canclini offers an important intervention by stripping it of religious, racial and populist overtones through his placement of hybrid thinking and practices within the context of societies in which these various systems of meaning circulate due to the logics of economic structuring and the technologies of the late twentieth century. According to him, the signification of culture no longer comes from the nation state, which is incapable of organizing or controlling cultural influences that come from both an extremely heterogeneous population as well as from increasingly influential transnational sources. Rather, meaning is created primarily in the act of consuming. That is, consumers are faced with a virtually infinite number of cultural choices. In this process, the sense of the popular is detached from an essentialist notion of what it means to be Mexican or Latin American, because popular artifacts circulate through different classes, and because the popular classes consume meaning-making goods that are not of popular or even national origin. These discrete cultural systems are not, and cannot be, pure, because their constant interconnection necessarily means that they share parts of each other as they evolve and as people use them to make sense out of the widely varying inputs they receive on a daily basis.

García Canclini's discussion of Latin American heterogeneity strips culture and identity of essentializing characteristics, placing the construction of culture squarely on the actual experiences of everyday life through his insistence that meaning is continually synthesized from the constant flow of cultural inputs. This move reflects disenchantment with both the nation-building projects of populism, which posited a unique national identity as essential to inhabitants of a nation, as well as neoliberal sensibilities, which posit the centrality of markets in the formation identities and cultural exchange. Cultural hybridity evolves out of the fusion and mutual transformation of all kinds of discursive inputs: state and non-state, market and non-market, global and local, modern and traditional. It is precisely in this fluidity and mutual sharing that García Canclini argues for the democratic possibility of a utopian future built on cultural hybridity. "Perhaps the central theme of cultural politics today is how to construct societies with democratic projects shared by everyone without making everyone the same, where disintegration is elevated to diversity and inequalities (between classes, ethnic groups, or other groups) are reduced to differences" (106). He holds out hope here that practices based on hybridity, on a commonly shared culture composed of difference, can lead to a more genuinely democratic process by providing the means through which diverse sectors of national and transnational societies can communicate and work with differences to build a common project.

This concept provides an avenue to explain how heterogeneous social movements can build through internally and externally diverse interests in order to articulate complex positions both within and against the grain of a larger system. Since, according to theories of hybridity, people already necessarily inhabit culturally heterogeneous spaces, their articulation of a specific cause draws simultaneously from the particularities of their circumstances as well as the universality of the system in which they are enmeshed. Contrary to some critics of social movements, the efforts of small, localized movements are not necessarily wasted by their acting in isolation just because their actions have little measurable systemic effects, rather, their efforts ought to be seen as their attempts at mobilizing aspects of ultimately widely shared symbolic and organizational systems. By calling attention to aspects of *their* specific culture or identity, they are also, necessarily, causing a revaluation of the larger shared, hybrid culture, by challenging perceptions about aspects and functions of *that* culture. It is a fundamentally communicative action in which some part (which may be an admittedly small part) of the larger cultural formation is brought into question and challenged. While movements, for instance, may make claims privileging local "traditions," there are usually strong connections to other outside systems inherent both in those traditions and within the movement itself. Indeed, the space occupied by local movements is necessarily the point of articulation of global, national and local discourses and practices. In Alberto Moreira's (1999) words, "there is no choice between particularism and universalism, because you get them both at the same time" (385). The time and space denoted as local is when and where discourses (local, national, global and hybrid) become enacted by particular agents, and made materially real. This "impurity," however, is not a hindrance to the success of the movement, rather it is a channel that allows for communication with the larger society (because of shared symbolic/cultural systems), as well as the importation of potentially useful strategies and discourses and their incorporation into the logics of local social dynamics.

Critics of cultural hybridity, however, point out that such theories are often vacant of notions of power. In his critique of García Canclini, John Beverly (1999) points out that in his theory of hybridity,

> The political as such as been partially displaced by a culturalist notion of social agency located in civil society. But social contradictions and struggles that are also struggles "in culture" and in civil society — for example, class struggles at the point of work, struggles for ethnic or community rights or for a more equitable national or regional situation within globalization (...), women's struggles for equality, even the micropolitics of the new social movements (...) — continue to depend on the logic of domination and subordination, contradiction and negation that characterizes subaltern identity as such, even as the social subjects involved may operate within the terrain of hybridization. They are *binary* rather than (or as well as) *hybrid* [129].

Although García Canclini recognizes an important differentiation in access to social goods (particularly access to means of communication), the theory of hybridity in a sense casts people as engaged in an equal exchange of meaning, by positing in people the ability to make sense of those symbolic inputs in ways that most benefit them. In a sense, he reduces the primary cultural contradiction to one between the state and civil society, without accounting for the competing cultural logics within civil society itself. There is little room to understand how socio-economic and political institutions work to structure meanings, nor of how an oppositional identity and practice can be articulated.

Questions of materiality and the conduction of power are elided in attempts to emphasize how different groups re-articulate various types of discourses and modes of culture. Ella Shohat (1992) argues that, "a celebration of syncretism and hybridity, per se, in not being articulated in conjunction with questions of hegemony and neo-colonial power relations runs the risk of appearing to sanctify the *fait accompli* of colonial violence" (109). The fluidity inherent in notions of hybridity can be read as either transgressive or reticent, that is as either subverting the dominant order by borrowing and transforming some of its ideological constructions or as capitulating, ultimately, to the logic of that dominant order (Moreiras 1999, 395). In its reticent mode, hybridity in and of itself does not necessarily provide a means of resisting attempts at domination by denying a concrete subject of domination. Rather hybrid subjectivity may instead be part of a strategy of neo-colonial domination because hybrid subjects are necessarily incapable of articulating difference (Mabardi 2000). If hybrid subjects continually combine and redefine themselves according to the discursive inputs that saturate their lives, then it would be impossible to clearly identify a "them" against whom an indefinable "us" might struggle. If hybridity leads to the disappearance of difference, how is that not the same as the acceptance of dominant, Eurocentric, modern sensibilities?[2] The success of contemporary neo-liberal hegemony, in fact, is based partially on its ability to accept, assimilate and commodify differences, making it difficult to ground opposition.

Since hybridity posits ambiguity as the defining characteristic of the process of cultural construction, can activists within social movements create themselves as distinct from the system against which they are struggling? Instead of allowing for the articulation of radical difference, which would seem to be necessary in the construction of an oppositional identity, hybrid thinking leads instead to an endless string of positional equivalencies, and not to a fundamentally antagonistic position in relation to systems of domination (Laclau and Mouffe 1985). In other words, if everybody is simply different, but no value is assigned to that difference, we are all essentially the same. Ethnicity, gender, class, sexual orientation etc. become labels of identification, that may be combined and altered, but they do not necessarily end in a profound understanding of how that difference relates to power and oppression, nor how opposition to an oppressive system might be articulated. If marginalized groups were caught in a system characterized *primarily* by hybridity, in which their unique cultural inputs are assimilated by the larger cultural system, while they simultaneously incorporate aspects of other deterritorialized symbolic systems, how would they define themselves as unique and their interests as different from dominant social groups? How do they find the grounding to reterritorialize those symbolic systems in ways that are meaningful to their historic experience and needs?

Floyia Anthias (2001) argues that debates about cultural hybridity are flawed, because "the bringing together of different cultural elements syncretically transforms their meaning, but need not mean that dialogue between cultural givens is necessarily taking place" (630). The juxtaposition and integration of different cultural forms and discourses does not automatically mean that there has been an equal transformation or blending of power between the cultural groups represented in the process of hybridization. The fault in much of the logic concerning hybridity is that "it privileges the domain of the cultural as opposed to the material or the political (restricting its sense to that of cultural products) and therefore depoliticizes culture. It loses sight of cultural domination: power as embodied in culture, disappears" (Anthias 2001, 630). The danger is that as hybridity is often theorized, difference disappears and the dominant sectors of society benefit from assimilating subcultural or marginalized groups into the overall logic ordering social relations. Anthia points out that this anxiety is empirically borne out by the "very little evidence of dominant white [elite and male, I would add] culture ceding its role in defining the cultural domain" (630). The point being that cultural mixing does not necessarily lead either to acceptance of colonized and marginalized cultural positions, nor certainly not to an automatic radical change in established social relations. In fact, hybridity thinking can itself create the very essentialized notions of identity, by creating reified categories of social positions against which it was initially deployed. To avoid these traps of hegemonic processes, theories of cultural hybridity, therefore, need to secure solid footing in paradigms of power.

Subalternity

The role of agency, particularly subaltern agency in creating cultural formations and articulating alternative proposals for organizing society, is one of the under theorized aspects of hybridity, limiting its usefulness in explaining social change. The disintegration of viable socialist projects has led intellectuals concerned with the ability of poor and marginalized people to transform their realities to reconsider the ways in which such groups define themselves and press more powerful adversaries for change. Toward that end, much attention has been spent recently in transposing subaltern studies from South Asia to Latin America.[3] Although a long list of resistance theories have circulated through the literature over the past twenty years,[4] the subalternists have most carefully theorized the relationships between power, exclusion and agency, by grounding theories of power in the acknowledgement that societies are thoroughly and simultaneously cut through by class, ethnic, gender and other types of divisions, and by arguing that resistance to those inequalities and the ability to make societal change rests precisely along those lines of division and in the very marginalization of those groups from the homogenizing impulses of dominant society.

Beverly (1999) insists that the study of social relations must ultimately be based on a dichotomy between domination and subalternity. He defines subalternity to be any category of exclusion from hegemonic structures. In this way, he is able to move beyond *class* as the only determinant to marginalization to be able to also consider race, ethnicity, gender, sexual orientation *et cetera*. Because these sectors are excluded (in one way or another and to greater and lesser extents) from elite hegemony, parts of their knowledge and experience are ultimately not representable through dominant discourses and institutions. It is this part of subaltern experience, the part which can not be appropriated by dominant sectors, which makes García Canclini's vision of hybridization impossible, because there must necessarily be part of "popular culture" that cannot by commodified or represented in order to be consumed in a meaningful way by middle and upper classes. According to this subalternist view, social relations are primarily binary, although within that binary system individuals may occupy several subject positions. In the end, however, marginalized groups are characterized more by their difference from the dominant groups than by their compatibility with them. In this sense, subalternity represents the negation of hegemonic discourses, because ultimately marginalized groups cannot be completely incorporated into the dominant system, since that system is based on the logic of their exploitation. From their positions at the peripheries of the hegemonic order, subaltern groups maintain and nurture other histories and other possibilities of societal relations. Subaltern groups, therefore, resist the universalist categories put forth by homogenizing discourses, because their identities and practices come, at least partially, from the particularities of their unincorporated experiences.

Politically, this distinction between dominant and hegemonic cultures implies that resistance to domination requires articulating clearly antagonistic positions between oppressor and oppressed. Since marginalized groups are relatively weak, effective social struggle depends not *only* on the success and promotion of micropolitical social movements, but the cohesion of those movements into larger oppositional coalitions. Groups advocating social change based solely on their own particular position are doomed to failure, because they cannot make viable counterhegemonic arguments based on the limitations of their own particularities. Using the Gramscian language of the national-popular, Beverly argues that subaltern groups, because they possess non-hegemonizable elements, can form what Laclau and Mouffe (1985) define as a "populist bloc." In other words, they can, theoretically, negotiate the intricacies of a hybridized cultural field to split that field into two antagonistic camps in which the "oppressed," the "oppressors" and the mechanisms of oppression are clearly defined. Failure to do so leads only to an infinite string of small unconnected social struggles that, while they may (or may not) successfully win certain concessions from the state or promote certain changes within civil society, will be unable to effectively articulate a fundamentally and structurally *different* state or regime of social relations.[5] The task, according to these subalternists is the articulation of a radical multicultural discourse in which group differences can be respected while commonalities are built between them and against the social sectors that oppress and marginalize them.

Gustavo Esteva and Madu Suri Prakash (1998) would argue that such a polarization of positions is indeed occurring as local communities are increasingly opting out of the globalization/modernization paradigm through a politics of saying "no." They note that communities of indigenous peoples, rural workers and marginalized urban dwellers have never been fully incorporated into the modern economic and political system. For them, promises of prosperity, democratic governance, respect for individual choices and other "benefits" of modernity have never materialized. In fact, modernization for them has meant just the opposite as it has disrupted social relations and communities, replacing ties of mutual responsibility with the logic of individual advancement. Rather than trying to catch up to those social sectors that benefit from contemporary arrangements, they argue that these communities, instead, are forging "a multiplicity of escape routes" from the false promises of neoliberal globalization. They reject the abstract institutions of state and transnational organizations, preferring instead to build politics on a more concrete, human level. Community based organizations' embrace of the particular has led them to reject the illusions of the universal proposed by modernist thought, in a process that the authors denote as localization.

Furthermore, they argue that the exclusion and continued antagonism between the social minorities and majorities, creates the logical basis under which the majorities, that is those who are in one way or another excluded from the benefits of modern society, develop a different consciousness. They see their living spaces and ways of life increasingly threatened and disrupted by the modernist project, while they themselves reap little benefit from the system. Given that historic paradigm, it is logical that the majorities would reject modernity and the liberal institutions that accompany them, in favor of other possibilities and other ways of thinking and being. They argue that these majorities have rejected the "...possibility of regaining the experience of human agency and autonomy by supposedly 'thinking' on the global scale to contend with the oppression of 'global forces.' No challenge to the proliferating experiences of people's powerlessness succeeds when conceived and implemented inside the institutional and intellectual framework which produced it" (20). By recognizing the impossibility of understanding, much less affecting, relations and institutions at the global level, local activists realize that we, as human beings, can only truly understand a small piece of the earth and meaningfully interact with a reduced number of people according to the specificity of cultural rules which have been developed (and continue to develop) through generations of social interaction.

Despite the pretensions of neoliberal economics to homogenize (or reform) markets and political systems, transnational corporations and the policies enacted on their behalf by national states and supranational organizations such as the IMF and the World Bank, take form and become reality only in local spaces. "Global powers can only have material existence and do the harm they are doing, in their local incarnations.... For the very logic of those 'global powers' forces them to leave places where they confront persistent, rooted and fiery local opposition" (Esteva and Prakash 1998, 34). People must attend actual physical markets in order to purchase the global economy's goods, just as they must be physically present somewhere to work or otherwise participate in social relations. It is at the local level, therefore, where the power of the global project can be most logically and effectively resisted or, as Esteva and Prakash suggest, simply ignored. This is a struggle for autonomy *vis a vis* the integrationist tendencies of the various aspects of globalized modernity. By rejecting the mono-culturalism of modernity, in favor of the heterogeneity of autonomous communities, each of which negotiate their relationship to each other and to global institutions, localized movements offer radically different ways of understanding and resisting the effects of postmodern conditions. This grounded politics replaces the abstractions of transnational space as a position of resistance with the concrete details of specific experience.

The desire, therefore of these majorities is to "...seek autonomy from the state so that local spaces may exert and govern themselves in their own cultural terms ... (and) to subvert the foundations of modern power structures" (Esteva and Prakash 1998, 153). Because they have been isolated from the abstractions of state power and because they have not participated in the benefits of modern society, people occupying these social positions have developed a consciousness attributable to their own traditions and experiences, which are necessarily completely different than those of the social minorities who control and benefit from modern economic, political and cultural institutions. Furthermore, this different consciousness is being increasingly manifested in actions through which people attempt to exert power over the system by refusing to participate in its diffusion, and by seeking autonomy to rule themselves according to their own cultural traditions. They advocate the recognition of the world as a heterogeneous pluriverse rather than a monolithic universe, thus negating the universalist pretensions of modern discourse, and privileging the unique and idiosyncratic logics produced through generations of marginality.

This concept of negation, however, is problematic because it implies not only the incapacity of the hegemonic system to incorporate subaltern discourses and practices, but it also implies an ultimately essentialized notion of the subaltern. It is assumes a type of purity of consciousness and purpose among marginalized communities that maintain a steadfast rejection of modernity and an almost automatic oppositional stance. Even if it could be argued that subaltern groups have an objective interest in overthrowing the currently and structurally exploitative economic/political/ social system, their social position does not necessarily translate into a particular ideology nor does it automatically become an oppositional practice. Esteva and Prakash, for instance, contend that marginalized people have an almost innate ability to perceive of different and radical social relations. They argue:

> It is not easy to explain why "common people" do not want to or cannot translate into formal discourse their actual practices. When asked to report their experiences and struggles in abstract terms, "the people" abandon their own modes of discourse and description. Perhaps people of the living word can neither describe nor orient their actions according to the intellectual logic of modern peoples of the text or *logos*. They use reason as a veto in exercising critical awareness. Following their impulses, coming from their gut, from their experiences in the flesh, from their cultures and long traditions, they seem to feel no need to produce abstract accounts of what they are doing for some unknown abstract audience. Even less do they seem to sense this need *before* they start to react to their difficulties with their oppressors [166].

Although it could certainly be the case that subaltern groups would neither have nor need the language of modern analysis, this representation by Esteva and Prakash of marginalized peoples attributes their actions not to reason, but to instinct, and not to an understanding of how the system works or how they can negotiate with it, but rather to its complete negation from their consciousness.

Given that culture, regardless of individuals' or communities' social location, is the result a dialogic process, they are inevitably marked by their contact, no matter how slight or antagonistic that contact may be, with other, competing cultural logics.[6] That is, culture, even that of marginalized groups, is fundamentally not "pure" but composed of various, sometimes competing, sometimes complementary, linguistic and cultural experiences. While some of those experiences are clearly not representable *to* or *in* other cultural codes, there is also no pure or essentially progressive core to popular culture that necessarily needs, wants or is capable of producing the kind of totalizing logic that a clearly counterhegemonic project would seem to need. Resistance to oppression, therefore, is neither a natural nor automatic response to being marginalized, but rather is due, in part, to an ability to actually understand *how* that system works in one's oppression. Furthermore, since virtually nobody lives in complete isolation from the project of modernity, the ideas and tools that they use in understanding and resisting those mechanisms of oppression, come in part from their participation, marginalized as it may be, in those systems.

It would be clearly erroneous to attribute a specific political or ideological position to otherwise heterogeneous groups of people, based solely on their marginalization from the hegemonic system. The fact of the matter is that most dispossessed people do not take individual or organized action against their domination. Just because some marginalized people are involved in certain social movements and at particular times do act, it is also imperative to remember that others occupying similar social positions do not. In his study of a working class, often times politicized *colonia* in Mexico City, Matthew Gutmann (2002) is interested in trying to explain action by divorcing a simple equation between class and resistance, noting that "class position and social behaving are not the same units of analysis" (116). He argues that the question of agency is key to understanding the ways in which marginalized people act to change their worlds as well as to understanding how they see themselves in the world. It is more complicated, however, than simply attributing agency to subaltern sectors, because it does not answer the question of *why* some people act in some circumstances and not in others. We can hold up social movement activists as exemplary models of subaltern agency, but why them and not all subaltern people? Why do most people, most of the time, simply not act? Why do some people believe their activism makes any difference, when there could clearly be made a case that it does little to change larger structures of oppression?

Gutmann takes aim at what he denotes as resistance theories that have evolved throughout the past twenty or thirty years alongside of the decline in the persuasiveness of socialist narratives of revolution and dramatic change. In most resistance theory, power is seen as pervasive, and, therefore, resistance to it is expressed in terms of oftentimes small, quotidian actions and attitudes. It is theorized that people in marginal social positions almost automatically attempt to resist their domination in a number of overt and covert means, and that those small steps will eventually lead to more comprehensive systemic changes. Gutmann contends however, "the fundamental flaw in much resistance theory is not that it lacks an account of utopian fancy among oppressed but rather that so many of these concepts about microresistance leading eventually to monumental transformations are one-sidedly idealistic" (116). If subaltern people resist domination *because* they are subaltern, then we really have very little room to understand the practices which lead to resistance, nor can we account for the ways in which oppressed people do not offer resistance, which in turn, makes it difficult to account for how and why people *do* decide to act. "As long as the poor and oppressed are tacitly treated as instinctual animals whose ignorance and knowledge is an involuntary consequence of their being poor and oppressed, questions of political and social consciousness will continue to be considered inappropriate, and discussion of illusions, delusions and fantasies will be seen as vulgar" (117).

The challenge, rather, is to chart the multidimensionality of individual and collective subjectivity, which can explain both successes and failures of resistance and of articulating different visions of society and different political practices. Clearly social position, particularly one of exclusion is a crucial part of subjectivity. The work of subaltern studies, therefore, is helpful in locating marginalization as a fertile ground for advocating different possibilities of sociability, precisely because it is from that exclusion that histories that challenge hegemonic systems can emerge. Furthermore, recognizing that subalterns occupy different subject positions within society, but are defined ultimately by their exclusion allows for the imagining of a radical multicultural politics in which alliances can be formed around difference and through which antagonisms can be articulated with dominant social structures. It keeps the discussion grounded in the material experiences of oppression and domination.

The danger, however, as Gutmann suggests is that such notions easily become romanticized, and to begin assuming that *because* people are poor they will therefore think and act in a certain way. Their position contributes toward forming who they are and how they act, but there are numerous other factors that influence the way people think, argue and ultimately act in the world. Subaltern thinking also assumes a *de facto* antagonism and binary relationship, which excludes the possibility that change and resistance may also be very much caught up in negotiation, compromise and collusion. It would seem, rather, that movements for social change are effective, in part, because participants understand, to at least some extent, the ways in which they are excluded from fully sharing in the benefits produced by society and on means through which they can negotiate with social, economic and political institutions. Their consciousness is created in part by that experience. But movements are also very much dependent on the particular circumstances of groups and individuals, political opportunities provided by openings in systems of control, and ultimately the sound (or at least perceived to be sound) arguments of others. They are built through the political and social work of their communities and their leaders. Members of subaltern groups debate political postures and courses of action in various ways. They do not develop naturally or automatically because of their social position. And, in an increasingly integrated world, successful movements and their leaders are able to move within and between different cultural orders, even as they are creating a new one, in order to make their cases, build alliances and retreat back to safety in moments of defeat.

Contingent Hybridity

The culture that both produces and is produced by the micropolitical social movements of Latin America needs to be understood as existing, therefore, somewhere in between the hybrid and subaltern positions. I agree with García Canclini that contemporary Latin American culture needs to be understood as an intensely hybridized field. The heterogeneity described (and celebrated) by postmodern theory seems almost transparent. And, certainly, exploring the different axes on which oppression occurs can only be beneficial in developing more comprehensive and viable strategies for liberation. On the other hand, however, we need to be careful not to become lost in some fog of difference or glorification of heterogeneity for the sake of heterogeneity. There continue to exist very real, material *structures* of oppression and an important part of the work of Latin American social movements is motivated around the need to alter those structures. Most forms of oppression, after all, can be traced to unequal access to the social and material value collectively created by society. And, although there is an extremely wide variety of movements in the region, what they have in common is an understanding that different sectors of society are being excluded from fully sharing in the benefits that society produces. The recent histories of populism and of socialist oriented political efforts suggest that the creation of identities based on master narratives of nation or class to the exclusion of other identities and agendas has been unable to articulate an oppositional bloc capable of dislodging capitalist, neoliberal hegemony, nor have they articulated a new vision of what kind of a project such an alliance would carry out.[7] The challenge, therefore, presented to and by social movements is their ability to articulate opposition at a systemic level while maintaining important internal differences. How can they articulate a political/cultural project that is simultaneously unique and coherent with the particularities of their histories while at the same time addressing their relationships to a variety of other groups and systems with which they necessarily have relationships?[8]

Moreiras (1999), following Laclau (1996), argues that moving beyond the transgressive and reticent options of hybridity can radicalize it as an effective analytical tool and not just a descriptive device. As a descriptor, hybridity neither contests nor subsumes itself to hegemonic formations. Its very ambiguity means that it can act in either way. "Hybrid subjectivity, through its very undecidability *qua* hybrid, pre-empts the closure of any discursive position around either identity or difference. Hybrid subjectivity, at its limit, does not sometimes allow for identity and sometimes for difference, but rather simultaneously undermines both identitarian and differential positions…" (396). If hybridity undermines both the ability to distinguish difference and the ability to recognize adherence to other systems, that is, it negates both subalternity and domination, how is it useful as an analytical tool to understand the cultural problematics of social movements in their challenges to hegemonic formations?

Part of the answer lies in the necessity for activists, while creating and living in hybrid cultures, to nevertheless be grounded in specific historic realities and narratives. Their linkage to particular circumstances means that even as their narratives change through their articulations with other outside discursive structures, they cannot completely lose their identity to those outside influences. This is particularly true in the case of social movement activists, who are building their (hybrid) identities in part in open antagonism with the "other" against which they are protesting. Laclau (1996) argues that "hybridization does not necessarily mean decline through the loss of identity: it can also mean empowering existing identities through the opening of new possibilities" (65). It is these new possibilities of which social movements can take advantage to create cultural and communicative frameworks that are simultaneously meaningful to the particularisms of their own community as well as to the outside communities and systems against which they are struggling or with which they are trying to build tactical alliances.

Thinking in terms of hybridity allows us to conceptualize the dynamics of the hegemonic system and the possible roles played by those resisting that hegemony, by highlighting the interdependent relationships of people occupying various subject positions within the system. Moreiras argues that hybridity ought to be understood as a double articulation. The first being the "hegemonic articulation between a discourse and a given

social force (the fictitious register) to a second articulation: the political
and theoretical articulation between the fictitious register itself and the
radical contingency of an affirmed subalternity, which is the negation of
what hegemony negates and thus the possibility of another history" (399).
Hybridity negates the possibility of absolute particularism or absolute
totality, because both extremes are mutually constituted. Since the first
articulation of hybridity is the linkage between a hegemonically recognized discourse with a particular social actor, the dominant system recognizes, even if to assimilate, that difference. It also underscores the
necessarily pluralistic functioning of the system. By arguing for the second articulation, that is the linkage now between this relationship between
the particular and the universal, what Morieras refers to as the fictitious
register, and "the radical contingency of an affirmed subalternity," Moreiras contends that the avowed marginality of that discourse negates its
possibility of complete assimilation, rendering hegemonic closure impossible and creating the discursive space for other histories. Hybrid thinking, in other words, allows us to understand social activists as being
inscribed within hegemonic discourses, but from the position within to
be simultaneously inscribed outside of the system itself. This double articulation allows activists to work within the communicative norms of dominant discourses and from that position introduce the negation of the
system itself, and offer other possibilities.

This varies markedly from a strictly subalternist position that would
posit marginalized thinking and practices to be completely outside of hegemonic structures. Rather, hybrid thinking opens the door to understanding the possibilities for social change by incorporating differences into a
potentially pluralistic system. When social agents, who are caught up in
communicative and power circuits inscribed by hegemonic projects, seek
to use that position to advocate a different history, they not only open the
possibility to communicating and working with other social groups, but
they also proclaim the impossibility of discursive closure on the terms
being imposed on them. From that discursive space created by hegemonic
projects, social activists affirm their differences both with the system and
with the particularities of other groups. Instead of leading to their continued isolation and marginalization, by insisting on their difference from
within the articulations of hegemonic discourses, they simultaneously challenge those hegemonic discourses, which seek to incorporate them, and
use those hegemonic discourses as a means of linking their positions with
the positions of other marginalized groups as well.

Such double articulation, it should be pointed out, however, is not
an automatic function of agents occupying subaltern positions, rather it

is the result of oftentimes hard social and political work, which is why I want to refer to this kind of politicized hybrid identity and practice as contingent. It is very much contingent on the specific historic circumstances and the talents of the people involved. As Moreiras observes, "social identities cannot be kept in storage and used for a resistant or a subversive end whenever the occasion arises: social identities are mere shifters, and they only mean what the present makes them mean" (382). The specific identities and practices that people develop, therefore, evolve through the intricacies of their particular histories. Each hybrid identity or hybrid culture, therefore, while circumscribed by the universalist grammar of hegemonic discourses, is uniquely defined by the specificities of historic difference. They take on meaning according to circumstances. Responding to moments of social crisis, therefore, talented activists are adept at making their hybrid cultures meaningful in ways that simultaneously articulate their grievances with dominant discourses and practices while maintaining themselves grounded in that which makes them different from the system against which they are struggling.

Contingent hybridity, therefore, describes the cultural practices embodied through the praxis of social movements. It is a subjectivity borne out of the concrete experiences of people as they confront material inequalities and attempt to articulate ideas and practices aimed at transforming those relationships. The cultural relations evolving out of these circumstances, in other words, are very much dependent on those very circumstances. It is neither a hybridity that results in the complete erasure or commodification of difference, that is Moreira's reticent hybridity, nor is it absolutely transgressive as it cannot completely escape or subvert hegemonic parameters. Rather, it is a cultural practice in which identities, which although always pliable, are maintained grounded in the unique experiences of individuals and communities. Those experiences are marked by inequality and by perpetual negotiation between local, regional, national and global discourses and social relations. Their marginality from dominant social relations serves to privilege belonging to other types of communities; likewise, their simultaneous incorporation (however marginal) into those very systems provides the means through which they are able to negotiate with dominant actors and institutions for recognition of their difference and for redress of material grievances.

Grounding Cultural Theory

In order for hybridity to be useful as a category of social change, it needs to be moved out of a purely theoretical discussion and grounded in practices. It is only through practice that ideas become politicized and agency can be exercised. Social movements provide one of the means through which people residing in the periphery demonstrate their abilities to advocate for change on their own behalf and through which they not only negotiate hybridized cultural terrains, but participate in creating them as well. As I have noted, people involved in social movements occupy already hybridized cultural spaces, yet certainly not all oppressed people negotiating such cultural terrain become activists, and not all communities automatically embrace the transgressive element of their hybrid cultures.

What makes for a successful social movement, therefore? History, political opportunity and the ability of activists to make their case simultaneously to local, national and transnational audiences, contribute to the potential success of movements, both in terms of winning particular concessions and in terms of building oppositional identities. Successful activists possess what Dubois would call double (or is it now multiple?) consciousness and can move between different cultural fields even as they create new ones based on those journeys. This multiple consciousness reinforces the notion that hybridity is contingent on both historic circumstance and the abilities and inclinations of particular agents and communities to act in the construction of that hybridity.

In their discussion of the role of culture in social movements, Alvarez, Dagnino and Escobar (1998) argue that culture is an incessant process of meaning creation, in which hegemonies are contested, negotiated and recast. While being aware that larger structures do impose constraints on the possibilities of enacting social change, they return repeatedly to the argument that culture is the terrain in which social movements operate and the field in which they are most likely to have a significant impact. These practices are manifest through the interactions of various networks and webs of individuals and groups, representing different subject positions, as they continually create meaning for themselves based on their lived experiences. This process is necessarily a political one as they coalesce into blocs that contest for power and come into conflict with other groups' meaning-making practices as well. Social movements in this sense, then, represent the attempts of marginalized groups to connect grounded representational practices with an explicitly political agenda, demanding greater political participation, recognition of fundamental rights, and/or more access to and control over basic economic activities. For the most part, however, these movements are not isolationist or essentialist. They have somewhat contradictory demands in that they simultaneously seek inclusion and autonomy from the system. They want to express and exercise their rights to self-determination, but also want to be included in national political processes and benefit from the material advantages of the economic system in which they participate.

Alvarez, Dagnino and Escobar further argue that these cultural/political formations "are the result of discursive articulations originating in existing cultural practices—never pure, always hybrid, but nevertheless showing significant contrasts in relation to dominant cultures—and in the context of particular historical conditions" (9). In other words, social movements make use of existing symbolic and representational systems that, because they originate in hybrid public and private cultural fields, contain elements from both dominant and marginalized sectors. Part of the role of the movement, therefore, is to operate within that hybrid field, in such a way that their cases can be understood by larger social sectors, but which accentuates important differences so as to make their local identities and demands paramount. This approach to studying social movements has two important effects. Firstly, it forces a reconsideration of exactly what politics consists of. It breaks with more orthodox political analysis, which tends to be focused on institutions and elite cultural brokering, while emphasizing non-elite struggles over the exercise of power. Incorporating non-elite concerns and actions into analysis allows for a more in-depth and potentially radical conception of politics, as it moves analysis beyond the realm of capturing power, to consideration of how power is understood and exercised. By conceptualizing social movements in this way, we are able to analyze them, not only as political formations, but also as important processes for preserving and renovating popular culture. Because of their work to win concessions on a variety of issues, they continually call attention to the existence of non-elites within dominant political and cultural discussions, while at the same time affirming the importance of those local, peripheral and non-modern cultural formations. Being in between these two cultural blocs causes social movements to be a mechanism for the articulation of new discourses which, while emphasizing the experiences and cultures of marginalized sectors also contribute to change within those sectors by introducing different ideas and possibilities of living.

Social movements, therefore, find themselves in the midst of a cultural field that is an incessant process of creating meaning. The study of how those meanings are created and why they matter, however, must be carried out not only by examining representations created by movement activists, but also through their practices. Culture must be understood, in other words, as material practices as well, because it is through those practices that relationships and meanings are constructed. Localized social movements provide in many senses a liminal situation in which existing relationships are challenged and new ones are formed. This process of changing relationships necessarily demands a rethinking of shared symbols, stories, understandings and both public and private social networks.

Part of the conflict in Mexico certainly has to do with distribution of resources and structural material and political inequalities, but part of the conflict clearly has to do with competing world visions and civilizational projects. Although some would stress that these projects are completely different, their relationship is more complicated than that. Individuals simultaneously participate in *both* projects, the problem then becomes how do they negotiate the terrain between these projects to establish and meet their goals as individuals and as communities. In the case of Tepoztlán and then later Atenco, not to mention the Zapatista autonomous municipalities in Chiapas, the contradictions between the two projects become evident, dramatic and even violent. The solution, however, is not simply resistance on the part of the oppressed groups, but also creative proposals on governance that reflect and contribute to the unique hybridity of those communities. They force the monocultural state to make concessions to the idiosyncratic demands of local communities, who themselves have incorporated and altered various types of political/cultural inputs to produce viable, meaningful and possible social relations, both internal to the community and with the larger networks in which they are inextricably enmeshed.

Chapter Notes

Introduction

1. See Wallerstein (1991) for a more detailed discussion on the uses of culture as the means through which hierarchies are consolidated and differences are flattened in the name of universality.

2. Throughout Latin America, mayordomos are men (usually, although increasingly some women have served as mayordomos in Tepoztlán) charged with overseeing the religious festivities of their communities. Although the actual responsibilities and selection process varies from community to community, people chosen as mayordomos are held in high regard by the community for their service. In Tepoztlán, mayordomos are selected annually by each neighborhood in an open assembly. They serve for a year, and organize the neighborhood's annual festival, maintain the chapel, organize communal work and serve as spiritual advisers. See Chapter 3 for more detail about their symbolic and functional work in Tepoztlán.

3. In addition to the support of various artists and intellectuals who reside in Tepoztlán, according to Rosas the movement received the active support of a number of groups including Greenpeace, the Group of 100, Espacio Verde, the Alejandro von Wuthenau Foundation, the Global Anti-Golf Movement, Multinational Monitor, the Guerrero Greens, 50 Mujeres por Morelos, Habitat, Huehheulcóyotl, Pacto de Grupos Ecológicos, Grupo de Estudios Ambientalistas, Consejo de Pueblos Nahuas del Alto Balsas, Comité Nacional para la Defensa de los Chimalapas, Slavemos al Bosque among others (1997, 65).

4. Ramírez Sáiz and de la Torre (2003), for instance, insist that conservative, middle class groups need to be considered in the construction of contemporary Mexican civil society. These groups tend to be ignored in studies of social change, but also represent attempts by non-state actors to organize themselves and to advocate both for material benefits and for recognition of their also unique identities within the Mexican nation.

5. The contemporary notion of subalternity was drawn most notably from a Gramscian reading of social theory by a group of South Asian, postcolonial scholars including notably Ranajit Guha, Gayatri Spivak and Dipesh Chakrabarty. In the mid to late 1990s, Latin Americanists frustrated by more orthodox Marxist approaches to the problems of inequality and social change in the Americas, began adopting some of the theoretical assumptions of their South Asian colleagues and transposing those theories onto the historic circumstances of Latin America. See, in particular, Rodriguez (2001) for a summary of their efforts.

Chapter 1

1. Throughout the twentieth century, the community of Tepoztlán has found itself to be the object of great interest among anthropologists and other social scientists. In the 1920s and 1930s, Robert Redfield conducted extensive ethnographic research among the town's inhabitants as Mexico

rebuilt from the devastation wrought by the Revolution. A generation later, Oscar Lewis built his in-depth studies of poverty and culture around families living in Tepoztlán and Mexico City. The late 1970s and 1980s found Claudio Lomnitz beginning his career through yet another detailed study of the town and a critique of some of Lewis's methods and conclusions.

2. The centralization of the system went much higher, of course, as the governor was picked by the president, who himself had been picked by the outgoing president under the tradition of the *dedazo* (or the big finger). In this way, the PRI as the central political authority was able to maintain vertical control over the entire political apparatus. Although this had been gradually changing with successful challenges from opposition parties in recent years, the tradition remained strong, and was certainly in effect in Tepoztlán prior to 1995.

3. Because of democratic reforms made to both institutions following the conflict of 1995–1997, they seemed better able to work in conjunction with one another, serving as institutional checks and balances, rather than being at odds over benefits from scarce resources.

4. Some of the newer residents complained of feeling threatened by the xenophobic atmosphere that existed during the height of the conflict, while others complained that even after the crisis passed, they felt that because they were not born in Tepoztlán, they would never by fully accepted into the community, nor have equal voice in community matters.

5. These projects include a golf course in the 1960s, a cable car in the 1970s, a highway in the 1980s and a scenic train in the early 1990s.

6. A poll conducted by *Reforma* in September 1995 found that 49 percent of residents cited water as their main reason for opposing the golf course (Giménez 1995).

7. After lengthy appeal processes, courts ruled in favor of the Tepoztecos, returning the disputed lands to the control of the Communal Landholding Authority in July 2001.

8. This last study suggested, instead, that the golf course would draw from an aquifer that fed into the Cuernavaca Valley instead of the Tepoztlán Valley. While this continued to be a disputed point, it also begged the question as to the impacts that draining that aquifer would have on the much larger population of Cuernavaca, which is also hampered by water shortages during the dry season.

9. Federal hydraulic officials were later allowed to reinstall the private water system, but they had to do so by drilling wells from a different source. Many people rejected the use of this water, claiming that the wells were drilled too close to the cemetery. As a result, Tepoztlán has two water supply systems, one that runs from the traditional spring and which is available from public taps and the other which is pumped from the wells and which is connected to private houses.

10. The officials held were the State Subsecretary "A," Victor Saucedo Pedromo, the State Director of Government, Armando Saldivar, Director of Transportation, Moisés Malpical and the municipal leader of the PRI, Diana Ortega.

11. At that time, state authorities directly supervised all police units. There were no municipal police, so expelling these units left Tepoztlán with no police "protection." Many citizens, however, noticed with a grin that crime rates plummeted after the police left town. Many implied that the police were generally responsible for criminal activity, while others suggested that crime dropped, because people were more aware of what was going on in their neighborhoods and mobilized to keep an eye out for one another.

12. Judicial police are detectives, assigned to state or federal jurisdictions who do not wear uniforms and who were generally pointed to as the prime violators of human rights in the state. Under the Carillo Olea administration, the state judicial police were associated with a kidnapping ring and with several murders, as well as the routine torture of suspects.

13. While it is arguable that Tepoztlán is not an indigenous community, their appeal to uses and customs suggests not only that the Zapatista movement has had a wide-ranging effect on the discourses of social movements, but also attests to the Tepoztecos' sense of being different from a suppos-

edly homogenous Mexico. The idea that communities should choose their leaders according to the idiosyncrasies of their histories and social relations also speaks to the depth of desire for local autonomy as an integral part of Mexico's political transition from authoritarianism.

14. See Olvera (2003) for a detailed description of Alianza Cívica and its impact on promoting democratic processes at a national level through the 1990s.

15. He uses the word *pueblo,* which could be translated either as people or as town or village. The connotation of "pueblo," particularly among leftists is the poor and/or the "true" people of a nation or community.

16. See "La Batalla de Tepoztlán" directed by Oscar Menéndez (*Batalla* 1995) for a filmed version of this ceremony.

17. This is, of course, within the parameters of debate set up by the assumption that everyone was opposed to the construction of the golf course. KS opponents effectively excluded the minority of residents in favor of building the golf course from the assemblies either through self-censorship or through intimidation.

18. Rosas (1997, 79) reports that this death, in the end, was suspect, because right before he died, he had seemed to be recovering. There are suspicions in Tepoztlán that he did not actually die, because no one in town was ever allowed to see the body and there are rumors that he was moved to a state in the north. They believe that the government faked his death in order to be able to increase the seriousness of its harassment campaign against movement leaders. Although these allegations have never been proven, the findings of the CNDH invalidate the testimony allegedly given right before his death and demonstrate that high ranking members of the State's Attorney General's office were actively involved in a conspiracy to frame Demesa.

19. Of course, given the human rights situation in Mexico, it could be argued that that was precisely the everyday relationship that the state had with civil society.

20. Besides the "normal" types of corruption, the Carrillo administration was linked to a kidnapping ring being run out of the state judicial police, and of drug trafficking. Press reports, attempted to link the governor's interest in the golf course with his need to launder narcotics money. His previous post as Salinas' head of drug interdiction, linked him with the drug cartels, which during his tenure as governor, increasingly used the state of Morelos as a safe haven and transshipment point (Meraz, García Flores et al. 1996).

21. This was the beginning of statewide organizing that would lead to Carrillo's removal from office in 1998.

22. In February 2000 Carrillo fled to the United States, allegedly to avoid prosecution in Morelos shortly after the National Supreme Court ruled that he could be officially impeached and stand trial for the various crimes with which he has been associated (Aranda 2000, 34–35).

23. In a March 1997 report, the Miguel Agustín Pro Juarez Human Rights Center noted, for instance, that while Carrillo Olea campaigned on a "law and order" platform, crime had risen markedly during his tenure. "Robberies, assaults, rapes and homicides have more than doubled. The participation of judicial agents and former police officers in these criminal activities is notorious" (Alvarez, Castillo et al. 4). Kidnapping, for instance, had become a somewhat important industry in the state under Carrillo's administration. Of the estimated 254 kidnappings that took place between 1994 and 1997, only two were solved. It was noted that, "the kidnappers use police techniques to carry out their operations which suggests the possibility that active or former police officers (were) involved" (7). In addition to these strong suspicions that the police were involved in criminal activity, there was a significant rise in human rights violations committed by those forces. "Complaints about human rights violations committed by police officials including torture, illegal detentions, and searches without warrants have increased 329 percent between 1993 and 1995, while the compliance of recommendations made by the State Human Rights Commission has declined from 78 percent to 28 percent in the same time frame" (Ortiz Pinchetti 1996, 12).

24. Seats on the Municipal Council were awarded according to a system of proportional representation, in which the party

with the most votes (the PRD) received the Presidency, the Secretary as well as two seats on the Council. Each of the other three parties each received one seat — thereby guaranteeing a voice to all factions, but allowing for governability by providing the winning party with at least a minimal majority of votes.

25. While this is particularly true of the PRI, which in turn means that the governor effectively names municipal presidents and a majority of the municipal council, it is also true in other parties. The nearby municipality of Huitzilac was involved in a serious political dispute in which an imposed candidate of the PRD won the municipal presidency in 1997, resulting in a sometimes-violent internal conflict over who should actually govern.

Chapter 2

1. Eugenia Echeverría (1994) notes that there are at least fifty major and minor festivals organized in Tepoztlán throughout the year, with Carnival and the Challenge to Tepozteco being perhaps the two most important ones organized at a municipal level. Indeed, the municipal government pays for a large part of the ceremonies out of the public purse, whereas other festivals are organized and paid for through voluntary donations. Thus, making the festival an important part of "official" Tepozteco identity.

2. The following is a summary of the legend that Zúñiga recorded in his 1995 book. All direct quotes come from this source. Some storytellers and scholars refer to him as Tepoztecatl and others as Tepozteco. Since Zúñiga prefers Tepozteco, that is what I use in this version of the story.

3. Zúñiga uses the term "guajalote" which means turkey, but which also has the connotation of "fool."

4. Other versions of the story have the neighboring kings immediately accepting the counsel of Tepozteco and being baptized right there.

5. Ehecatepetl, besides being the name of the wind god is also the name of one of the mountains which surrounds Tepoztlán.

6. During relatively recent renovations of Colonial Churches throughout the state of Morelos, for instance, small stone gods have been found inside many of the walls. It is believed that indigenous builders secretly placed these representations of their deities in the church wall and then placed statues of Catholic saints outside of them, so that it would appear to Spanish officials that they had in fact been converted and were praying to the Catholic saints. This part of the Tepozteco story would seem to be a narrative version of "hiding" older deities within Christian structures. It also reflects the ability to merge two seemingly contradictory belief systems into a single, meaningful one.

7. See Sánchez Ascencio (1998) for a more complete history of Tepoztlán.

8. According to Sánchez Ascencio (1998), the Anenecuilco papers were written in Nahuatl, which Zapata had translated by the Tepozteco priest, Pedro Rojas Zúñiga, so that he could use them in court. This provided some of the first contacts between Tepoztlán and the fledgling Zapatista movement.

9. I have cited the narratives of various Tepoztecos and collected by Marcela Tostada in this chapter, because all of these testimonies concerning local stories of Zapata, and festivals were produced at the end of 1994 and the beginning of 1995 (although not published until the end of 1998). This is very convenient for my argument, because it shows the sensibilities present and circulating in Tepoztlán on the eve of the golf course conflict. In other words, it shows what movement activists were working with, rather than what they created, as may be the case in testimonies collected after the crisis.

10. Except where specifically noted, all information regarding the construction of Zapata as a local icon is drawn from composites of interviews conducted in Tepoztlán between 1998 and 1999, as well as from some published sources (Lewis 1968; Womack 1968; Gallo Sarlat 1988; Warman 1988; Zúñiga Navarrete 1995; Sánchez Ascencio 1998; Tostada Gutiérrez 1998).

11. See in particular the work of Lomnitz (1982; 1992; 2001), for a more detailed discussion of the role of this residual campesino ideology in Tepozteco politics.

12. This means that the land is technically

"communal" land and not "*ejido.*" The *ejidos* were created and administered by the state after 1920 as the result of expropriations from large landholders who had illegally acquired the lands in the previous century, or from owners who would not cooperate with the land reform process. As a result, communities receiving land from the *ejidal* authorities were more bound to state officials, than those communities, like Tepoztlán, which never lost their property to begin with.

13. In 1992, new textbooks were introduced into the school system, by then Secretary of Education, Ernesto Zedillo, which, reflecting the decidedly neoliberal turn in the Mexican state, portrayed Porfirio Díaz as a somewhat enlightened dictator, responsible for great economic prosperity and "modernization," even if prone to some understandable excesses in the exercise of his authority. Zapata, by contrast, was portrayed as a much more problematic revolutionary with a dark past and less than "pure" and "saintly" motives.

14. Spanish colonial practices often left local indigenous leadership more or less intact. Indigenous leaders themselves, therefore, became more important and powerful based on their abilities to mediate between their populations and Spanish government and church officials.

15. One community leader explained to me that although the *mayordomías* and the municipal authorities were two very separate entities (even under the electoral rules established since 1995), the *mayordomos*, based on their authority and respect they receive from neighbors, do interact with municipal authorities to attempt to win certain services. In the neighborhood in which I was living in 1999, for instance, as the result of a series of neighborhood assemblies, the *mayordomo* was able to solidify enough commitments from residents to leverage support from the municipal government for a major water works project. The *mayordomo* promised, and delivered, the necessary labor and the municipality provided the material for the neighborhood to improve the tubing and water collection station in the neighborhood. Although some people complained that it was the municipal government's responsibility to provide all of those services, most were pleased to be able to cooperate to substantially improve this fundamental service to their homes.

Chapter 3

1. The contradiction, of course, between all states and nations is that they do not necessarily correspond, as states often times encompass many nations. This is particularly true in the case of decolonized countries, whose boundaries were artificially drawn by colonizing powers. In virtually all cases, however, states administer the relations between many different cultural groups. In the current process of globalization and weakening of the state, states' abilities to maintain their control over and create an imagined national community has seriously eroded, leading to the kinds of ethnic and religious conflicts which have characterized much of central and eastern Europe, parts of Africa and Latin America.

2. See Lomnitz (1992) for a detailed discussion of the non-racial implications of *mestizaje* in contemporary (particularly regional) cultural production.

3. Besides the obvious negative effects of global capitalism, Esteva and Prakash are particularly critical of the international human rights movement for attempting to impose the western modern cultural sensibility of individualism on all people, in the guise of helping secure certain liberties and protections for all individuals. They argue that this is modernity's "Trojan horse" which seeks to create abstract "citizens" endowed with certain rights, at the expense of the social relationships that already exist among many community members.

4. This process of identity creation is important to consider, because it outlasts the spatial and temporal limits of the movement itself. While identity, is of course, contingent and part of an ever-changing process, it nevertheless has a certain permanency to it. That is, people look for and attempt to create stability in their identities. While the types of positions that people develop in the course of a political conflict or the life of a movement change or fade with time, their involvement with that process creates a permanent part of their

identities and thus, their position within the structuring of social relationships.

5. This also helps to explain Lomnitz's (1999) observations about the state's difficulty in incorporating such movements. Not only are they small and not necessarily sector related, but they also correspond to a break in the homogenizing epistemology of states and seek to build upon and strengthen identities of difference.

6. Keck and Sikkink identify human rights, environmentalism and the ending of violence against women as the most important of these current issues.

7. One of the most contentious issues at the 1992 UN Earth Summit in Rio de Janeiro, for instance, was precisely this question of equity. Less industrialized countries demanded (and got vague promises for) serious concessions from more industrialized countries as the price for switching to more environmentally sustainable and costly practices.

8. See Keck and Sikkink (1998) for a detailed description and analysis of this process.

9. Aguilar (1994) notes that while Morelos is a prime area for the development of eco-tourism, because not only of its mountain ranges, but also the many rivers and springs in the valley, most of these projects end up as failures because of a lack of regulation of development. With an eye to short term profits, communities and corporations, build quickly and haphazardly, often times infringing on environmentally sensitive areas and spoiling what had made the site so promising to begin with (i.e. a clean river or a mountain view).

10. Sensing that it was losing the support of public opinion in Tepoztlán, KS even chose to take up the cloak of environmentalism, claiming that its "industry without smokestacks" would bring prosperity without pollution, and that the opening up and maintaining of green spaces would improve the local environment. Finally, they even offered to build holes into the bottom of the walls that would surround the project so that local animals could continue to migrate (more or less) freely.

11. According to Lomnitz (1999) land in Tepoztlán is among the most highly valued in the entire country.

12. Activists explained that during the height of the conflict, residents did effectively police themselves from committing unacceptable building projects. As the pressure waned, however, it became more difficult to oppose community members' intentions to develop their property.

13. The CNDH, unfortunately, has little autonomous power and its findings result only in recommendations. Despite its findings in Demesa's case, for instance, that he was not present at the time of the murder and that the testimony given by the victim was inadmissible because it was taken while he was in the hospital under the influence of narcotics, and that there were any number of legal irregularities in his arrest and the subsequent investigation, Demesa was not released until Carrillo had left office and the electoral issues in Tepoztlán had been resolved. In essence, this recognized that he was being held as a hostage to the negotiations. Nevertheless, the finding is important in that it is an admission on the part of the state itself that flagrant violations of rights occurred in this conflict.

14. Keck and Sikkink (1998), for instance, argue that the efficacy of human rights networks depends on their ability to produce and disseminate accurate information. They attribute this to a long history of informational politics that movements, dating back to the anti-slavery movement in the 18th and 19th centuries, have used in order to further their causes. The human rights movement has used this technique to circumvent silences and evasions by states accused of systematic abuses.

Chapter 4

1. This political entrepreneurship can be seen particularly among "dissident" members of the PRI elite. A number of governors and former governors led by Manuel Bartlet of Puebla, for instance, openly challenged the PRI's presidential selection process in 1999. Bartlet and his "club" certainly did not represent a "democratizing" wing of the PRI; in fact, they were just the opposite. Their public challenge to the technocratic control of the upper PRI structures and their running of candidacies against the wishes of the PRI leadership

represented the inability of the PRI structure to control not only a wide array of social movements, but even of elite factions within the party itself. (See Cornelius (1999), for a more in depth discussion of these dissident governors.) Furthermore, other relatively high-ranking PRI officials have left the party and run either as independents or have joined the PRD to run for higher office. Some of these moves seem to be based on principal, where as others seem to be based on the politician's inability to advance within the PRI hierarchy. In either case, it represents the capacity for political operatives to defy the PRI or to work outside of it all together.

2. To exemplify this antagonism, Zapatista armies' habitually burned municipal archives because they contained land titles, which in their view had been the means through which the state had protected the interests of large landholders against those of the community.

3. The Salinas administration (1988–1994) developed the National Solidarity Program (PRONASOL) as an attempt by the federal government to directly patronize marginalized sectors. Designed as a public works and anti-poverty program, the federal government directly funded projects developed and supervised by local "Solidarity Committees." While this was officially a means to break dependence on government bureaucracies and to allow local communities some control over development projects, critics charged that funds were directed to politically sensitive areas as a means to undercut non-governmental and oppositional organizing in marginalized sectors. Like other anti-poverty programs, however, PRONASOL did not outlive the administration and was effectively defunded when Salinas left office. See Dresser (1991)for an in-depth analysis of PRONASOL's political implications.

4. A poll conducted in 1995 found 93 percent to oppose the project; 1 percent to support it and 6 percent to have no opinion (Fierro Symonds 1995).

5. For a thorough discussion of Mexican Civil society see Olvera (2003)

6. *Subcomandante* Marcos of the EZLN, for instance, writes many letters addressed to "Dama Sociedad Civil," in which he asks her for assistance. Although some-what of a joke, this is an enlightening statement, because it illustrates the way in which "civil society" is referred to as a social actor rather than a field in which social actors operate. It is an important ideological position, which organizations such as the EZLN create so as to polarize the debate.

7. This also highlights Olvera's (2003) argument that the growth of civil society depends on the state's respect for the rule of law. Under constant fear of reprisal, organizations and individuals are unlikely to propose or enact autonomous projects. The clear lack of a rule of law in Morelos in the mid 1990s, seriously hindered the growth of civil society and of regional public spheres, forcing movements like the one in Tepoztlán to take extreme measures (barricading the town and expelling state officials) in order to protect themselves. It also contributed to a climate of intolerance for dissent from the movement, in that dissenters were seen as potential "traitors," rather than people with an honest difference of opinion.

8. Of particular importance in this effort were the human rights organizations. While a prisoner, Gerardo Demesa received support from Amnesty International and numerous national human rights organizations. In his book documenting his experience, he found this support so important that he reproduced letters and cards that he received from all around the world in support of his case.

9. In order to protect his identity, Carlos is a pseudonym.

10. Mendez Arceo was, and knew he would be, replaced by a very conservative bishop who was intent on disarticulating the network of radical base communities that he had so painstakingly encouraged during his thirty-year term as bishop.

11. Padre Fili was transferred to another parish at the beginning of 1999. Members of the Base Ecclesial Communities believed that he was moved as a punishment for his having defied church authorities and having become too involved in political matters. They saw his transfer as part of the ongoing struggle within the Church to eliminate liberation theology and for the hierarchy to regain control over church

members. In their analysis, the CEBs had become too dangerous for the political establishment (as evidenced by their roles in Nicaragua and El Salvador in the 1970s and 1980s and Chiapas in the 1990s.) At the same time, however, some less radical parishioners were relieved when Fili left, and complained that they felt "forced" to listen to political speeches from the pulpit with which they did not agree.

12. I make these observations with a keen awareness that my gender most probably influenced the kinds of discussions that I was able to elicit from women in Tepoztlán.

13. Rubin, for instance, has found that in Juchitán, Zapotec women, who are historically seen as strong and autonomous because of their control over the local market, created and acted in public spheres associated with everyday life in the market and in family patios. Although most officially elected leaders were men, women wielded enormous influence through the public spheres defined by these informal networks. In other research that I have conducted in Xoxocotla, Morelos, male public leaders continually pointed to the importance that women have in struggles, by forcing the male leadership to go further than they think wise, and by not backing down from police threats. Also, see Lynn Stephen (1997) and Vivienne Bennett (1995) for a more in depth analysis of the ways in which women activists work both through publicly visible as well as informal networks to shape and carry out movement decisions. All of these cases point to important communicative networks in which women engage in debate and decision-making that is not visible in the more commonly reported "public spheres."

14. In 2003, for example, the Mayordomía of the Santa Cruz neighborhood organized a Day of the Dead celebration for the town's children and encouraged parents to not let their children celebrate Halloween as it was a from of cultural imperialism and not part of "our traditions."

15. This observation is borne not only by this case, but also the struggle over "autonomous municipalities" in areas of Guerrero and Zapatista influence in Chiapas, and the almost regular post-electoral struggles throughout the country in which the losing side (usually the PRD) claims fraud and occupies municipal offices.

16. This tactic, pioneered by COCEI in Juchitán (Fox 1994; Rubin 1997), has been emulated in several other cases as well, particularly with movements allied with the PRD.

17. This tension also highlights an important ambiguity within the PRD itself. The party has a sort of schizophrenic personality being partially composed of movement activists and partially composed of professional political operatives (usually ex-priistas). Many PRD activists refer to these two distinct tendencies as the "movement" and as the "structure," respectively, and seem rather divided as to the possibilities of reconciling them.

18. Lomnitz (1999; 2001) discusses how Tepoztlán is part of a series of center-periphery relationships that make it increasingly dependent on outside economic, political and social actors.

Chapter 5

1. Fundamental contradictions between official, national culture and specific and diverse communities throughout the country were exemplified most clearly by the Zapatista leadership's march to Mexico City in March 2001 to demand greater autonomy for indigenous communities. Although their presence failed to convince the Congress to pass the reforms outlined in the San Andres Peace Accords of 1996, their ability to mobilize large numbers of supporters seems to indicate that the transition continues to be a contested process in which the state has not found adequate ways of providing representation to the country's pluricultural population.

2. *Ejiditario* is a member of the collective farms, *ejidos*, established by the land reform of the Mexican Revolution. *Ejido* land, until reforms in 1992, were inalienable, meaning that they could not be sold, mortgaged or rented and could only be transferred to family members, effectively tying families to their land while protecting them from the possible loss of their lands to investors. While Ejidal Councils, selected by *ejido* members, are the governing body of the lands, the federal government is the actual owner of the land.

3. Unless otherwise noted, all interviews in this chapter took place in San Salvador Atenco between July and November 2003, and all translations from Spanish are mine.

4. The government did eventually offer some compensation to the family, but never acknowledged responsibility for his death.

5. See Sánchez Gómez (1999) for more complete history of Atenco.

6. See the debates in *Metapolítica*, July 2003.

7. Showing that these networks continue to grow and expand beyond the immediate conflict, Nacho del Valle and other Atenco activists and activists from Tepoztlán, were arrested and injured in January 2004 while protesting the violent repression of an autonomous government in the indigenous town of Tlalnepantla in the state of Morelos.

Appendix

1. The concept of *mestizaje*, for instance has been an integral part of understanding Latin American cultural make-up. Similarly, the notion of syncretism has been applied to the study of colonial religious experiences, as the Catholic Church incorporated some indigenous practices, and indigenous people incorporated Catholic practices and names to their own beliefs.

2. This is particularly important especially given Floya Anthias' (2001), observation that "there is little evidence of dominant white culture seceding its role in defining the cultural domain" (630).

3. See especially the collection of debates around subalternity edited by Rodríguez (2001).

4. See Gutmann (2002, 109–142) for a detailed discussion and critique of resistance theories.

5. Arguably, this is an accurate description of what has transpired through the transition process in Mexico, where various social movements have forced some change, but have been unable to create a fundamentally different state that would represent the diverse communities of the country.

6. In arguing against a monoglot, state-centered language and cultural project, Bakhtin attributes the constitution of culture to a complex and rich process of heteroglossia.

7. Perhaps the most recent attempt at such an endeavor can be seen in the Zapatista attempts at organizing civil society in Mexico through the latter part of the 1990s. Under such slogans as "a world in which all worlds fit" "everything for everyone, nothing for us," and such projects as the National Consultation (1999), the Intercontinental Gathering For Humanity and Against Neoliberalism (1996) and the National Democratic Convention (1994), the EZLN and its unarmed, national wing the FZLN, have consistently proposed a reorganization of the state (along the lines advocated by Beverly's conception of a new kind of state), and a locally based national coalition of civil organizations dedicated to respecting internal differences but committed to articulating a program of profound change which includes, among other things the satisfaction of basic human needs as the first priority of any society. Nevertheless, and in part certainly due to the political realities of Mexico and global economic pressures, it has been difficult to put such a plan into action or to mobilize organizations deeply and long enough to carry out this struggle. There still lacks, in other words, a viable, totalizing vision caught between the universalizing needs of a new kind of state and the particular needs of local communities and groups.

8. The case of the Argentine *piqueteros*, who successfully dislodged various presidents at the end of 2001 is instructive here. Working under the slogan of "*que vayan todos*" ("throw them all out"), the movement organized thousands of people into street demonstrations and neighborhood assemblies to express their dissatisfaction with economic crisis, corruption and political paralysis. But, because they did not articulate a broader vision of what to do after the politicians were all thrown out, the politicians regained control of political institutions within two years, without having to make substantial institutional or economic changes.

Bibliography

Aguilar Benítez, Salvador 1994. *El ecoturismo en el Estado de Morelos*. Cuernavaca: Centro de Estudios Históricos y Sociales del Estado de Morelos.

Aguilar Rivera, José Antonio 2003. El legado del autoritarismo. *Metapolítica* 7(30): 23–28.

Alonso, Jorge 2003. Los miedos a la democracia. *Metapolítica* 7(30): 14–22.

_____, and Juan Manuel Ramírez Sáiz, eds. 1997. *La democracia de los de abajo en México*. Mexico City: La Jornada Ediciones, Consejo Electoral del Estado de Jalisco, Centro de Investigaciones Interdisciplinarias en Ciencias y Humanidades/UNAM.

Alvarez, Rafael, Alfredo Castillo, et al. 1997. *Morelos: Tan lejos de la justicia*. Mexico City: Centro de Derechos Humanos Miguel Agustín Pro Juarez, AC.

Alvarez, Sonia, Elverina Dagnino and Arturo Escobar, eds. 1998. *Cultures of Politics, Politics of Cultures: Re-Visioning Latin American Social Movements*. Boulder, CO: Westview Press.

Anthias, Floya 2001. New Hybridities, Old Concepts: The Limits of Culture. *Ethnic and Racial Studies* 24(4): 613–641.

Aranda, Julio 2000. Jorge Carrillo habla desde San Francisco. *Proceso*: 34–35.

Ayuntamiento Libre, Constitucional y Popular del Municipio de Tepoztlán 1996. *Historia breve de la lucha del pueblo de Tepoztlán*. Tepoztlán.

La batalla de Tepoztlán 1995. Oscar Menendez, dir. Cuernavaca: Video Cine Independiente.

Bauman, Zygmunt 1998. *Globalization: The Human Consequences*. New York: Columbia University Press.

Benet, Raul 1996. Tepoztlán: saldos de una lucha social. *La Jornada* (Mexico City), 23 Feb.

Bennett, Vivienne 1995. *The Politics of Water: Urban Protest, Gender, and Power in Monterrey, Mexico*. Pittsburgh: University of Pittsburgh Press.

Beverly, John 1999. *Subalternity and Representation: Arguments in Cultural Theory*. Durham NC: Duke University Press.

Bocanegra Quiroz, Laura Adela (Deputy for the Second District for the State of Morelos) 1999. Personal Interview. Tepoztlán: 31 May.

Bonfil Batalla, Guillermo 1987. *México profundo: una civilización negada*. Mexico City: Giralbo.

Brecher, Jeremy, and Tim Costello 1994. *Global Village or Global Pillage*. Boston: South End Press.

Brito Velázquez, Enrique 1997. Sociedad civil en México: análisis y debates. *Sociedad Civil: Análisis y debate* 1(2): 185–206.

Bruhn, Kathleen 1999. PRD Local Governments in Michoacán: Implications for Mexico's Democratization Process. In *Subnational Politics and Democratization in Mexico*. Wayne Cornelius, Todd Eisenstadt and Jane Hindle, eds. La Jolla: Center for U.S.–Mexican Studies, University of California, San Diego.

Brysk, Alison 2000. Globalization: The Double-edged Sword. *NACLA: Report on the Americas* 24(1): 29–33.

Bueno Castellanos, Carmen 2000. Diversidad en lo global. In *Globalización: una cuestión antropológica*. Carmen Bueno Castellanos, ed. Mexico City: Centro de Investigaciones y Estudio Superiores en Antropología Social, Miguel Ángel Porrúa Grupo Editorial.

Calderón, Fernando 1995. *Movimientos sociales y política: la década de los ochenta.* Mexico City: Siglo Veintiuno Editores.

Castillo, Jaime, and Elsa Patiño, eds. 1997. *Cultura política de las organizaciones y movimientos sociales.* Mexico City: La Jornada Ediciones, Centro de Investigaciones Interdisciplinarias en Ciencias y Humanidades/UNAM.

_____, _____, and Sergio Zermeño, eds. 2001. *Pobreza y organizaciones de la sociedad civil.* Puebla: Editorial de la Red Nacional de Investigación Urbana, Universidad Autónoma de Puebla, Consejo Nacional de Ciencia y Tecnología.

Cedillo Méndez, Asciano (Council Member for the Constitutional Council of Tepoztlán, 1997–2000) 1999. Personal Interview. Tepoztlán: 14 Apr.

Cohen, Jean, and Andrew Arato 1992. *Civil Society and Political Theory.* Cambridge: MIT Press.

Comisión Nacional de Derechos Humanos (1997). *Recomendación No. 114/97: Sobre el caso del Comité de la Unidad Tepozteco.* Mexico City.

Cornelius, Wayne 1999. Subnational Politics and Democratization: Tensions between Center and Periphery in the Mexican Political System. In *Subnational Politics and Democratization in Mexico*. Wayne Cornelius, Todd Eisenstadt and Jane Hindle, eds. La Jolla: Center for U.S.–Mexican Studies, University of California, San Diego.

_____, Todd Eisenstadt and Jane Hindle, eds. 1998. *Subnational Politics and Democratization in Mexico*. La Jolla: Center for U.S.–Mexican Studies, University of California, San Diego.

Corona Caraveo, Yolanda, and Carlos Pérez y Zavala 1999. *Tradición y modernidad en Tepoztlán: Historias y leyendas de un pueblo en resistencia.* Mexico City: Universidad Autónoma Metropolitana — Xochimilco.

de la Peña, Guillermo 1980. *Herederos de promesas: agricultura, política y ritual en los altos de Morelos.* Mexico City: Centro de Investigaciones Superior del INAH; Casa Chata.

Demesa Padilla, Gerardo 1998. *Tepoztlán, la lucha del pueblo tepozteco contra la imposición de un megaproyecto.* n.p.

_____ 1999. Personal Interview. Cuernavaca: 21 January.

Díaz-Barriga 1998. Beyond the Domestic and the Public: *Colonas* Participation in Urban Movements in Mexico City. In *Cultures of Politics, Politics of Cultures: Re-visioning Latin American Social Movements*. Sonia Alvarez, Elverina Dagnino and Arturo Escobar, eds. Boulder CO: Westview Press.

Dresser, Denise 1991. *Neopopulist Solutions to Neoliberal Problems: Mexico's*

National Solidarity Program. La Jolla: Center for U.S.–Mexican Studies, University of California, San Diego.

Durand, Jorge, ed. 2002. *Movimientos sociales: Desafíos teóricos y metodológicos*. Guadalajara: Universidad de Guadalajara.

Echeverría, Eugenia 1994. *Tepoztlán: Que viva la fiesta*. Cuernavaca: Dirección General de Culturas Populares— Unidad Regional Morelos.

Esteva, Gustavo, and Madhu Suri Prakash 1998. *Grassroots Postmodernism: Remaking the soil of cultures*. New York: Zed Books.

Fierro Symonds, Raquel 1995. Tepoztlán: sobre el Club de Golf. *Ventana*: 7.

Flores Ayala, Victor 1998. Tepoztlán. In *Tepoztlán, nuestra historia: testimonios de los habitantes de Tepoztlán, Morelos*. Marcela Tostada Gutiérrez, ed. Mexico City: Instituto Nacional de Antropología e Historia.

Flores Pérez, Malaquías 1998. Mi vida, mi familia y recuerdos vagos de mi pueblo. In *Tepoztlán, nuestra historia: testimonios de los habitantes de Tepoztlán, Morelos*. Marcela Tostada Gutiérrez, ed. Mexico City: Instituto Nacional de Antropología e Historia.

_____ 1999. Personal Interview. Member, Ayuntamiento Constitucional de Tepoztlán 1997–2000. Tepoztlán: 4 May.

Foweraker, Joe, and Ann Craigs, eds. 1990. *Popular Movements and Political Change in Mexico*. Boulder CO: Lynn Rienner.

Fox, Jonathan 1994. The Difficult Transition from Clientalism to Citizenship: Lessons from Mexico. *World Politics* 46(2): 151–184.

_____, and Luis Hernández 1992. Mexico's Difficult Democracy: Grassroots Movements, NGO's and Local Government. *Alternatives* 17 (Spring): 165–208.

Frente de pueblos en defensa de la tierra (2002). El discurso de los ejidatarios de Atenco de este 11 de marzo, ante la ausencia por segunda ocasión de Vicente Fox en el Auditorio Nacional, donde fue emplazado a debate público por los ejidatarios. Atenco, Photocopy.

_____ (n.d.). Manifiesto del Frente de pueblos en defensa de la tierra. Atenco.

Gallo Sarlat, Joaquín 1988. *Tepoztlán: personajes, descripciones y sucedios*. Mexico City: Talleres Gráficos de Cultura.

García Canclini, Nestor 1995. *Hybrid Cultures: Strategies for Entering and Leaving Modernity*. Minneapolis: University of Minnesota Press.

García de Leon, Antonio 1999. Commentarios. Presentación del libro *No al club de Golf*, Tepoztlán, Morelos.

Gilly, Adolfo 1971. *La revolución interrumpida*. Mexico City: Ediciones Era.

_____ 1994. *El cardenismo, una utopía mexicana*. Mexico City: Cal y Arena.

Giménez, Rafael 1995. No al club de golf. *La Reforma* (Mexico City), 16 Sept. p. 1.

Gómez Guerra, Sergio 1998. Preparan amnistía para tepoztecos. *Unión de Morelos* (Cuernavaca), 15 Oct., p. 1+.

Greene, Kenneth 1997. Complejidad, cohesión y longevidad en un movimiento urbano popular: Asamblea de Barrios de la Ciudad de México. In *Movimientos sociales e identidades colectivas*. Sergio Zermeño, ed. Mexico City: La Jornada Ediciones, Centro de Investigaciones Interdisciplinarias en Ciencias y Humanidades/UNAM.

Guidry, John A., Michael D. Kennedy, et al. 2000. Globalizations and Social Movements. In *Globalizations and Social Movements: Culture, Power, and the*

Transnational Public Sphere. John A. Guidry, Michael D. Kennedy and Mayer N. Zald, eds. Ann Arbor: University of Michigan Press.

_____, eds. 2000. *Globalizations and Social Movements: Culture, Power, and the Transnational Public Sphere*. Ann Arbor: University of Michigan Press.

Gutmann, Mathew 2002. *Romancing Democracy: Compliant Defiance in Contemporary Mexico*. Berkeley: University of California Press.

Habermas, Jürgen 1987. *The Theory of Communicative Action, Volume Two: Lifeworld and System: A Critique of Functionalist Reason*. Boston: Beacon Press.

Harvey, David 1993. The Nature of Environment: The Dialectics of Social and Environmental Change. In *Social Register 1993: Real Problems, False Solutions*. Ralph Miliband and Leo Panitah, eds. London: Merlin Press.

Hernández Chávez, Alicia 2002. *Breve historia de Morelos*. Mexico City: El Colegio de México, Fideicomiso Historia de las Américas, Fondo de Cultura Económica.

Hernández Cortés, Eduardo 1994. Nota preliminar. In *Tepoztlán ¡Qué viva la fiesta!* Eugenia Echeverría, ed. Cuernavaca: Dirección General de Culturas Populares—Unidad Regional Morelos.

Hernández López, Julio 2003. Astillero. *La Jornada* (Mexico City), 7 July, p. 1.

Hernández Navarro, Luis 1999. La revuelta de los globalizados. *La Jornada* (Mexico City), 2 Dec., p. 2.

Icaza Longoria, Pedro A 1995. D.O.O. DGNA 03279. Resolución Número 1256. Mexico City: Instituto Nacional de Ecología, Dirección General de Normatividad Ambiental.

Johnston, Hank, and Bert Klandermans, eds. 1995. *Social Movements and Culture*. Minneapolis: University of Minnesota Press.

Keck, Margaret, and Kathryn Sikkink 1998. *Activists Beyond Borders: Advocacy Networks in International Politics*. Ithaca NY: Cornell University Press.

Labastida Martín del Campo, Julio, and Antonio Camou, eds. 2001. *Globalización, identidad democracia: México y América Latina*. Mexico City: Siglo Veintiuno Editores, el Instituto de Investigaciones Sociales—UNAM.

LaBotz, Dan 1995. *Democracy in Mexico: Peasant Rebellion and Political Reform*. Boston: South End Press.

Laclau, Ernesto 1996. *Emancipation(s)*. London: Verso.

_____, and Chantal Mouffe 1985. *Hegemony and Socialist Strategy: Towards a Radical Democratic Politics*. London: Verso.

Lajous, Alejandra 2003. *¿Dónde se perdió el cambio?* Mexico City: Planeta.

Lands, Yes! Airplanes, No! 2002. Greg Berger, Constantino Miranda and Adan Xicotencatl, dir. Mexico City: Arte y Comunicación Social.

Lechner, Norbert 1997. El malestar con la política y la reconstrucción de los mapas políticos. In *Culturas políticas a fin del siglo*. Rosalia Winocur, ed. Mexico City: Juan Pablo Editor; Facultad Latinoamerican de Ciencias Sociales.

Levy, Daniel, and Kathleen Bruhn 2001. *Mexico: The Struggle for Demcocratic Development*. Berkeley: University of California Press.

Lewis, Oscar 1968. *Tepoztlán: un pueblo de México*. Mexico City: Editorial Joaquín Mortiz.

Lomnitz, Claudio 1982. *Evolución de una sociedad rural*. Mexico City: Fondo de Cultura Económica.

_____ 1992. *Exits from the Labyrinth: Culture and Ideology in the Mexican National Space*. Berkeley: University of California Press.

_____ 1999. *Modernidad indiana: Nueve ensayos sobre nación y mediación en México*. Mexico City: Planeta.

_____ 2001. *Deep Mexico, Silent Mexico: An Anthropology of Nationalism*. Minneapolis: University of Minnesota Press.

Mabardi, Sabine 2000. Encounters of a Heterogeneous Kind: Hybridity in Cultural Theory. In *Unforseeable Americas: Questioning Cultural Hybridity in the Americas*. Rita De Grandis and Zilá Bernd, eds. Atlanta: Rodopi, B.V.

Manrique Mendoza, Janeth 2003. *Atenco: Un acto de rebeldía*. Mexico City: Imagen Mexiquense.

Martin, JoAnn 1993. Contesting Authenticity: Battles over Representation of History in Morelos, Mexico. *Ethnohistory* 40 (3): 438–465.

Martínez Zúñiga, Ricardo (General Secretary for the Council of Tepoztlán, 1997–2000) 1999. Personal Interview. Tepoztlán: 1 Feb.

Melucci, Alberto 1995. The Process of Collective Identity. In *Social Movements and Culture*. Hank Johnston and Bert Klandermans, eds. Minneapolis: University of Minnesota Press.

Meraz, Fernando, Celia García Flores, et al. 1996. Narcolavado detrás del club de golf El Tepozteco: DEA. *El Financiero* (Mexico City), 28 Apr., pp. 1, 18.

Meyenberg Leycegui, Yolanda, ed. 2001. *El dos de julio: reflexiones posteriores*. Mexico City: Facultad Latinoamericana de Ciencias Sociales, Universidad Autónoma Metropolitana — Iztapalapa, Instituto de Investigaciones Sociales — UNAM.

Meyer, Lorenzo 1998. *Fin de régimen y democracia incipiente: México hace el siglo XX*. Mexico City: Oceano.

Miller, Byron 1993. Collective Action and Rational Choice: Place, Community, and the Limits to Individual Self Interest. *Economic Geography*: 22–42.

Miranda Rodríguez, Justino 1995. El conflicto en Tepoztlán. *Ventana*: 3–7.

Monografía del Estado de Morelos 1990. Mexico City: Secretaría de Educación Pública.

Monsiváis, Carlos 1987. *Entrada libre: crónicas de la sociedad que se organiza*. Mexico City: Ediciones Era.

Moreiras, Alberto 1999. Hybridity and Double Consciousness. *Cultural Studies* 13 (3): 373–404.

Morris, Aldon D., and Carol McClurg Mueller, eds. 1992. *Frontiers in Social Movement Theory*. New Haven CT: Yale University Press.

Olvera, Alberto, ed. 2003 *Sociedad civil, esfera pública y democratización en América Latina: México*. Mexico City: Fondo de Cultura Económica, Universidad Veracruzana.

Ortiz Pinchetti, F 1996. En Morelos, pese a los militares en la policía, el general Carrillo Olea está perdiendo la guerra contra el crimen y la impunidad. *Proceso* (1014): 12–15.

Ortiz Rivera, Sergio (Director for Environmental Protection) 1999. Personal Interview. Tepoztlán: 19 Apr. 1999.

Peñaloza Rojas, Benito 1998. Relato sobre la muerte del general Emiliano Zapata. In *Tepoztlán, nuestra historia: testimonios de los habitantes de Tepoztlán, Morelos*. Marcela Tostada Gutiérrez, ed. Mexico City: Instituto Nacional de Antropología e Historia.

Poot Capetillo, Efraín Eric 2000. La renovada participación ciudadana: elecciones, organizaciones cívicas y nuevas formas de gobierno municipal. In *Cambio político y participación ciudadana en México.* Juan Manuel Ramírez Sáiz and Jorge Regalado Santillán, eds. Mexico City: Centro de Estudios de Política Comparada, Centro Univeristario de Ciencias Sociales y Humanidades de la Universidad de Guadalajara.

Quero, Morgan 2003. El Arte de la Asociación — o una periferia que puede ser centro— Sociedad civil y gobernabilidad en Morelos. In *Sociedad civil, esfera pública y democratización en América Latina.* Alberto Olvera, ed. Mexico City: Fondo de Cultura Económica, Universidad Veracruzana.

Quiroz Acevedo, Mario Antonio 1998. Fiestas de Tepoztlán. In *Tepoztlán, nuestra historia: testimonios de los habitantes de Tepoztlán, Morelos.* Marcela Tostada Gutiérrez, ed. Mexico City: Instituto Nacional de Antropología e Historia.

Rabasa, José 2001. Beyond Representation? The Impossibility of the Local (Notes on Subaltern Studies in Light of a Rebellion in Tepoztlán, Morelos). In *The Latin American Subaltern Studies Reader.* Ileana Rodríguez, ed. Durham NC: Duke University Press.

Ramírez, Carlos 2003. Transición: Volver a empezar. *Metapolítica* 7 (30): 29–39.

Ramírez Sáiz, Juan Manuel, and Renée de la Torre 2003. Conservadurismo, sociedad civil y gobernabilidad. Nuevas grupalidades en Guadalajara. In *Sociedad civil, esfera pública y democratización en América Latina: México.* Alberto Olvera, ed. Mexico City: Fondo de Cultura Económica, Universidad Veracruzana.

Robertson, Roland 1992. *Globalization.* London: Sage Publications.

Robles Bladeras, Humberto (Council Member for Social Welfare and Human Rights) 2001. Personal Interview. Tepoztlán: 6 Aug.

Rodríguez, Ileana, ed. 2001. *The Latin American Subaltern Studies Reader.* Durham NC: Duke University Press.

Rodríguez Araujo, Octavio, ed. 1996. *Transición a la democracia: diferentes perspectivas.* Mexico City: La Jornada Ediciones, Centro de Investigaciones Interdisciplinarias en Ciencias y Humanidades UNAM.

Rodríguez Castañeda, Lázaro 2001. Personal Interview. Municipal President, Tepoztlán Morelos: 1995–1997; 2000–2003. Tepoztlán: 21 July.

Rosas, Maria 1997. *Tepoztlán: crónica de desacatos y resistencia.* Mexico City: Ediciones Era.

Rubin, Jeffery 1997. *Decentering the Regime: Ethnicity, Radicalism and Democracy in Juchitán, Mexico.* Durham NC: Duke University Press.

Russell, James 2003. Land and Identity in Mexico: Peasants Stop an Airport. *Monthly Review* 54 (9): 14–25.

Salazar Garrido, José 1998. Semblanza de una tradición. In *Tepoztlán, nuestra historia: testimonios de los habitantes de Tepoztlán, Morelos.* Marcela Tostada Gutiérrez, ed. Mexico City: Instituto Nacional de Antropología e Historia.

Salazar Peralta, Ana María Las mayordomía: el caso de Ixcatepec, Morelos. Photocopy of an article in the archives of the National Institute of History and Anthropology Museum, Tepoztlán.

Sánchez Ascencio, Pilar 1998. *Antología histórica de Tepoztlán.* Cuernavaca: Instituto Nacional de Antropología e Historia, Morelos.

Sánchez Gómez, Martín Abraham 1999. *Atenco: Monografía Municipal.* Toluca, Mexico: Instituto Mexiquense de Cultura.

Schedler, Andreas 1999. Civil Society and Political Elections: A Culture of Distrust?

The Annals of the American Academy of Political and Social Sciences (565): 126–141.

Shohat, Ella 1992. Notes on the "Post-Colonial." *Social Text* (31/32): 99–113.

Snow, David, and Robert D. Benford 1992. Master Frames and Cycles of Protest. In *Frontiers in Social Movement Theory*. Aldon D. Morris and Carol McClurg Mueller, eds. New Haven CT: Yale University Press.

Soler Frost, Pablo 1997. *Cartas de Tepoztlán*. Mexico City: Ediciones Era.

Stavenhagen, Rodolfo 1998. Identidad cultural y globalización. In *Visión crítica de la globalida*. Mexico City: Centro Latinoamericano de la Globalidad.

Stephen, Lynn 1997. *Women and Social Movements in Latin America: Power from Below*. Austin: University of Texas Press.

Stolle-McAllister, John 2004. Contingent Hybridity: The Cultural Politics of Tepoztlán's Anti-Golf Movement. *Identities: Global Studies in Culture and Power* 11(2): 195–213.

_____ 2005 (forthcoming). What Does Democracy Look Like? Local Movements Challenge the Mexican Transition. *Latin American Perspectives*.

Subcomondante Marcos 2001. Speech, 11 Mar., Mexico City.

Tavera-Fenollosa, Ligia 1999. The Movimiento de Damnificados: Democratic Transformation of Citizenry and Government in Mexico City. In *Subnational Politics and Democratization in Mexico*. Wayne Cornelius, Todd Eisenstadt and Jane Hindle, eds. La Jolla: Center for U.S.–Mexican Studies, University of California, San Diego.

Torres, Gabriel 1999. The El Barzón Debtors' Movement: From the Local to the National in Protest Politics. In *Subnational Politics and Democratization in Mexico*. Wayne Cornelius, Todd Eisenstadt and Jane Hindle, eds. La Jolla: Center for U.S.–Mexican Studies, University of California, San Diego.

Tostada Gutiérrez, Marcela, ed. 1998. *Tepoztlán: Nuestra historia: testimonios de los habitantes de Tepoztlán, Morelos*. Mexico City: Instituto Nacional de Antropología e Historia.

Urías German, Gregorio 2003. *La democracia en México después de la alternancia: retos y posibilidades*. Mexico City: Porrua.

Vélez-Ibáñez, Carlos 1983. *Rituals of Marginality: Politics, Process and Culture Change in Central Urban Mexico, 1969–1974*. Berkeley: University of California Press.

Vilas, Carlos, ed. 1994. *La democratización fundamental: El populismo en América Latina*. Mexico City: Consejo Nacional para la Cultura y las Artes.

Villamil Ortiz, Enrique 1998. Pasajes de mi vida. In *Tepoztlán, nuestra historia: testimonios de los habitantes de Tepoztlán, Morelos*. Marcela Tostada Gutiérrez, ed. Mexico City: Instituto Nacional de Antropología e Historia.

Villamil Tapia, Enrique 1961. *El origen del carnaval en el pueblo de Tepoztlán*. n.p.: n.p.

Villoro, Luis 2001. Un nuevo proyecto de nación: los acuerdos de San Andres. In *Globalización, identidad y democracia: México y América Latina*. Julio Labastida Martín del Campo and Antonio Camou, eds. Mexico City: Siglo Veintiuno Editores, el Instituto de Investigaciones Sociales/UNAM.

Wallerstein, Immanuel 1991. *Geopolitics and Geoculture. Essays on the Changing World-System*. London: Cambridge University Press.

Warman, Arturo 1988. "*...y venimos a contradecir": los campesinos de Morelos y el* *estado nacional.* Mexico City: Secretaría de Educación Pública; Centro de Investigaciones y Estudios Superiores en Antropología Social.

Williams, Heather 2001. *Social Movements and Economic Transition: Markets and Distributive Conflict in Mexico.* New York: Cambridge University Press.

Womack, John 1968. *Zapata and the Mexican Revolution.* New York: Alfred A. Knopf.

Yudice, George 1998. The Globalization of Culture and the New Civil Society. In *Cultures of Politics and Politics of Cultures: Re-Visioning Latin American Social Movements.* Sonia Alvarez, Evelina Dagnino and Arturo Escobar, eds. Boulder CO: Westview Press.

Zaragosa, Juan Manuel (n.d.). The Community Organizes, Tepoztlán: National Example of Municipal Democracy. Cuernavaca: n.p.

Zermeño, Sergio, ed. 1997. *Movimientos sociales e identidades colectivas.* Mexico City: La Jornada Ediciones, Centro de Investigaciones Interdisciplinarias en Ciencias y Humanidades/UNAM.

Zúñiga Navarrete, Angel 1995. *Breve historia y narraciones tepoztecas.* Tepoztlán: Secretaría de Educación Pública.

_____ 1998. El Tepoztlán legendario a través de los siglos. In *Tepoztlán, nuestra historia: testimonios de los habitantes de Tepoztlán, Morelos.* Marcela Tostada Gutiérrez, ed. Mexico City: Instituto Nacional de Antropología e Historia.

Index